151
FOLK TALES OF INDIA

151
Folk Tales of India

Compiled by
KANWARJIT SINGH KANG
DILJIT KAUR KANG

1988

AJANTA
PUBLICATIONS

ISBN 81-202-0180-9

Illustrations by
Diljit Kaur Kang
Rachanjit Kaur Kang

Published by
Ajanta Publications (India)
Jawahar Nagar,
Delhi - 110007

Distributor
Ajanta Books International
1-UB, Jawahar Nagar, Bungalow Road,
Delhi-110007

Printed at
S. Narayan & Sons, Delhi - 110006.

Dedicated to
DR. ATTAR SINGH

FOREWORD

Folk Tales are valuable heritage and must be documented and preserved. It is a pity that the studies of folk-lore in India were much delayed and even now these have not picked up to meet the danger of the vanishing oral traditions bequeathed to the generations from time immemorial. But for the pioneering work of European scholars who made compilations in different parts of India of the great folk-tales of the sub-continent, much more would have disappeared. The professional story-tellers who once formed a valuable source of the Indian society, and were much sought after, have become extinct ; and our present-day grandmothers remember much less of traditional folk-tales compared to what was committed to memory of their great-grandmothers. I feel, therefore, that there is a sense of urgency for recording these tales before they disappear altogether.

This volume, compiled by Dr. Kanwarjit Singh Kang and Mrs. Diljit Kaur Kang, presents those wonderful old legends that mostly have their origin in Northern India and give the readers an insight into the culture and civilization of the ancient and medieval periods, indicating the customs, traditions, manners, habits, rites, castes, games, apparels, ornaments, myths and morals, religion and popular beliefs. These stand answers to the primitive inquisitive mind that sought to incorporate itself in its milieu for questioning and answering. I am sure this book will be welcomed by all those who would like to have a peep into the folk realm of Indology.

January 20, 1988

Mrs. S. BHATIA
President,
Lalit Kala Akademi, Punjab

PREFACE

We had ventured to compile an analytical bibliography of North-West India, a bibliography of an all encompassing nature, that would cover all aspects of the art and culture of the region, not merely listing of books that refer to history or history of art and culture alone. The stupendous task was still in its infancy when the sources tapped suggested potentials of much broader dimensions and a scope that would not fit in a' bibliography initially aimed at.

While going through old publications we came across hundreds of folk tales, legends, myths, riddles, proverbs, sayings and other similar observations that have a direct bearing on the folklore heritage of this vast country, and the relevant references were recorded in research notes forming the basis of the proposed bibliography, referred to above. It was simultaneously felt that, a bibliography being a reference book, the compilation of the scattered matter on particular themes be made to form separate books and work on preparing the analytical bibliography be continued steadily. The first attempt has resulted in the form of the present volume : *151 Folk Tales of India,* which were first recorded nearly a hundred years ago in the *North Indian Notes and Queries,* under the editorship of the illustrious William Crooke.

The selection of one hundred and fifty-one folk tales is arbitrary, however an attempt has been made to select tales that are fascinating and tend to keep the readers enthralled with their exciting narrations. Each folk tale carries an illustration attempting to capture the spirit of its version and thus adding to its appeal visually. Since most of the old publications are becoming rare day by day and it is invariably hazardous to use these for instant reading, this volume, it is hoped, will prove quite handy to readers, old and young.

KANWARJIT SINGH KANG
DILJIT KAUR KANG

CONTENTS

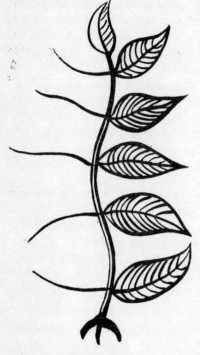

1

THE MAN WHO FOUGHT WITH GOD

Once upon a time there was a Musalman who was very poor, and used to earn four pice a day by wood-cutting. Now he heard that whoever gives charity gets double in return. So he used to give a pice daily in alms, one pice to his wife, kept a pice for his own food, and laid by one pice.

After some time he thought he would see if his store had doubled, but to his disgust, when he counted his savings, he found he had only just as much as he put by. So he said :—"I will go and fight God, because He has not doubled my pice."

So he shut up his house and started off, and when his neighbours asked him where he was going, he said :—"God has written in His book that whatever a man gives in charity He doubles, but He has not done so; so now I am going to fight Him." So his friends advising him, said :—"You fool! has any one ever fought with God ?" He said :—"No matter. I am going all the same."

On the road he met a man and the same conversation passed. So the man went to the King and said :—"There is a traveller here who says he is going to fight God." The King said :—

"Bring him before me." Then the King asked him :—"Where are you going ?" And he made the same answer.

Then the King said :—"You might as well, as you are going, ask God one question. My kingdom goes on all right during the day, but is burnt up at night. Why is this so ?" At first he refused to do what the King wished, but finally, after great persuasion, agreed. As he went on he felt very thirsty, and seeing a well, approached it, and found that it was full of filth, in which a man and woman were submerged. When these people saw him they asked him who he was, and where he was going. He said :—"I am going to fight with God." Then they said :— "When you meet Him, ask Him either to kill us, or to take us out of this well." He agreed and went on.

When it became very hot he sat under a tree, but the tree was dry and did not keep off the glare. Then he said :—"What is the use of this tree ? It is only cumbering the ground." Then the tree asked him who he was, and he replied :—"I am a Musalman, and am going to fight with God." The tree said :— "You might ask Him either to make me green again, or cut me down because I am useless to weary travellers." So he agreed and went on.

Then he saw a great fire burning in the jungle. As he was considering how to avoid the fire, he found that the blaze proceeded from an Angel (*firishtah*). The Angel asked him where he was going, and he said :—"To fight with God." Then the Angel asked :—"Has any one ever fought with God ?" "What matter," replied the traveller, "I will do it all the same." The Angel said :—"Well ! stay here and I will inform God." Then God sent the Angel back to enquire what the man wanted to say. The man answered :—"In such and such a land there is a King, and his kingdom goes on well by day, but it is burnt up at night. What is the reason of this ? *Secondly*, on a certain road there is a man and a woman in a well who want to be killed, or relieved of their trouble. *Thirdly*, there is a tree in a certain place—why has it withered. It wants either to be cut down, or made green again." But he forgot to tell his own complaint to the Angel.

Then God answered his questions by the mouth of the Angel :—"The reason why the King's kingdom thrives by day and goes to ruin at night is that the King has a daughter. All day she amuses herself with her companions, but at night her breath becomes cool (*thandi sans bharti hai*), and then everything goes wrong. When the King gets her married this will cease. And as regards the two persons in the well—they are great sinners, and are now receiving their punishment. So when you reach this well throw a pinch of clay into it, and it will gradually fill up, but when the earth rises to the top, place a large stone upon it. As to the tree—at its root there is a great snake in whose belly are two sapphires : near this tree is a smaller tree. Take the root of this, and dig a little near the foot of the large tree. The snake will then appear. Put the small root near his nose : he will vomit up the jewels and escape. Then the tree will become green again."

So the man did as he was directed. When the snake appeared he was insensible, but when he smelt the root he vomited up the sapphires. Then he came to his senses and disappeared, and the tree became green again. But the man touched not the sapphires. When he came to the well he said to the man and woman :—"You are being punished for your sins." Then he threw a pinch of clay into the well and it became filled with rupees. But he took none of them, and closed the well with the stone.

Then he came to the King and told him that if he got his daughter married, the trouble in his kingdom would cease. So the King said :—"Where can I find a better husband for my daughter than yourself ?" So he had them married. And from that day the trouble in his kingdom ceased. The Musalman went back, dug the treasure out of the well, and brought away the sapphires. And thus by the grace of the Almighty became exceedingly rich and the son-in-law of the King, and after his death reigned in his stead. So in this way his charity was rewarded.

2

MR. GOOD AND MR. EVIL

Once upon a time Mr. Good and Mr. Evil made friends and went off in search of employment. They came to a stream. Mr. Evil drew water and Mr. Good went for firewood. Meanwhile Mr. Evil opened his companion's bag and stole his provisions.

When Mr. Good came back and found his bag empty he told Mr. Evil, who said :—"It must have been your wife stole your food. My wife often does the same when she does not want me to go out."

Mr. Good suspected his friend and said nothing.

Mr. Evil cooked his food, but gave none to his companion.

They went on till they came to the cross roads, and there Mr. Good said to Mr. Evil :—"Friend, we had better part, as we cannot get work if we stay together."

So they separated, and Mr. Good being hungry went on into the forest. At last he saw a hut, and going in—what does he see—four animals,—a tiger, a jackal, a snake, and a mouse,— were sitting, each in one corner of the hut. They took no notice of him, and he sat down in the middle.

Now, Mr. Good knew the speech of animals, and presently he heard them talking.

The tiger said to the jackal :—"What a lot of treasure the snake has in the house ! If any one would come and dig it up while he is away looking for food what a good thing it would be; for we should then be no longer forced to guard it for him."

"Indeed, I do wish it were so. But, brother, do you know that there lives in the city of Ujjain a Raja who is stricken with leprosy, and he has promised to give his daughter and half his kingdom to the man who cures him ?"

"Is it really so ?" asked the tiger.

"It is so, indeed," answered the jackal.

"And how could he be cured ?" was the next question.

"If any one," said the jackal, "were to get some of the dung of a swan (*hansa*), mix it with oil and rub it over him with a feather of the eagle Garuda, he would be cured of the disease."

Mr. Good heard all this and started for Ujjain.

Then he walked through the market crying :—

"A physician, he ! Does any one want a physician ?"

The Raja sent for Mr. Good and he prescribed for him as the jackal had said, and he was cured. So Mr. Good married the princess and became lord of half the kingdom.

Then he went back to the hut and dug up the snake's treasure.

"Can I do anything more for you ?", asked the tiger.

"Well, if you would devour the next person who comes here, I would feel obliged," said Mr. Good. Soon after Mr. Evil, wandering about in great poverty, came to the hut, and the tiger at once killed him.

So this was the end of Mr. Evil.

May Paramesar so reward right and punish wrong !

3

WHICH IS GREATER—RAMA OR KHUDA

A Hindu and a Muhammadan fakir were once disputing. The Hindu said that Rama and the Muhammadan said that Khuda was the greater. So they went to Raja Vikramaditya to decide the dispute. The Raja ordered the Hindu to climb up a palm tree and jump down. As he jumped he thought of Rama and was not hurt. When the Muhammadan went up seeing how the Hindu had escaped he began to think that he had better invoke both the deities. So with an invocation to Rama and Khuda he jumped and was dashed to pieces.

So Kabir Das writes :—

Do nawa na chariye ;
Doka phatke biche giriye.

"Do not sit on two boats when crossing a stream. You will fall between them and loose your life."

4

THE GODDESS OF POVERTY

There was once a Brahman so poor, that he could scarcely support himself by begging. The goddess of poverty had beset him. One day he was bathing at the Ganges, when a friend advised him to go to the Raja, who would surely relieve his wants. He went to the Raja, and when he stood before him he cried out :—"Victory to the Raja," and the Raja gave him ten thousand rupees. As he was going home with the money the goddess of poverty met him in the guise of the Raja and ordered him, on pain of his life, to surrender the money, so he laid it down and went home empty-handed.

Next day he went to the Raja, got the same present as before and lost it in the same way. And so it happened a third time also. Then the Raja was surprised and determined to go himself and see what the Brahman did with the money. When he saw the goddess take the money he went to her and asked her who she was. She answered :—"I am the goddess of poverty, and I am now besetting this Brahman. Whatever he receives I take from him." The Raja asked if there was any way by which this poor Brahman could be relieved, and she said :—"If you take me upon yourself, then he will be relieved." The Raja agreed and the goddess came to live with him, and when he went home the Brahman found all the money which the Raja had given to him at his house. When the Raja returned to his palace he sent the Rani with her children to her mother's house and he stayed at night in the palace. Suddenly a terrible storm arose and the palace was demolished, and all the horses, elephants and other goods of the Raja were buried beneath the ruins. So next day the Raja started for the jungle and another Raja ruled in his stead. The Raja went along begging his bread, and at last he came to a city and began to cut wood, which he used to sell daily to a confectioner. When the confectioner cut up the wood a lot of diamonds came out of it, whereat he was much pleased. He offered some to the Raja, but he said that they were of no use to him, and that all he wanted was the bare price of the wood. The confectioner wished to give him a share, so he put some of the jewels in a *laddu* (sweetmeat) and gave them to the Raja. On the way he met a Brahman, who asked for alms, and to him he gave the *laddu*. The Brahman did not care for the *laddu*, so he brought it back to the confectioner and changed it for some parched barley flour. When the confectioner examined the *laddu* he found the diamonds within it; so he said :—"It is my fate to keep them."

The Raja then went out to the jungle. There some thieves were planning to commit a theft and they, thinking the Raja to be a *Sadhu*, bowed before him and asked him to bless their enterprise. After committing a burglary in the palace they returned to where the Raja was, and by force made him accept a diamond necklace which was part of the booty. He left it lying near him and the thieves went away. Meanwhile some sepoys of the Raja, who were in pursuit of the thieves, came up and finding the necklace with the Raja seized him and brought him before the Raja. He protested that he had no share in the robbery, but without further enquiry the Raja had both his hands struck off.

In this miserable state the Raja took refuge in the house of an oilman who, when he heard what had befallen him, said :— "I cannot give you charity; but if you will sit on the beam of my mill and drive the ox, I will give you food."

There the Raja remained many days. Meanwhile the Raja of the land was performing the *swayamvara* of his daughter, and the Raja having by chance gone to the assembly, the princess put the garland of victory round his neck. They tried to make her change her mind, but she refused; and they were married, and the Raja, her father, allotted a mansion in which they lived.

This went on for three years, and one day a pair of swans came and sat on a tree, near where the Raja lived. They began talking together and the male said to his mate :—"This is a very virtuous Raja, who has taken upon himself the poverty of another man." His mate asked :—"Is there any medicine by which he may be cured ?" "If he procure a certain root from the jungle, and having powdered it apply it to his hands, they will be restored." The other swan said : "It is impossible for him to get the root, unless you go and fetch it." So the swan fetched the root and the Raja, who knew the speech of birds, heard what they said, and having applied the root, his hands were restored to him.

When his father-in-law heard of his recovery he enquired into his case, and then he gave him a great army and he returned and won his kingdom from the other Raja and lived with his Rani and children many years in happiness.

5

WHICH IS BETTER—WEALTH OR WISDOM ?

Two men were once disputing which was better—wealth or wisdom. They went to the Emperor to decide the case, and he sent them with a letter to the King of Balkh. In the letter it was written— "Hang these men at once." So they were thrown into a dungeon. The advocate of wealth admitted to the other that he could do nothing save their lives. The other said : "Write these words on a piece of paper and I will procure our release." So he demanded an audience with the King, and when he came in the presence, he said : "Does not your Majesty know why we have been sent hither ? The Emperor of Hindustan is your greatest enemy, and his astrologers have foretold that if our corpses are buried in your city it will become a ruin. It is for this reason that he desires to have us executed here." When the King of Balkh heard these words he released them. The advocate of wealth then admitted that wisdom was superior.

6

HOW TO PLEASE EVERYBODY

One day Mahadeva and Parvati were travelling through the world together and Parvati asked her spouse : "How can a man so rule his life as to escape the blame of others ?" "No man" he answered "can pass his life free of blame. If he does good or if he does evil he is blamed." Parvati asked Mahadeva to illustrate this. So he said : "I will mount my ox Nandi and you can follow on foot." Soon they met a party of men on the road who said : "What a knave this old man must be. He rides himself and lets his wife follow on foot."

Then Mahadeva dismounted and made Parvati ride the ox. Soon they met another company who said : "What a fool this old man must be. He lets his wife ride and trudges along on foot himself."

Then Mahadeva mounted the ox and took Parvati behind him. By and by

some men said : "What a brute this old man is to ride with his
wife on this unfortunate ox."

Then Mahadeva led the ox by the halter and both he and
Parvati went on foot. Soon some people said : "What a stupid
old man this is. He pampers his rascally ox and he and his
wife march afoot."

Then Mahadeva said to Parvati : "You see now what an
evil place this world is. Whatever you do you cannot escape
the tongue of censure."

So they left this world and went to their abode in the
Himalayas and were so disgusted that they never visited this
world since.

7

THE CHARITY OF THE
LORD SOLOMON

The Lord Solomon (on whom be peace !) was so renowned for
his charity that no suppliant ever left him unsatisfied. One
day a starving *faqir* came to his Court and Solomon conferred
upon him precious stones and robes and gold. As he was
going away he met a second *faqir* in worse case than his own
and to him he gave the gifts which he had received from
Solomon.

Next day he again went to Solomon who rewarded him as
before, and again as he left the palace he met a starving *faqir*
to whom he gave his gifts. In this way he went five times to
Solomon and received lordly gifts which he immediately gave to
some beggar poorer than himself.

At last when Solomon heard his case he said : "For you it only remains to pray to God for blessing. Man gives not and receives not ; the Lord is the giver and he is the cause of charity."

8

THE OLD MAN'S WISDOM

It happened once that a rich man betrothed his daughter much against his will, and though he was very anxious to break the engagement he was bound by his word. Finally he sent a message to the bridegroom to come with exactly one hundred young men with him when he came to fetch the bride, and that if any of them failed to comply with the conditions imposed, the match should be broken off. The young man selected his companions, but had the wisdom to bring one old man with him concealed in a drum.

When they arrived at the bride's house her father produced a hundred goats and gave one to each of the party, and said that if each man could not eat his goat without leaving any scraps the marriage would not take place. They were all confounded until the bridegroom went and consulted the old man. "You must do this", he said ; "first kill one goat and serve out a little to each of your men; then kill a second goat and act in the same way until all are consumed." In this way the condition was satisfied and he won his bride.

9

THE FRUIT OF CHARITY

The Lord Moses, on whom be peace, was once going into the court of the Almighty, when he met a poor man who said : "Find out what is to be my fate in this life." So Moses asked the Lord Almighty, and he answered : "His fate is to receive seven dirams in this life, of which he has received half already." So when Moses came out from the presence, he gave the poor man three and a half dirams and said : "This is awarded thee by the Lord Almighty."

With the money the poor man bought a cow and he used to give of her milk in charity; so he prospered and his income came to be seven dirams daily. Then the Lord Mosses came to the Almighty and said : "You promised this man seven dirams in his whole life and now he makes seven dirams daily. How is this ?"

"This," said the Lord Almighty, "is the fruit of charity."

10

THE CONTEST OF
GOOD AND EVIL

The two brothers Neki and Badi (Good and Evil) were one day disputing. Neki said : "The result of good is good and evil is evil". Badi denied this, so they agreed to appoint an arbitrator, and whichever of them was defeated was to have his hands and feet cut off. When they had gone some distance they saw a nim tree and Badi said : "Let us refer our case to the tree. Many travellers sit daily beneath its shade, and it must have wide experience." When they referred the case to the nim tree it said : "In my opinion the result of good is evil and of evil good, because every one sits under my shade and they are refreshed ; but when they are going away one says, 'What excellent fire-wood this old tree would make ;' and another says, 'I will come some day soon and cut it down to make a box.' Thus do they return me evil for good."

When Badi heard the judgement of the nim tree, he promptly cut off Neki's hands and feet and left him there. In his agony he rolled himself to a well close by and threw himself in. Now in that well there was a couch and on each of its legs sat a Deo. They used to go out in search of food and meet in the well at midnight. That night, when they met, Neki heard them talking. They were asking each other where they had been and what they had seen. One Deo said : "Brothers ! I have seen to-day a field the clay of which has this virtue, that it can restore the limbs of a cripple." The second said : "I have seen a treasure which is buried in such and such a place. I watch it all night long and leave it during the day when there is no dan-

ger of any one touching it." The third Deo said : "The Raja
of this land is sick unto death. There is no man in the world
who knows that if he were to bring a he-goat from such and
such a village and sacrifice it and pour a drop of the blood on
the Raja he would recover."

Neki heard what the Deos were saying, and soon after a
man came to the well and helped him out and then on promise
of a reward took him on his shoulders to the field of which the
Deo had spoken. When he touched the earth of the field his
limbs were restored whole as before. Then he dug up the
treasure and cured the Raja by means of the goat as the Deo
had said. The Raja was so pleased that he gave him half
his raj. Some time after Badi happened to come to the city
where Neki ruled, and when he saw his prosperity he was
forced to admit that the fruit of good is good and the fruit of
evil is evil.

11

HOW BHAGWAN GAVE A LESSON TO NARAD MUNI

Once upon a time Bhagwan and Narad Muni were walking in
the jungle and came upon a wild pig with twelve young ones.
Narad asked Bhagwan : "Does the pig love all her offspring
equally or not ?" "She loves them all alike," answered Bhagwan.
"Then," objected Narad, "if that is so, you must love all human
beings alike, the just and the unjust". Bhagwan said nothing
and they went on.

Then Bhagwan created a tank and asked Narad to bathe in
it. As Narad was diving under the water Bhagwan turned him
into a lovely woman and he himself took the shape of a Kewat
and sat on the bank. In a short time Narad, in the form of a
woman, came out of the tank and asked Bhagwan who he was.
Bhagwan answered that he was a Kewat, and he asked her if
she would marry him. She agreed, and they settled down in a

village where they lived as husband and wife for a hundred years, and Narad in that time bore to Bhagwan sixty sons.

Then Bhagwan turned himself into a Sannyasi and created another Kewat in his original shape and put him to live with Narad. Next day Bhagwan in the shape of Sannyasi came to beg at Narad's house. Narad offered him some rice which he refused. Then Narad asked : "What then will you take ?" "I want one of your sons," said Bhagwan. Narad answered : "Be off, you scoundrel. I have seen many rogues like you ! Will any one give his son as alms ? You have twenty fingers and toes which you got without any trouble to yourself. Will you give one of them in alms ? And yet you have the impudence to ask for my son." Bhagwan answered : "Why then did you deny that the wild pig loved all her off-spring equally ? If you love all your sons equally, the pig does the same, because she has feelings like your own." Narad was silent through shame, and Bhagwan, having taught him this lesson, transformed her and himself into their original shapes.

12

THE VIRTUE OF FAITH

There once lived a Sannyasi in the jungle and his disciple lived with him. Now the Sannyasi had promised his disciple to teach him a *mantra* by means of which he could do anything he pleased. He served him for twelve years but he was never taught the *mantra* ; at last one day when the holy man was washing, the disciple came and said : "I have served you now for twelve years and you have not taught me the *mantra* as you promised ; kindly teach it to me now."

The saint was wroth at being addressed on such a subject at such a time and said : "*Tanain jana na jaghai jana, na junai jana,*" that is to say, "You paid no heed to my state of ceremonial impurity, nor to place nor time." The disciple did not understand what his master was saying and thought that this was the *mantra* which he had promised to teach him. So he went away quite contended.

One day soon after while the saint and his disciple were sitting, together, a party of men passed by carrying a corpse and when they saw the saint they asked for fire to burn the body. When the disciple heard this he asked them where the corpse was ; they said that it was under yonder tree. He told them to bring it. When the saint heard this he was angry because he feared lest they might ask him to revive the body and if he failed his reputation would suffer. So he told his disciple not to allow the men to approach ; but he paid no attention to his words. When the men brought the body the disciple muttered over it the supposed *mantra* which he believed the saint had given him and the dead man rose immediately. Every one was surprised and none more so than the saint himself. When they had all gone away, after thanking him profusely, he asked his disciple what *mantra* he had used and when he heard it he smiled and said *Vishwas phal dayakum*. "It is faith that gives the fruit."

13

ENTERTAINING
ANGELS
UNAWARES

'Once upon a time Mahadeva and Bhagwan were making a visit
to the world and in the evening they came to the house of a
poor Brahman and asked for shelter.   He asked them to sit
down and as he had nothing wherewith to entertain them, he
sent his son to pledge his *lota*, and with the money thus obtained he supplied them with food. The gods were much pleased
with his devotion and Mahadeva said : "My friend, I wish to
have your son married." The Brahman answered : "O good
guests, I am so poor that I can hardly support myself. How can
I provide for a daughter-in-law ?" Mahadeva did not heed his
words and sent a Brahman and a barber to find a bride for the
son of the Brahman. They arranged the match in the family of
a very rich and respectable man. They returned and informed
Mahadeva that the marriage had been settled and a day fixed for
the ceremony.

On the fixed date the Brahman, accompanied by Mahadeva, and the planets Shukra (Venus) and Sanischara (Saturn) went with the bridegroom to the house of the bride. When her father saw how small their number was, he asked Mahadeva why the marriage procession was so mean. Mahadeva said : "The others are coming behind." And when he looked he saw thousands of men and a splendid equipage approaching. When all was ready, the ceremony was duly performed and the party sat down to the marriage feast. Mahadeva said : "Let these two men, named Shukra and Sanischara, be first fed." The house master took them first inside and they at once devoured all the provisions. The Brahman returned to Mahadeva and said : "There is no more food for the other guests and my honour is lost." Mahadeva said : "Shut the door of your food closet and open it again" ; and when he did so, lo, he found it full of the most delicious food ! So all the guests were fed, and when the bridegroom brought home his bride he found that his poor hut was changed into a palace of gold, with a lovely garden, and gems lay about it like the sand on the river bank. When his neighbours asked the cause of his prosperity, he answered :

"Tulasi ya jag aike sab se miliye dhaya,
Kya janen kehi bhes men Narayan mili jaya ?

"Tulasi says : 'When you come into this world be kind to every one. Who knows in what guise Narayan may appear ' "

14
THE LESSON OF THE SADHU

There was once a Raja whose habit was whenever a Sadhu came to him for alms he used to put to him this question : "Which is better, the life of the house-holder or that of the ascetic ?" If he answered "The ascetic's life is better," he would say : "Then why do you come to the house of a house-holder ?" But if he said, "The life of the house-holder is the better," he would answer : "Then why have you become an ascetic ?" In this way he confounded all the Sadhus who came to him for alms.

After many days a Sadhu came to the Raja. The Raja put the usual questions to him and he said : "First give food and then I will give an answer." When he had eaten, he was again brought before the Raja, who called on him to solve the difficulty. The Sadhu answered : "Maharaj ! You need not seek an answer from me. To-morrow early ride towards the south and go on riding up to noon ; then your question will be answered."

The Raja was so anxious to test the words of the Sadhu that he lay awake all night and longed for the dawn. Then he mounted his horse and rode steadily on towards the south until noon ; but he met no man who could answer his question. When it was noon he angrily turned back thinking that the [Sadhu had deceived him. As he was returning he lost his way and came into a very thick forest. He tied his horse to a tree and sat down and there he remained the whole day and night without food or water. He feared an attack from wild beasts ; so he collected some dry leaves and with his sword and a bit of flint he managed to strike a light and made a fire. Just then a pair of birds came and perched on the tree beneath which the Raja lay. The male bird said to the female : "You see that this man, who is a worthy prince, is dying of hunger. You know that we are all mortal and this body of our's will soon be reduced to ashes and be of no use to any one. If you agree I will throw myself into this fire and this man who is an eater of flesh will be saved." The female replied : "As a virtuous wife I cannot prevent you from doing an act of piety. You can do as seems fit to you." The male bird then threw himself into the fire and was roasted and the Raja ate his flesh. Then the female bird thought within herself : "My husband has devoted his life to perform an act of the greatest piety. I am left a widow and for me life is now unendurable. I had better follow the example of my husband and help to save this man's life." With these words she too threw herself into the fire and was roasted and the Raja ate her flesh.

By this food the Raja's strength revived and he managed to ascend the tree, from the top of which he saw a city which he reached in a few hours. There he saw a number of men assembled round a cauldron by which a woman was sitting. The Raja asked the cause of this assemblage and they said : "This woman has vowed that she will be his who passes through a cauldron of boiling oil for her sake." When the Raja saw her he was enamoured of her beauty and he told her that he was a Raja and that if she would agree to go with him he would keep her in the greatest comfort. But she said : "I care not whether you are prince or peasant, I will go only with that man who passes through the ordeal for my sake." The Raja feared to undergo the terrible test ; but he was so fascinated that he could not leave the place. Meanwhile a Sadhu appeared and when he heard the conditions he at once plunged into the cauldron and passed through. The woman immediately started with him.

As the Sadhu was taking her away with him, the Raja followed him. The Sadhu asked him why he did so. The Raja replied : "I am a Raja ; you are a Sadhu ; what use have you for this woman ? Give her to me." The Sadhu asked the woman if she was ready to go with him." She answered : "I am your property , you can dispose of me as you please." The Sadhu gave the woman to the Raja and he took her home with him.

When he returned he sent for the Sadhu to whom he had originally propounded the question and called on him for the answer. Then the Sadhu made him describe all that had happened to him. Then the Sadhu said : "The pair of birds which gave their lives for you represent the house-holders among men and the Sadhu, who gave you this woman, notwithstanding all she had cost him, was an ascetic of the highest type. If a house-holder is charitable as these birds were, he need not covet the life of the ascetic ; and the true ascetic is as free from covetousness as was that man. If all house-holders and ascetics are like these examples they are both equal." The Raja was satisfied and laid his forehead at the feet of the Sadhu. The Sadhu dismissed him with a blessing.

15

THE WORTH OF
LEARNING

There was once a raja who had a son, and when he was growing up he consulted his wazir as to what he should be taught. So the wazir selected a pandit, who trained the boy in all kinds of wisdom. One day the boy went to the shop of a greengrocer and said : "Take some of my learning and give me some fruits and radishes in exchange". But the greengrocer answered : "What do I want of your learning ? Bring me pice and you can buy what I have in my shop."

The boy went home and told the raja of this, and said : "What then is the use of wisdom ?" His father gave him a handful of pearls and said : "Take these to the greengrocer."

When the boy took them to the greengrocer he said : "What use are these worthless stones to me ?"

The boy came back and told the raja what he had said. His father said : "Take them to the jeweller and see what he says."

When the jeweller saw the pearls he readily exchanged them for a large sum of money. Then the raja said : "You see by this that those who are ignorant have no sense of the value of wisdom."

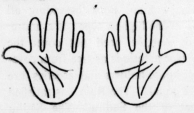

16

FATE IS MIGHTIER
THAN WISDOM

Once upon a time Fate and Wisdom (Vidya and Bidhata) had a dispute as to which was the greater. So they agreed each to enter a man and test their powers. Both men attended the court of a Raja. Wisdom's man sat at a distance and the representative of Fate went close to the royal cushion. The moment he sat down he made a blow at the Raja's turban and knocked it off. The courtiers rushed and seized him, but immediately a venomous snake came out of the turban and was killed by the attendants. The Raja thanked his deliverer and sat down, when the man caught him by the legs and dragged him into the court-yard ; the courtiers again seized him, but all of a sudden the roof of the council chamber fell in and the Raja barely escaped with his life, so Wisdom had to admit that Fate was greater than he.

17

JAI KO BURHO, TAI KO KURHO—THE COUNSEL OF THE OLD IS BEST

With this proverb is told a story of a man who promised to marry his daughter to a young man, provided he brought no old man in his marriage procession, but should be accompanied by one hundred young men who should perform any condition he imposed. This was agreed on, but one old man was brought in the marriage drum. When they arrived at the girl's house her father made it a condition of the marriage that if they should eat a goat, a ser of *ghi* and half a ser of rice the marriage might proceed. In their perplexity they consulted the old man, and he advised them to eat each a little and spit out the rest unobserved. They [did so, and fooled the girl's father, and got the girl married.

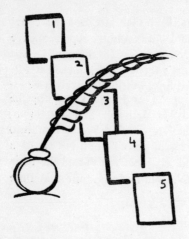

18

THE NAWAB AND THE
BRAHMAN BEGGAR

There was once upon a time a poor Brahman who made his living by begging. One day his wife said to him :

"The children are starving and you must make money somehow. What you make to-morrow we will spend in pens, paper and ink."

Next day the Brahman bought these things and handed them to his wife, who wrote five sayings— "The father of a worthy son :" "The mother of an undutiful son :" "A Brahman in prosperity :" "A friend in poverty :" "He who lies awake, gains ; he who sleeps, loses."

She gave this paper over to her husband, and said :

"Take it to the market-place and sell it for two lakhs of rupees."

The Brahman hawked it all over the place and could get no one to buy it. At last the Nawab of the place came out for an airing and asking the price of the paper, was told "two lakhs of rupees." He bought it at once and ordered his treasurer to pay the price.

The Nawab determined to put these principles to a test; he showed the paper to his father, who said : "What a fool you are ! you had better leave the house." Having tested the first precept he went to his Mother ; she said :

"If your father has given such an order there is no help for it. But here is a jewel worth nine lakhs of rupees. Take this with you in case you want money."

Having tried two precepts, he went to the town where his sister was married. He sent a message to her by her maid-servant. His sister enquired how many attendants were with him and when she heard that he had come on foot alone and in poverty she said :

" He can put up with the potter. When I have time I will see him."

In the evening she sent for him and scolded him.

"Why did you come in this miserable state. You have disgraced me before my neighbours. Go away at once."

Thus three precepts were tested. Then he came to a village where lived a friend of his. When he heard of the Nawab's approach he hastended to meet his friend and gave him food and a change of raiment. He pressed him to stay so eagerly, that at last he had to go away by stealth. He then came to his father-in-law's house, where his wife was still with her father. There he passed himself off as a faqir and sat before a fire close by.

One day he saw a horseman with a number of attendants riding by, and he asked some one who this was.

"This is Chief Constable of the city, and he is in love with the daughter of the man who lives opposite."

The Nawab was stunned at this news, and, when he saw the Chief Constable making his second visit he attracted his attention, and was sent by him to bring a pice worth of betel from the bazar. He arranged the leaves into packets, and in one packet he put his ring and placed that packet below all the others. His wife found the ring with the name of her husband on it, and in her anger she wrote to the Chief Constable to have her husband put to death. He was delivered to the executioners, who were ordered to put out his eyes.

As they were about to kill him, he said : "Take this jewel which is worth nine lakhs of rupees and spare my life."

The executioners took this jewel and liberated him, and having killed a deer took its eyes to the Chief Constable and pretended that they were the eyes of the Nawab. He sent them to his paramour.

Next day the Nawab came to the city of Jhunjhanapur, which was ruled by a Princess. It was her custom that whoever first passed by her palace in the morning was allowed to sit on the throne that day and share her couch at night. But whoever did so always died, and his body used to be thrown next morning into the river. By chance the Nawab was the first man to pass the palace and was selected. He ruled for one day and at night went to the room of the Princess. He kept walking about to prevent himself from falling asleep, and at midnight he saw two female snakes come out of her nostrils and creep about on the couch where they used to find their victim. He drew his dagger and slew them, and covering them with a piece of cloth placed them under the couch. He lay awake all night through fear, and in the morning when the Princess woke and found him alive, she was astonished, and asked how his life had been spared.

When the news spread, all the people praised his bravery, and he was married to the Princess and ruled the kingdom.

He then started for home, and was suitably entertained at the house of his father-in-law and sister : and when he convinced his father of the truth of the Brahman's precepts, he ordered that they should be painted on the wall of his chamber as a perpetual memorial.

19

THE BRAHMAN'S RIDDLE

There was once a Brahman who was very poor, but who had a very clever wife. One day she said to him :

"We must really do some thing to live. I hear that Raja Bhoj gives a lakh of rupees for a good Sanskrit verse. Why don't you compose one ?"

"But I can't," he answered. "Well," said his wife, "I will write one, and if he asks for the interpretation, let him come to me for it."

And this was the riddle she made—

"It has no legs, yet it walks.

It terrifies the world.

It is fair-complexioned and dark.

It always rests on the earth."

The Brahman took this to the court of Raja Bhoj and made it over to a gate-keeper. He determined to appropriate it himself, but he had to go away and handed it to his companion, who gave it to a third. So when the riddle was read there were four claimants, and all four were asked for their interpretation.

The first gate-keeper said :

"The meaning is a snake. It has no legs, but it walks. It frightens the world. It is black above and white beneath. It always rests on the ground."

The second said :

"It is the cloud. It has no legs, but it moves. It roars with the tempest. It is white and it is black. It feeds on the mountains as the sheep pasture."

The third said :

"It is the water which moves, though it has no feet : roars in the torrent : is white and black, and rests upon the earth."

At last the Brahman was asked :

"Your Majesty must go to my wife for the answer," he replied.

So the Raja went to the Brahmini.

"The answer is my poverty," she answered.

"It has no legs, yet it has come to me. My clothes were once white ; now they are black. It is fearful, because it drives away my friends : and it ever lives on earth."

The Raja was pleased and gave her a present double that he conferred on the other interpreters.

20

THE WISE PANDIT

There was once a Raja who was blessed with a son in his old age, and when the boy grew up his father appointed the most learned Pandits to instruct him ; but in vain, because the boy took to disorderly courses and spent all his time flying kites and pigeons and other disreputable amusements. At last the Raja promised a large reward to any Pandit who would reform his son. One day a Pandit passed through the city and seeing the notice agreed to attempt the task. So he bought a lot of pigeons and used to spend the whole day flying them. At last the prince struck up an acquaintance with him one day he said : "Panditji tell me a story." The Pandit said :—"The words of the elders should be obeyed as you will learn from the following tale :— There were once seventy pigeons who lived on a tree and one of them was their *guru*. One day a fowler came to the foot of the tree, scattered some grain there and laid a snare. The pigeons were about to fly down and pick up the grain when the *guru* warned them ; but they would not mind his words and when they flew down the fowler drew the string and they were all caught in the net. When they were caught they implored the *guru* to save them and at last he said : 'My advice is this. The net weighs only a quarter *ser* of thread, you had better all rise at once and fly away with it to an island beyond the ocean.' "

So the pigeons flew away with the net and where they alighted was the hole of a rat. So they implored the rat to cut the net with his teeth and when he had done so all the pigeons were released. Thus you may learn to obey the advice of the experienced.

Again the Pandit related another tale :—"In a jungle lived many elephants and one of them was their *guru*. One day he saw two chameleons fighting on a tree and he said to the other elephants : 'Brethren, fighting has commenced here and we would do well to leave this forest !' But one said : 'Why should we leave this excellent forest for fear of these small creatures ?' So they stayed there and as the chameleons were fighting one of them was defeated and ran for shelter into the trunk of one of the elephants to whom he caused excruciating pain. The elephant in terror went to the *guru* and implored his protection. At last the *guru* said : 'Go into yonder deep tank and draw up a quantity of water with your trunk. Then discharge it violently and you will get rid of the chameleon.' He did so and got relief. By this you should learn to obey the advice of the wise."

When the boy again asked the Pandit for a story he put him off on pretence that he was too much occupied with his pigeons. The boy was angry at this and sold all the pigeons he possessed and finally induced the Pandit to do the same. Thus, by the cleverness of the Pandit he was induced to give up his evil companion, and devote himself to the acquisition of wisdom.

21

THE BRAHMAN'S LUCK

There was once a Brahman
who lived in a forest; his wants
were small and as he possessed
all the desired he was quite
happy. One day the Raja went
into the forest to hunt and
being hungry he halted at the
house of the Brahman, who
entertained him with fruits and
water. As he was going away
the Raja wrote down his name
and said : "If you are ever in
want and it is in my power to
relieve you, I shall gladly do
so."

Time passed and the Brah-
man became so poor that he
had nothing left but his *lota*.
At last his wife asked him why
he did not go to the Raja who
had promised to help him in
his need. The Brahman answered : "I do not wish to come
as a supplicant to a man whom
I once obliged." But his wife
told him of many great men who had gone to Rajas in their hour
of need, and at last the Brahman went to the Raja's palace and
craved an audience. The Raja received him with honour and
seated him beside him. When he learnt his case, he loaded a
cart with money and goods and gave it to the Brahman to take

home to his wife. As he was driving home with the cart, he halted at a tank to bathe and left the cart and bullocks on the bank. When he had done bathing and returned, he found that they had disappeared. He went home to his wife lamenting his bad luck, and as his troubles increased, his wife induced him to go to the Raja a second time. The Raja was as kind as before and this time gave him a horse laden with gold. As he was going home he came to the same tank as before and went to bathe. When he came out of the water the horse and money were nowhere to be seen.

His wife forced him to go to the Raja a third time, very much against his will. The Raja said : "My friend, these are your evil days. I will now give you four thousand rupees and you can trade with them." The Brahman started a business with the money and at the end of a year he had made a profit of one pice. When, he told the Raja, he laughed, and said : "Now your luck is changing. Trade with this one pice and see what is the result " He put the pice into his business and made two pice, and so he by degrees made a large fortune. Then he started for his home and on his way he came to the same tank and there he found his cart and horse and all his money safe. Thus his bad luck left him and he lived for many years in great prosperity.

22

THE GREEDY BRAHMAN

There was once a Brahman who was so greedy that whenever he was going out to a dinner at the house of one of his clients

he used to tell his wife to make his bed ready and when he
came home surfeited he used to throw himself upon it and lie
there for a couple of days till he worked off his indigestion.
One day as he was going off to a dinner he did not as usual
give his wife instructions about his bed and she began to laugh.
When he noticed this he asked her why she was laughing.
She said that she was laughing because he had given no orders
about his bed. "To-day," said he, "I am going to have an
extra good dinner and in any case I shall have to be brought
home on a bed, so there is no need of arranging one for me."

He went to the dinner and there he ate so many sweetmeats
that he became senseless and the people seeing him in this condition put him on a bed and brought him home to his wife. When
she saw him, she went off to the grocer and brought two seeds
of the myrobalan (*harra*) and asked her husband to take them.
"What a fool you must think me," said he. "If I had room
for two myrobalan seeds don't you think I would not have
eaten two more sweetmeats ?" And with that he died and no
one lamented him.

23

THE BRAHMAN'S SONS
AND THE GUSAIN

Once upon a time there was a Brahman who had a wife and two
sons. When the Brahman went to beg, it was so with him that
whether he begged for an hour or for the whole day, he never
got more than a small basket of grain. So one day he consulted
his wife and said :—"We are both starving. We had better make

over our boys to some one to teach. When they are able to write and read, we will take one and leave the other with their teacher." This was agreed on, and the Brahman went out to beg and got his basket of grain which he brought home and told his wife to cook at once, and give him the boys to dispose of. So he went off a long way with the children until night fell. Then they rested and ate their supper and went on again. At last they came to a forest, where they saw a Gusain sitting in his hut. The Gusain said :—"Maharaj ! where are you going ?" The Brahman told him of his difficulties. Then the Gusain said :—"Well ! give me the boys. I will teach them. When they are educated you can have one and I will keep the other." The Brahman agreed, and made over the children to him. Then the Gusain taught the elder boy carefully, but gave him very little food, while he taught nothing to the younger boy, but fed and clothed him well, and used to take him about. His object was that the elder should remain thin, and when the time came for his father to select a boy he would chose the younger, and leave him the elder who was well versed in magic.

Meanwhile, when he came home after leaving the boys, the Brahman attended a funeral of a rich man and got a cow as a gift. This cow had a calf, and the Brahman and his wife lived well on milk and cream. After four years had gone his wife said :—"The boys must be educated by this time. You had better go and fetch one of them." He agreed, and told his wife to prepare some curds and milk to take with him for the boys. She did so, and he started next morning. When he reached the forest he saw his elder boy up a tree breaking wood, a piece of which fell in the curds. He called out, and the boy recognizing his father, said :—"O father ! I am dying. The Gusain gives me only half enough to eat." His father hearing this wept, and gave him the curds. When the boy had eaten it he told his father how the Gusain had fattened up the younger boy. "If you choose him," said he, "six months will finish you off in supporting him. But if you take me I will support you all your life." Then the father said :—"All right ! I will choose you." So the son said :—"You better stay here. If we come together the Gusain will kill us both." The father stayed behind and the son went back. In the evening the Brahman went to the Gusain,s hut, who received him kindly, and made him sleep near him for the night. In the morning the Brahman said :—"I am going to take one of the boys." Then the Gusain made both of them stand before him and said :—"Take whichever you like." Then the Brahman took his elder son by the hand, and the Gusain said :—"You are wrong. This boy will cause you trouble and expense. You had better take the younger : at any rate you can live on the jewelry he is wearing for a whole year." But the Brahman said :—"His mother told me to bring the elder boy." "All right," said the Gusain, "but you will live to repent what you are doing." So the two went off together, and at last the boy said to his father :—"You must be tired. Look behind you." When he looked round he saw that his son was turned into a horse, which said :—"Mount on my back, and ride me into the town and sell me. Go away then, and when I get the chance I will turn into a man and come to you." So the father sold him for Rs. 100 and went away. When his owner tied him up and left him, the boy immediately took his former shape and came back to his father and said :—"It was well you took me, or you would not have made this money so easily." But as he looked round he saw the Gusain, and warned his father to go home, and said :—"I am off, and will bring my brother with me. If I don't go you will never see my face again." So he turned round, and, seeing a tank there, turned himself into a fish and went into the water. When the Gusain came up and saw the father alone he opened his book of spells to find out what had become of the boy. He discovered that he was in the tank in the form of a fish. So he turned himself into paddy-bird (*bagula*) and began to devour all the fish in the tank. Meanwhile an oilman brought his ox to water at the tank; and the Brahman's boy at once went into the stomach of the ox. When the Gusain had finished off all the fish in the tank and could not find the boy, he looked in his book again and found that he was in the stomach of the ox. Then he hastened to the oilman's house and offered him any price he liked for the animal. At first the oil-man declined to sell the ox, but finally the Gusain so worried him that he sold it. Then the Gusain carried it off and killed it, and began to cut it in pieces and separate the bones. But the boy made the bone in which he was concealed jump away, and

a kite seized it and carried it to the river bank where the Rani
was bathing. The kite dropped the bone on her clothes, and she
called to her servants to pitch it away. But the boy from within
the bone implored her to save his life. So the Rani took the
bone and shut it up in her box. Meanwhile the Gusain worked
his spells again, and traced the boy to the Rani's box. Then he
went to the Raja and said :—"Your Rani has stolen my bone."
The Raja was fiercely angry and struck the Gusain, but he
said :—"Beat me as much as you please, but I won't leave this."
Then the Raja asked his Rani about it. The Rani said :—"It is
not a bone at all, but a Brahman's son," and told the Raja the
whole story. Then the Raja said :—"It is a bad business. The
bone must be given up to the Gusain." "At any rate," urged
the boy, "if you must give me up, sprinkle a little sesamum
(*sarson*) about the place. But please break the bone first." Then
the Rani did, and immediately the Gusain turned himself into a
pigeon and began to eat up the sesamum. But the Brahman's
boy became a cat and ate up the Gusain. Then he went off to
the hut, recovered his brother, seized all the Gusain's treasure,
and the two boys lived happily with their father ever after.

24

THE BRAHMAN AND
MOTHER GANGES

There was once a poor Brahman who lived by begging, and all
the alms he got in a day would hardly fill a lamp saucer. One

day as he was going about begging, he came to the door of a Chamar (currier).

The Chamar seeing him, said :—"Maharaj ! What has brought you here ?"

"I am starving," said the Brahman, "give me alms."

"If you will take an invitation for me I will pay you handsomely," said the Chamar.

The Brahman agreed, and the Chamar gave him a betel-nut, and said :—"Take this and present it to Mother Ganges."

The Brahman went to Ganga Mai and gave her the betel-nut which she accepted and said :—"Tell the Chamar that I will come at the appointed time, and here ! take this bracelet of gold, and give it to the Chamar, telling him that Ganga Mai has sent it as a present for his wife."

The Brahman took the bracelet, and after saluting Ganga Mai, went back. On the road he was overcome by covetousness, and instead of giving the bracelet to the Chamar, he hid it in his loin cloth and merely said :—"Ganga Mai accepts your invitation. Now give me the present you promised."

The Chamar told his wife to give the Brahman a ration (*sidha*) of five *sers* of grain.

The Brahman went home, well pleased at his good luck. His wife, too, was delighted, and gave him an excellent dinner. Then he made a plan and thought he would give the bracelet to the Raja, who would be sure to reward him handsomely. So he went to the Raja, and after giving him his blessing (*asirbad*), asked for alms. The Raja rose from his seat and asked the Brahman to sit down.

The Brahman said :—"Maharaj ! I have been supported by you for many years. So I have brought you a present which I got from a charitable client (*jajman*) of mine."

The Raja was much pleased, and took the bracelet into the inner room to the Rani. She was very much delighted, and said to the Raja :—"It is very nice indeed, but I must have a pair to it."

The Raja thought to himself that if he rewarded the Brahman he would never bring the second bracelet; so he said to the Brahman :—"Go and bring a pair to this and I will give you a reward."

The Brahman went home very sorrowful, and at last told the whole story to his wife. She comforted him.

"Don't fret yourself. She who gave you one bracelet will give you another, if you ask her."

The Brahman returned to the Chamar, and with great penitence told him what had happened. The Chamar said :—"You had better take my invitation again. But whatever Ganga Mai says to you, you must tell me."

The Brahman went to Ganga Mai and gave her the Chamar's invitation. She accepted it, and said to the Brahman :—"Go and pour a *ser*-and-a-quarter of *ghi* on the ground in my name."

The Brahman promised to do so, and when he came to his house, told his wife that Ganga Mai had ordered her to pour a *ser*-and-a-quarter of water on the ground in her honour.

The Brahmani replied :—"Bad luck to you and Mother Ganges ! You have spent the day wandering about and brought nothing home, and now you are telling me to pour water on the ground in the name of Ganga Mai ! Why should I pour water on the ground which I have been toiling all day to drag from the well ?"

The Brahman returned to the Chamar and told him what Ganga Mai had said. When she heard the message, the Chamar's wife bathed, put on clean clothes, and poured five jars of *ghi* on the ground in the name of Mother Ganges.

Then the Brahman said to the Chamar :—"Brother ! my life is at stake. Give me a bracelet. If you refuse the Raja will have me hanged."

"I have no bracelet to give you," answered the Chamar. "When Ganga Mai gave you a bracelet you never showed it to me."

The Brahman was plunged in grief, and sat at the Chamar's door, saying he would die there.

At last, after a couple of days had passed in this way, the Chamar said :—"Come aside and I will tell you something."

The Chamar took him behind his house and said :—"You are a rogue, and your wife is such a fool that she cannot spare even a pot of water for the gods and goddesses. How can you

expect ever to become rich ? I and my wife are charitable, and
see how we prosper. Take a lesson from us."

Then the Chamar took a wooden kneading dish (*kathwat*),
filled it with water, and put it at his door, and told the Brahman to say :—"When the heart is pure even the Ganges comes
into a platter."

The Brahman repeated this verse and then put his hand into
the water and pulled out a pair of the golden bracelet. He took
it to the Raja, who gave him five villages and much wealth,
and the Brahman changed his manner of life and lived happily
ever after.

May Paramesar change us as he changed him !

25

THE TIGER, THE
BRAHMAN, AND THE
COVETOUS GOLDSMITH

There was once upon a time a poor Brahman who used to
get his living by begging. One day in his wanderings he came
to a stream in the jungle near which a tiger had his den, and it
was guarded in turns by his four servants—the swan, the parrot,
the jackal, and the crow. On that day the swan and parrot
happened to be on duty. When they saw the Brahman approach
they called out—

"Miserable Brahman! make your escape while you can. If the tiger knows you have come he will surely devour you."

"I throw myself on your protection," said the Brahman. "You can eat me or spare me as you will."

The swan and parrot, pitying him, went to the tiger and said :—

"Master! a beggar Brahman is standing outside. What is thy pleasure regarding him ?"

The tiger answered :—"If he is really hungry, you can open my treasure-house and let him have as much as he pleases."

The Brahman was taken into the treasure-chamber, where he loaded himself with as much wealth as he could carry. He took it home, thanking Bhagwan for his mercy, and lived in prosperity for a long time.

He had a friend, a jeweller, who went to him one day and said :—"Panditji! as we are friends let me have a share in your good luck."

The Brahman agreed and offered to take the goldsmith with him when he next paid the tiger a visit.

They started, though the Brahman's wife advised her husband not to go. By ill-luck the jackal and the crow were on guard that day. When they saw the pair approaching they said one to the other :—"Let us tell the tiger and he will kill these people, and then we can have a good feed."

Meanwhile the tiger called out to the Brahman—

"The parrot has gone to the forest of Nanda,

The swan to Mana Sarowar lake :

The crow and jackal are my ministers.

For you the times are evil."

The goldsmith asked the Brahman what this warning of the tiger meant.

The Brahman replied :—"The times are changed and the guards are different. Escape at once if you value your life."

The goldsmith said :—"You can run away if you please. I will steal in through the back of the den and get hold of some of the treasure."

The Brahman went away and the goldsmith crept into the back of the den.   But the jackal and the crow saw him, and informed the tiger who jumped out and killed him.   The Brahman returned home, and that was the last visit he paid to the tiger.

26

THE TALE OF THE
FOUR FOOLISH
PANDITS

There were four Pandits in a village.   One was a physician, the second a grammarian, the third a logician, and the fourth an astronomer.   The four went to seek employment at the Court of a Raja.   When they arrived to his capital, they thought it wise to eat their dinner before they attended on the Raja.   They decided to make arrangements for their food, and said to the grammarian : "If you will act as cook, your knowledge of grammar will come of use."

As the physician was skilled in botany, he was asked to purchase the vegetables.

To the logician was entrusted the purchase of the *ghi*, as his skill in argument would aid him in making a good bargain.

The astronomer was asked to select an auspicious time for the meal.

All four accepted the tasks assigned them, and set about doing them.

When the rice began to boil, a sound came out of the pot like *bhad-bhad*.

The grammarian called out "This is not the correct word. It should be *bad-bad.*" So he threw a handful of dust into the pot.

The physician said : "I do not like the vegetables in the market. But there is nothing so good for a man as *nim* leaves." So he bought a lot of them.

The logician purchased some *ghi* in a leaf saucer, and as he was going home he began to think : "Does the *ghi* protect the saucer, or the saucer the *ghi* ?"

To remove his doubts he upset the saucer and spilt the *ghi.* So, regretting his folly, he came back empty handed.

The astronomer by his calculations found that the only lucky time for eating was midnight. At midnight the four Pandits sat down to dinner, and finding the food spoilt had to go to bed hungry.

Then the astronomer said :—"This is the only lucky hour to call on the Raja."

They went to the palace, and finding the gates closed made their way in through a drain. By this they dirtied their clothes, so they determined to have a bath. They could find no water, and one said : "The Raja's wife is as pure as mother Ganges. Let us touch her and we shall be cleansed." So they went into the room where the Rani was asleep with the Raja. The four of them jumped on her, and her screams woke her husband. He had them put under guard. Next morning he heard them, and finding that they were only fools, laughed and dismissed them with a present.

They hired a bullock cart to take home what they had got. On the way the cart began to creak, and the physician said : "I am sure that the wheels are sick." So he felt the axle-box, and finding it hot, said : "This is in strong fever. I must cauterise it."

He applied a hot iron, and the cart and its contents were burnt to ashes. The Raja heard of this, and admiring the skill of the physician, gave them more presents and sent the four fools home in charge of his servants.

27

THE GOLDEN-HAIRED
RANI AND THE JOGI

There was a king who had seven sons. When he died and his eldest son succeeded him, the seven brothers determined to marry, but the wife of the youngest was the loveliest of all and her hair was of gold. One day she was sitting on the house-top, drying her hair, when a Jogi passed by and sat down below. When he began to beg the king told his servant to give the Jogi some alms, but he refused to take alms from the hands of the servant. Then he asked the Jogi :—"From whose hand will you take alms ?" He replied :—"Let all who are in the king's house come, and I will take the alms from whom-ever I select." The king was informed of this, and in his anger said :—"Turn him out." But the Jogi said :—"You may kill me, but I won't go." The king at last asked his youngest brother to give the alms, but he would not take it from him ; and the same was the case with all the brothers. Then the king and his wife and the wives of all the brothers, except the youngest, went, and they too all failed. At last the Jogi said that if she with the golden hair came he would take alms from her hand. But the king said :—"She cannot come," and again gave orders to drive away the Jogi. But the Jogi would not stir. Finally, the servants proposed that a cloth should be hung up and the youngest Rani be asked to pass out the alms from behind it. Still the Jogi would not agree. At last the golden-haired Rani came, and the moment the Jogi saw her,

he pronounced a spell (*mantra*) that she was turned into a
bitch and began to run after the Jogi. Then the Raja seized
her and tied her with a golden chain, but the Jogi turned her at
once into a horseman (sawar), and took her home, when she
became a woman again. Now this Jogi by his spells had
killed all the people of the land in which he dwelt, and the only
persons who survived were two, who equalled the Jogi in their
knowledge of magic—a Brahman and an old woman—the latter
of whom lived in the Jogi's house. The Jogi was a great
gambler, and he and the Brahman used to play. Whenever
Jogi went to gamble he used to cut off the Rani's head and
hang it by a rope to the roof, while he put her body to sleep
on a couch. When he came back he used to fix her together
with a stick, and then she came to life again. Some time after
the Raja and his brothers determined to go and recover the
little Rani. So with great difficulty they reached the Jogi's
house where the old woman met them. They told her the
whole story, and asked her to show them the little Rani. She
said :—"This is the Jogi's dinner hour. Wait till he goes, and
I will do what I can." So she turned them into flies and hid
them in the house. When the Jogi returned, he said :—"I
smell a man, I smell a man." The old woman said :—"What
a fool you are ! There is not even a man's shadow here." So
the Jogi was pacified and ate his dinner. So when he went
away the old woman turned the king and his brothers into men
again, and taking the stick ordered the Rani's head to descend
and join her body. She came to life again. Then they put her
into a carriage and took her home. By ill luck the Jogi
saw them departing, so he asked the Brahman for a grain of
sesamum (*sarson*), and with it blew a spell upon them, so they
all had to come back to the Jogi's house, and then he killed
them all except the little Rani, to whom he gave a sound
beating.

Now one of the seven wives had borne a son, and when he
was grown up and playing with the other boys, he used to speak
of his father and his uncles. But the boys laughed at him and
said :—Where have you a father or uncles ?" So he was distressed and asked his mother, and she told him the whole story.
Then though all his friends warned him, yet he determined to

go and rescue them. So he rode off to the Jogi's house, and
there the same old woman met him. She asked his business,
he enquired :—"Have not my aunt and my uncles come
here ?" So she told him that the Jogi had killed all his
uncles, but that his aunt was living. He said :—"Show me
my aunt, for I want to take her home." She said :—"I will
show her to you, but take her home you cannot." So she
showed him the head and body of his aunt, and gave him the
magic stick with which he restored her to life. She asked :—
"Who are you ?" He answered :—"I am your nephew, and
I was born after the Jogi carried you off. Now you must come
with me." She said :—"This is impossible. Why are you risk-
ing your life ?" The boy answered :—"Whatever happens I
must do it. But when the Jogi comes you must find out from
him in what his life remains." So he cut off her head again
and hung it up and went and hid himself. So when the Jogi
returned the Rani asked him where his life was. First he said
it was in the fire, but she would not believe this, and so he
tried to deceive her many times. At last he told her :—"Beyond the seven oceans is a forest watched by a tiger and tigress
and a guard of nine hundred witches. In the midst is a sandal
tree, on which hangs a golden cage containing a diamond
parrot. In this is my life." When the boy heard this from
his aunt he started at once, and with great difficulty crossed
the seven oceans. The moment he came into the forest the
tiger rushed at him, to whom the boy said :—"Good morning,
uncle !" (*mamu salam.*) Then the tiger said :—"You have been
twelve years coming, but still you are my brother :" so he
spared him, and conducted the boy as far as his jurisdiction
reached. When he got so far the tigress charged him, but she
also spared him and conducted him to her borders. When he
reached the witches' border they called out :—"We will eat
human flesh to-day." But when he approached he bowed to
each and said :—"Good morning, aunt." Then all said :—
"Why, this is our nephew !" Then he told them that the Jogi
had sent him for the diamond parrot. So they gave him the
parrot, and when he returned he came to the Jogi's house and
called out—"Jogi ! buy the parrot ?" When the Jogi saw the
bird, he saw at once that this contained his life. So he rushed

down to seize the bird, but as he was coming down the staircase the boy broke one of the parrot's legs, and immediately one of the Jogi's legs broke too. But be continued to run on one leg, so the boy broke the other leg of the parrot. Then the second leg of the Jogi broke, and he fell on the ground imploring the boy to spare him. Then the boy said :—"You have killed my father and uncles. You must bring them to life." So the Jogi did so. Then he said :—"You must restore to life all the people of the land." This too the Jogi did. Then the boy crushed the parrot to death, and as it died the Jogi died too. Then he took the magic stick and revived his aunt, the golden-haired Rani. So they all went home and lived happily ever after.

28

THE WICKED QUEEN AND HER STEP-CHILDREN

A certain king had a son and a daughter, and when he married a second time their step-mother was displeased with them and induced their father to get rid of them. So he called the snake-catchers and told them to catch the smallest snake they could find. They brought a very little snake and this the king had put in the water goblet used by the children. When they returned from school the girl went to get a drink and soon after returned to her brother and said : "As I was drinking something went into my stomach." He said "nonsense ! You drank too fast and so thought that something had gone down your throat."

So the children left home in grief, and wandering on they knew not where, came to a great jungle and there saw a great house, the door of which was shut.   There they sat weeping. Now in front of the house a cow was tied and she took pity on the children and prayed to God (*khuda*) "O God ! Give me only the power to speak and I will comfort them." So God heard her prayer and gave her the power of speech. The cow asked "why are fyou weeping ?"   The children told her who they were and how they had been driven from home.   The cow said :—"I will open this house for you, stay here. Give me a little grass now and then and I will supply you with as much milk as you want." So the cow opened the house and then she lost the power of speech.   The children slept in the house and in the morning milked the cow : they drank some and put the rest on the fire to boil.   Then the boy said :—"Sister ! I am going out to get grass for the cow and search for some fruits in the jungle." So he went out leaving his sister alone, and she lay down to sleep. Then the snake came out of her stomach and drank all the milk, and then went down her throat again. When the boy returned he woke his sister and said :—"Bring the milk, I am hungry." She said :—"I am hungry too," but when she went to look what did she see ? that all the milk was gone. She told her brother and they had to fast till evening. In the evening they milked the cow and made their supper on milk and some fruits which the boy had brought. The rest of the milk they put in the fire to boil and when the girl went to sleep, the snake came again out of the stomach and drank the milk.

So it went on for many days. At last the boy thought "I will sit up and catch the thief who steals our milk." So he watched and saw the snake come out of his sister's throat, drink the milk and go back again. Next night he armed himself with a club and sat up again. When the snake came out the boy struck it with a stick and killed it. Then he took the dead snake and threw it into a pit, and went to cut grass for the cow.

When his sister got up and saw that the milk was safe she told her brother. He said :—"I killed the thief to-day." She asked—"What thief." "A snake" he answered "used to come out of your mouth and drink the milk." "I told you" she said, "the day we left home that something went down my throat." "This must be the same snake," he said. After that the milk was not stolen. One day the girl said :—"I am very lonely while you are away. Take me with you." He agreed. So they went out together to cut grass for the cow, and as they were returning the girl happened to look into the pit into which the boy had thrown the snake. But the snake had turned into a tree on which a beautiful flower was growing. When the girl saw the flower, she said to her brother, "Pull it for me." When he saw the flower he suspected that it was the snake, and thought that if he plucked it injury might result. So he began to make excuses to his sister. At last as she insisted he had to give her the flower. She was very tired and said :—"Brother I am very tired." So he took her on his back, and as they went on she said to him :— "If I put this flower in your turban you will look so handsome." She then put the flower in his turban and he was immediately turned into a snake. As he was crawling away his sister kept calling out "Oh my brother ! O my brother !" but he paid no attention to her, and at last they came to a river into which the snake jumped. His sister sat on the bank weeping until in three days she became dumb from dint of crying.

At last on the third day a king's son came up to the place, and saw the girl sitting there weeping. He asked her the cause of her distress, and she signed with her hand that her brother had been turned into a snake and had jumped into the river. But he could not understand what she meant, and pitying her took her home and said to his mother :—"This seems to be the daughter of some nobleman (*amir*) because though she is dumb she is very beautiful." At last he fell so much in love with her that he married her. On their marriage day her tongue was loosed, and she told how she was the daughter of a king and detailed the whole story and how her brother had become a snake and jumped into the river. Then the king of the land had many large earthen vessels (*nand*) sunk in the ground and filled with milk and made proclamation to the snake-catchers that whoever should seize the snake which the girl pointed out, would receive a great reward.

The first day many snakes came out of the river to drink the milk, but her brother was not among them. She looked at all the snakes and said :—"My brother is not here." Next day the King had the vessels again filled with milk and many snakes appeared, but even then her brother did not appear. On the fourth day, however, her brother came out of the river and the moment she saw him she cried out :—"This is my brother." At once the snake-catchers trapped him and lo ! the snake had a long loch (*chonti*) on his head. The moment the snake-catchers pulled this out he turned into a man again, and embraced his sister.

The king asked him :—"How far is your home from here ?" The young man replied :—"a week's journey." So the king took the brother and sister with him to their home. When the young man saw his father he said :—"Hail father !" (*bap jan, salam* !) and his father said :—Why do you call me father ? I had only two children, and these I turned out of my house. And when I heard that they were innocent I was much grieved and searched for them. Nay, I promised half my kingdom to whomsoever would recover them. But from that day to this there is no trace of them. The youth answered :—"I am the son whom you expelled from home." Then the king embraced his son and daughter and had his wife killed. Some days after he sent off his daughter with her husband. The youth remained with his father, succeeded to the kingdom on his death, and ruled his kingdom with wisdom and valour.

29

THE TALE OF THE TWO QUEENS

There was a Raja who had two wives, one of whom bore a son but the other was barren. One day while the mother of the boy was absent, the barren Rani choked the boy and each laid the blame upon the other. The Raja was at a loss how to discover which of them had killed the boy, so he said :

"Whichever of you will stand naked before the whole Court I will be sure that she speaks the truth."

The murderess agreed to do as he ordered. Then he said : "Shameless wretch ! if you have no regard for your honour and mine you must have killed the boy."

So he handed her over to the executioner.

30

SHAIKH CHILLI
AND THE FAKIR

One day Shaikh Chilli was very sick and he vowed that if he got well he would feed a fakir. When he recovered he went out and meeting a fakir he said:—"Will you kindly eat at my house to-day ?"

The fakir agreed and when the Shaikh asked him what he would eat, he said he would like an ounce of mung pulse. Shaikh Chilli went back to his wife and said :—

"A fakir will eat here to-day. Cook an ounce of mung pulse and you can give it to him. I perhaps shall not be home as I am going to the mosque to pray."

She cooked the food and gave it to the fakir and then she asked :—

"Do you ever go to Khuda ? If so perhaps you can tell me how my parents are getting on."

"I go every day to Khuda," he replied, "and see your parents. They are miserable and get only bones to chow ; but the parents of your husband get plenty of *pulao*."

So she gave him five hundred rupees and said : "Please take this money to my parents and let them get better food in future."

When the Shaikh came back his wife said :—

"It is very hard that my parents should have to chew bones while yours get plenty of *pulao*."

When the Shaikh heard this he got on his horse and pursued the fakir. When the fakir saw him he climbed up a tree. The Shaikh climbed after him and shouted :

"Where is my money, you rascal ?"

The fakir went out along the branch and the Shaikh followed him. When he came over the place where the horse was tied the fakir jumped on it and rode away. When he came back his wife said : "Where is the horse ?"

"When I heard" said he "that my parents had such high rank in heaven, I thought it only proper that they should have a horse to ride there. So I sent them mine."

31

THE TALE OF THE WICKED STEPMOTHER QUEEN

Once upon a time there were in a certain country four youths, one the son of a king, the second of a wazir, the third of a banya and the fourth of a black-smith. The four were great friends, and one day they determined to go on their travels. So they all started and reached a jungle. There they saw a goat, which they seized, and when they milked her she gave four *sers* of milk. So they drank a *ser* each, and as they could not get out of the jungle they slept under a large tree. When it was midnight the goat changed herself into an ogress (*deoni*) and devoured the son of the banya, and then became a goat again and sat down.

Next morning the remaining three youths supposed that the banya's son had deceived them and run back home. The wazir's son said : "I am hungry. Let us milk the goat." When she was milked she gave only three *sers* of milk, and each of them drank a *ser*.

Again night came, and they milked the goat again, and the blacksmith's son cooked some cakes. Then they went to sleep under a tree, and again at midnight the goat became an ogress and devoured the blacksmith's son.

Next morning when the sons of the king and the wazir found themselves alone they remarked : "This is the way with

low-born people. They can never be trusted. Our friends have
left us. At least they might have said they were going." The
wazir's son milked the goat, and this time she gave only two
sers of milk. At this they were much surprised, but they went
on and could not get out of the jungle. At night they said :
"We two must not part. Let us tie ourselves together and lie
down. Then neither of us can run away." So they did, and
at midnight the goat, turning into an ogress, tried to carry off
the son of the wazir, but the king's son woke, and then the
ogress retreated and turned herself into a lovely girl. The two
youths untied themselves and got up into a tree.

Next morning by chance a king was passing by. When he
saw the ogress he said : "Damsel, why are you here and what
are you doing ?" She replied : "That youth (pointing to the
king's son in the tree) has married me and has taken me into
this jungle intending to abandon me." The king said to the
king's son : "Why do you ill-treat her ? Give her to me, and
I will give you a lakh of rupees." The two youths willingly
agreed to sell her, and having received the money hastened to
make their escape.

The king with great delight took the ogress to his palace.
Now he had ten other queens, who lived in separate rooms,
and when the ogress saw them she was inflamed with rage and
began to plan how she could destroy them. At midnight she
got up quietly and went into the royal stable and devoured a
horse.

Next morning there was a great outcry that some one had
stolen one of the king's horses. The king punished all the
sentries and guards, but the horse could not be traced. When
the morning meal came up, the orgress ate only a couple of
grains of rice, and the king thought she was out of sorts. Again
in the evening she ate only a couple of grains, and getting up
at midnight went to the stable and ate another horse.

Next day the king again punished his guards, but the horse
could not be found. Thus at meals she used every day eat only
one or two grains of rice, and every night devoured one of the
king's horses.

When the king found that his horses were being destroyed he
became much distressed, and was sitting in great grief, when the

orgress came to him and said : "Why are you grieving ?" He
said : "I am in grief because no matter what guards I lay my
horses are being taken." The orgress replied, "I engage to
find the thief this very night." The king said : "How can
you find the thief when so many officers of my army have been
unable to catch him ?" The ogress replied : "Let all the
guards be removed from there to night and I will catch the thief,
but whatever punishment I prescribe you will have to impose
upon the offender." So the king removed all the guards from
there, and again at midnight the orgress came and devoured
another horse. But she put aside a little flesh and blood, and
going to the houses of the other ten queens she threw a little
flesh and blood before the door of each, and after spreading a quantity of blood all over the stable, she returned to the
palace.

Next morning she went to the king and said : "I have
caught the thief, and it turns out that your ten queens have
stolen your horses. I was sitting quietly in the stable when they
all came at night and killed a horse, and after sharing the flesh,
took it home with them. Whatever was left they threw out
into the verandah of their rooms." So the king sent his servants
to see if this were true or not, and when they saw in the verandah of the queens' rooms a little blood and flesh, they brought
it and laid it before the king, who was filled with wrath and
said to the orgress : "What punishment shall be inflicted on
them ?" The orgress replied : "Let the eyes of all be torn out,
and let them be taken and thrown into a pit in some desolate
jungle." The king ordered his soldiers to take out the eyes of
the ten queens and bring the eyes before him, and then to throw
the queens into a pit in some desolate jungle. The soldiers
obeyed him and brought the queens' eyes to the king, and taking the queens threw them into a deep pit in the forest.

Now all the queens were in child, and they lay starving in
the pit, and to one of them a child was born, which all the
others devoured. But one of them said : "I will not eat any one
else's child, nor when my child is born will I allow any one else
to eat it." So she used to eat earth, and all the others whenever a child was born used to eat it. So only one child of the ten
queens remained. And when this boy began to grow up, he

used to go out of the pit and pluck wild fruits, on which all
these ladies lived. One day, when the boy came out of the
pit, he saw a huntsman pursuing a deer and as the deer ran
before the boy, he took up a clod and struck the deer with it,
so that it died. When the huntsman saw the cleverness of the
boy, he was much pleased and gave him a bow and an arrow
the peculiarity of which was that, whichever way the arrow was
discharged, it infallibly struck the mark, because of course this
arrow was made by the power of magic.

Now the boy with this bow and arrow used to kill game
every day and give it to his mothers. One day the king who
was the boy's father, was hunting a deer in the forest. The boy
saw the deer and discharging his arrow at it killed it. The king
wondered at the skill of his shot; and saw him kill many other
animals besides. So he was much pleased and said to the lad :
"I have many other huntsmen in my service, but none can
shoot like you. If you take service with me, I will give you
high pay and treat you kindly". The lad answerd : "I will
first ask my mother whether I can take service with you or
not". The king replied : " Well tomorrow I will come to this
place again; meanwhile ask your mother about it."

But the boy forget and next day the king met him and asked
him whether he had consulted his mother or not. The boy
answered : " Excuse me, I forgot to do so." The king replied :
"Well, I will come again to-morrow; be sure to consult her to-
day." The lad again forgot to do so, and for the third time,
when the king met him and asked him, he begged to be excused. The king answered : "This time I give you an arrow of
gold; keep it by you and you will remember my words." When
the lad went into the pit and was about to put away his bow
and arrow, he remembered the golden arrow, and going to his
mother said : "Mother, for the last three days a man has been
meeting me who has been asking me to take service with him
and promises to give me high pay and treat me kindly." His
mother asked "What is the appearance of this man and what
clothes does he wear?" The boy described the appearance and
clothes of his friend. Then his mother said : "Alas, this is your
father ; you may take service with him, but be very cautious
regarding the queen. If she comes to know that you are my son

she will certainly plan your death and destroy you." The lad replied : "Don't be anxious about her. I will revenge myself on her." So when the king met him and asked him the lad replied : "My mother agrees that I should serve you." So the king took him home with him, and there the lad hired a house, and stealthily removing his mother and the other queens from the jungle entertained them there ; and the lad used to hunt with the king, and the king was much pleased with him. One day by chance the ogress saw the lad and knew that he was the son of the queen. So she began to plan his death, but found no means to destroy him. So one day she pretended to have a bad headache, and the king was much distressed and gave her much medicine, which did not cure her. At last the king asked : "What remedy will cure you ?" The ogress answered : "When I was with my father, I used to get pains like this ; then my father used to send for the milk of a tigress and I used to rub it on my head, and the pain disappeared." Then the king called all his huntsmen and said : "Whoever brings the milk of a tigress will receive a great reward." But no one accepted the duty. At last this lad undertook to do it, and taking his bow and arrow, went into the forest, and lo ! he saw a tigress suckling her four cubs. The lad fixed his arrow in his bow and was about to fire at her, but the tigress began to wag her tail and raised her foot. So the boy refrained from discharging the arrow, and when he went close to her, what did he see that in the foot which the tigress was raising up a great thorn was imbedded. Then the lad went close to the tigress and pulled out the thorn, by which she got great relief. Meanwhile the tiger came up and was about to spring upon the boy, who aimed an arrow at him, but the tigress stopped him and said to the tiger : "Do not kill this lad, who has given me great relief." Then the tigress said to the lad : "I will give you whatever you ask." The lad replied : "I want nothing but one thing if it be not impertinent on my part to ask it : I only want a little milk, which was what I came into the jungle to fetch." The tigress replied : "I will gladly give you as much as you require. " So the lad milked a *lota* full of her milk but then began to think : "If I take the milk with me perhaps the orgress will say this is not tiger's milk at all, and all my labour will be lost." So he told this to the tigress, and she said : "Well, can you suggest a plan ?" He answered : "I have a plan if you only trust me." She replied : "I fully trust you and will do whatever you say." So the boy said : "Let me take your young ones with me. I will take the greatest care of them and bring them back to-morrow : by this I shall be able to satisfy the ogress that in truth it is tiger's milk I have brought." So the tigress gladly allowed him to take her young ones with him, and when he took the cubs and the milk to the king, he was much pleased and gave him a great reward. But the ogress was inflamed with rage that he had succeeded in his mission and not lost his life. So she rubbed the milk on her head and recovered. And next day the lad took the cubs and returned them to the tigress.

Then the ogress made another plan to destroy the lad, and took another woman into her counsel and told her to go to the lad and say : "You are a great hero ; you ought to go and bring a cow such as is not found with the king, and I will tell you where such a cow can be found. Now there are three mountains close together and between in the direction you go an open space, in which the cows are grazing, and they have no owner, so you may drive away as many of the cows as you please." So this woman went to the boy, and the plan pleased him and he asked the king to give him a few day's leave and without thinking of the danger took his bow and arrow and went to fetch the cow. When he reached the place of which he had been told, what did he see, that on three sides there were such lofty mountains that their tops reached unto heaven, but no man met his view, and many cows were grazing there. He thought : "If I drive away all the cows, I shall have great trouble." He tied ten of them together with a rope and was about to drive them home, when he heard shouts from behind—"Seize him ! this is a thief ; he is stealing my cows." And when he looked back, he saw many demons (*deos*), pursuing him, and he that was in the middle was the tallest of all and appeared to be the leader. So the lad thought : "Now my life is lost ; but if I kill the leader, perhaps I may save myself". So he aimed his arrow at the demon who was leader of all, and the arrow struck the demon in the ear. Then the demon said :

"Thousands of men have tried to kill me and thousands of arrows and guns have been discharged against me but I was never wounded : now this lad has struck me on the ear : he must be some special person, the son of a *jinn* or a fairy (*pari*) I must kill him". But the other demons advised him not to kill the lad. So he called the lad to him and gave him back his arrow, and said : " You are a brave boy : take away not ten, but a hundred cows." The lad replied : "Perhaps I alone cannot drive away a hundred cattle." The demon answered : "I will give you my servants to help you : and they will drive the cattle to your house." So the boy made him a *salam*, and the demon sent his servants and a hundred cows with him. That night the lad reached his home. The demon's servants tied up the cows and went back and the lad lay down to rest. In the morning, when people saw the cows, they were much astonished and went and informed the king. He himself came to inspect the cows, and when he saw them was greatly pleased and asked the lad to sell some of them to him. But the boy replied : "They all belong to your majesty ; take as many of them as you please." So the king took ten of the cows for himself.

When the ogress heard of this, she was consumed with rage. "Next time for certain I will kill him ; for if he continues to live, he will certainly take my life." Again she pretended to be sick and said to the king : "I am certainly dying." So the king asked her : "Is there any remedy that will save you ?" The ogress answered : "If any one was to go to my mother and bring from there the water of gold, and I was to drink, I should recover." The king asked his people if any one would consent to go to the house of the queen. But when they heard that they had to traverse desolate jungles all of them refused to go and said : "No-one can do but the huntsman boy." So the king sent for the lad and said to him : "My queen is sick unto death and there is only one remedy for her, which her mother can give, and by this her health will be restored : if not, she will die. None of my servants agrees to go fetch it". The lad at once said : "I will go." The king was much pleased, and went to the queen and said : "My huntsman lad agrees to go." The ogress answered : "I was going to tell you myself that he alone can fetch it because he is a hero, and I will give him a letter, which if he shows to my father or mother they will at once give him water of gold." So she wrote a letter addressed to her father and mother to this effect : "This lad is my deadly enemy ; when you see him devour him at once : if you spare him some day he will take my life : let him never return." So she gave the letter to the lad and said : "When you give this letter to father or mother, they will entertain you kindly in their house ; so take this letter with you, and do not forget to return to me."

So the lad took his bow and arrow and tied the letter in his turban and started for the house of the ogress. He travelled for many days, and at last reached a thick jungle, where, as it was night, the unfortunate lad lay down to sleep. When midnight came, Adam and Eve were flying over this jungle, and Eve noticed the boy, and asked Adam : "Whose lad is this and how does he come to be living in this forest ?" So they both went near him, and they saw the letter in his turban, and when they took it out, they said : "This is the work of some enemy, who wishes to kill him." So they took the letter and tore it up and wrote another letter to this effect : "This is my son, whom I am sending to you ; take the greatest care of him : if anything happens to him, it will cause me great distress : entertain him as long as he wishes to stay, and when he wishes to return, do not detain him." Then Adam and Eve tied this letter in his turban, and both of them flew away.

When morning broke the lad arose and marched on. When he went a little distance he saw that a great mountain was in front. But when he went a little further, what does he see that, in spite of himself, he is advancing towards the mountain, and no matter how much he tried to stop himself, he could not. When he got close up, he perceived, to his astonishment, that it was not a mountain at all, but a demon, who was dragging him by his breath towards himself. Then immediately he took the letter from his turban and handed it to the demon : then the demon said : "What sort of letter is this ? I will first read it, and then I will devour him." So he shut his mouth for the time and the lad approaching the demon, gave him the letter. When the demon read the letter, he remarked : "Alas ! I was nearly eating my own grandson." Then the demon embraced him and said : "If you had not shown me the letter, I should certainly have eaten you ; now go to your grandmother, and she will take care of you." So the demon wrote a letter to his wife, and the lad took both letters away with him. When he had gone a little distance the old ogress met him. The lad said : "Good morning, grandmamma," and gave her the letter. When she had read it she also embraced him, took him into her house and gave him food and drink and received him with great affection.

One day the lad was looking about its grandmamma's room and in a cupboard he saw two little boxes. He took them up, and asked his grandmamma what was in these boxes. His grandmamma in confusion said : "You are a great rogue ; have you opened them or not ? The lad answered : "No grandmamma, I have not opened them." Then his grandmamma said : "Be careful, child, never open these boxes, for when one is opened, a great tempest arises, and when the second is opened, the rain falls with such violence, that everything is washed away." The lad answered : "All right, grandmamma ; give them to me ; I will put them away quietly." So he put away the boxes, and began to look about the room. There in another cupboard he saw something tied up in a piece of cloth. He took up the parcel and said : "Grandmamma, what is in this." The old ogress replied : "Child these are the eyes of your father's ten queens." The boy inquired : "Can these be fitted on again, that you are keeping them." She answered : "Yes ! In the evening I will take you into the garden and there show you the water of gold. If this is mixed with water and poured upon their eyes, they will become right again." The lad was much pleased at heart, but said nothing. So when evening came, he said : "Come grandmamma, and show me your garden." The old ogress took him with her. When they reached the garden, and he saw the water of gold, the lad said : "How beautiful this water is." The ogress said : "Child, the power of this water is such, that if a little water be placed in a vessel, no matter how large it be, the vessel will become filled with water, which, however much it be used, cannot be exhausted." The lad made no reply, and went on a little further. When he reached the middle of the garden, he saw a birdcage

hanging on the tree, and in the cage was a beautiful parrot.
The lad asked : "What is the name of this parrot ?" She
answered : "Child, in this parrot is the life of thy mother ; if
this parrot's leg be broken, then your mother's leg will break,
or if its wing be broken, then your mother's hand will break :
and if any one kills this parrot, then your mother will die."
The lad said nothing, but went back quietly to the house and
began to think in his mind how he could succeed in carrying of
the two boxes, the eyes of the queen, the water of gold and the
parrot.

Some days after his grandmother said : "Child, I am going
to see a friend of mine : you look after the house, while I am
away." The lad was inwardly delighted, but he said : "Grandmamma, come back as soon as you can." The old ogress said :
"Yes, child, I will return soon." So when the ogress went away,
the lad took the two boxes and eyes of the ten queens and
tied them in his waistcloth and filled the bottle full of the water
of gold and taking up the parrot's cage, ran away from there.
He had gone a short distance, when the old ogress returned,
and when she saw that he was carrying off the cage and the
bottle of water, she became much displeased and pursued the
lad. When he saw that he was being followed he quickly
opened the tempest box, and such a severe storm arose, that all
the trees were torn up from the roots. Then the ogress held on
to an immense fallen tree and sat down. Then the lad opened
the box of floods, and the rain began to fall so violently, that all
the trees which had been torn up and the ogress with them was
swept away.

The lad escaped from there and reached home after some
days. When he returned, he poured some of the water into a
large vessel and sorted all the eyes in it, and the eyes all recovered. Some water he sent to the king, and taking the parrot to
the ogress queen shewed it to her. When the ogress saw the parrot in the hands of the lad, she raised her hands in supplication
and said : "Give the parrot to me." He replied : "I will now
take my revenge on you." Then the ogress prayed to the king
to give the parrot which the lad had brought. The king said
to the lad : "My wife wants this parrot." The lad replied : "I
will give it with pleasure, but on one condition, that you call

all your servants to some appointed place and go there yourself, and call the queen there too. Then I will give her the parrot." The king agreed and appointed a place. And there all his servants attended.

The king too came himself ; the ogress queen came also in her litter, and the lad followed after. The queen called out from her litter : "Give me the parrot." Then the lad broke one leg of the parrot, and immediately one leg of the queen broke too. Then she began to weep, and still asked for the parrot. The lad went a little further, and broke the second leg of the parrot. Immediately the second of the queen broke also. Similarly he broke both the parrot's wings, and as he did so, both the arms of the orgess broke also. Still she went on asking for the parrot. Then the lad said to her in the presence of all : "Put out your hands and take it." But she could not do so, as her hands were broken. Three times he said the same, and then he took the parrot out of the cage, twisted its neck and flung it on the ground. So the parrot died and the ogress died also. The king said : "What have you done ?" The lad answered : "Your majesty, this is an ogress ; it was she devoured all the horses ; her father and mother are demons also." Then he went on to tell how he had deceived her mother and brought away the parrot and all the other things. Finally he said : "I am the only remaining son of your majesty's ten queens, and I have brought all their eyes from the house of the ogress ; and have so treated them, that now they have all recovered." The king on hearing his story, embraced him ; sent for the ten queens and all of them lived in happiness ever after.

32

THE TASKS OF THE WITCH-QUEEN

Once upon a time a Raja went
to hunt. By chance he came
into a desolate jungle. He sent
his servants to search for
game. They went off. They
saw a light burning in a grove,
near which an old woman was
sitting. She asked them what
they wanted. They said:—"We
have come in search of game."
The old woman gave them two or three deer. When they cooked
the deer they found they were nothing but eyes. So they conten-
ted themselves with the broth.

When all of them started with the King the old woman
turned herself into a lovely girl and pursued the King. As she
pursued him the King's horse was tired. The woman caught
the horse's tail. The King jumped off and got up a tree : just
at the moment a second King came up, and seeing the woman,
fell in love with her. She agreed to go with him. So he took
her home and treated her as his Queen. Now her custom was
at midnight to steal out and eat one of the best horses of the
King. The King tired to detect the thief. The Queen heard
this and took some of the horse's flesh and put it on the bed of
the other Queen who was in child. In the morning she pointed
to the young Queen as the thief. The King said :—"How are
we to punish her ?" The wicked Queen said :—"Put out her
eyes and abandon her in the forest." This was done by the
King's orders.

While the young Queen remained in the jungle a mysterious
jar of milk used to come for her every day, and when her son

was born the milk was increased two-fold. One day when the young Prince grew up he wandered away and met a horseman. He asked the horseman for some food which he got. He took the food to his mother. One day he wandered to his father's Court. The King gave him service, and put him to tend his most vicious horse. The Prince tamed the horse. The wicked Queen discovered who he was. She pretended to be sick, and no medicine would do her any good. The King said :—"Is there any medicine you would like ?" She said :—"If I had tiger's milk I would get well." So the King ordered the Prince to bring tiger's milk.

He went off having got a lakh of rupees from the King for his charges. He gave the money to his mother and went off to the jungle. There he met a tiger's cubs and made friends with them by feeding them on sweets. They became attached to him, and at his request brought him a little of their mother's milk. When the tigress heard of this she died of grief, and the Prince took the Cubs and the milk. He brought the milk to the wicked Queen. She said :—"Now I want the milk of a goat which belongs to a Demon (*Deo*)." Then she wrote a letter to a certain Demon, which she gave to the Prince, and said :—"When you show this letter you will get the milk." But she wrote in the letter :—"When this son of man (*adamzad*) comes to you kill him at once." He went off with the letter after taking a lakh of rupees for his road expenses, and coming to his mother, he gave her the money, and went off to search for the milk. But before he started he took the precaution of getting the letter read, and when he knew the contents, he threw it away and got another letter written to the Demon to the effect that when this man reached him he was to receive him with great courtesy and assist him in every way.

With this letter he went to the Demon. He was very civil to him, and said :—"I am going about some business. You stay here. But take care not to loose the goat which is tied to this tree, or a witch (*Dain*) will appear and eat you up." As an experiment the Prince loosed the goat. The witch jumped out of the tree. The Prince said :—"There is a great storm coming. We had all better cling to this tree, which will not be broken, and for this reason I untied the goat." The witch was satisfied, and the Prince hung her and the goat to the tree, and then broke the witch's neck.

When the Demon came and saw what had happened to her he was sore afraid, and said :—"I make you a present of the goat. Take it away." The Prince came with the goat to the King's Court.

The Rani said :—"I want the hair of the horse Shyam Karan." The Prince with a lakh of rupees went off at once in search of the horse. He came to the same Demon again. He asked his errand. He said :—"I want the Shyam Karan horse." The Demon said :—"This horse is in my charge and I will never tell you of it." Then the Prince threatened to serve the Demon as he had served the witch. Then the Demon said :— "Go and sit in a *pipal* tree near a certain tank. Many horses came to drink there. One horse stays apart from the others and is always jumping about : be sure that this is the horse Shyam Karan. Mount him, and no matter how much he plunges, never let him go, and make him agree to bear you." The Prince did so, and the horse said :—"All right : I will come to-morrow, and then you must recognize me." Next day this horse came in the form of a miserable worn-out animal. The Demon also appeared there in disguise and pointed this horse to the Prince. The Prince caught this miserable horse. The horse made many attempts to escape, but the Prince held on to him, and finally he brought the horse to his mother, and took the hair of it to the King. The King gave it to the Rani.

She said :—"There is a kind of flower which grows in the ocean. This I must have." The Prince again started with a lakh of rupees, which he gave to his mother. Then mounting Shyam Karan he went again to the Demon. The Demon said:—"Ride to the shore of the ocean. But the peculiarity of this flower is that when any one comes near it, it turns into a woman and kills him." But the horse Shyam Karan said :— "Remain behind me. I will catch the flower for you." The Prince did so, and when the flower advanced to attack him, Shayam Karan caught it in his mouth.

The Prince brought the flower to the Demon. It turned into a woman, and said to the Prince :—"This Rani, who is always imposing tasks on you, is a witch and sister of this

Demon. It was she who had your mother blinded, and she is planning to take your life. There is a parrot here which you must take. The life of the witch remains in this parrot. When you kill it you will kill her at the same time." Then the Prince took the parrot with him and the flower-woman.

When he came to his mother he said to the flower-woman, "laugh ;" and when she laughed a flower came out of her mouth, which he took to the Rani. Then he said to the King :—"Come with me and I will show you a strange sight : but don't bring the Rani." Then the Rani took the form of a witch and came to kill the Prince. He at once wrung the parrot's neck. When it died the Rani died too.

Then he told the King the whole story, married the flower-woman, and they passed their lives in happiness, till the Separator of all things removed them from this world.

33

PHULMATI RANI

A King was returning home after marrying his son. In the bazar he saw an old woman selling a handkerchief, which he purchased for Rs. 500. One day the Raja's son saw the handkerchief, and suspecting it to be the work of a Raja's daughter, asked his mother where it came from. She referred him to the old woman whom he found selling a similar handkerchief in the bazar. She told him that it was embroidered by a Raja's daughter. He asked

her to procure him an interview, and she advised him to wait
at a temple, where the Princess used to go every night to worship
Devi. There he met her, and they fell in love. The Princess
advised him to secure one of her father's camels which could go
300 *kos* (600 miles) in the day. By mistake he selected a camel
which could go only 200 *kos*. They started together, but the
father of the Princess overtook them on the swift camel, and
then she made a bow and arrow out of some reeds which grew
near the road and killed her father. She then took the swift
camel and went on. When they got to a city the Princess gave
her lover a ring to sell. He took it to the shop of a one-eyed
Banya, who knew at once that it was a Princess' ring, and telling
the Prince to wait, went out by the back way, and inducing the
Princess to believe that he was taking her to her lover, brought
her to his house and locked her up. The Prince searched for
her in vain, calling out, "O lady of the handkerchief" (*rumal
wali*), all over the city. Then he, being in distress, took service
with a bangle-maker (*churihar*), and went about selling bangles.
One day he went to the Banya's house and recognized his sweet-
heart. She took two bags of the Banya's money and told him
to go and buy two horses. He brought the horses and they went
off : but the stupid Prince fell asleep and the Princess went
ahead. Meanwhile the Banya came up, and suspecting that the
Prince had taken the Princess, though he did not recognize
him, began to beat him. But the Prince convinced him
that he was innocent, and the Banya took him as his
servant, and they went on in search of the Princess. As
Princess Phulmati went along five Thags met her and began to
dispute who was to have her to wife. She said :—"Whoever can
shoot an arrow ahead of mine shall marry me." But they all
failed, and she took them all before the King of the land
dressed as a youth. The King adopted her as his son, and
when she took her seat on the throne, she sent for the seven
men who were following her on the road, and among them she
at once recognized the Prince, her lover. She dressed him in
royal robes and married him.

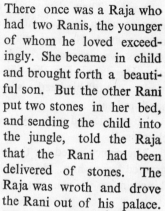

34

THE RIVAL QUEENS

There once was a Raja who had two Ranis, the younger of whom he loved exceedingly. She became in child and brought forth a beautiful son. But the other Rani put two stones in her bed, and sending the child into the jungle, told the Raja that the Rani had been delivered of stones. The Raja was wroth and drove the Rani out of his palace. She wandered into the jungle and found a child lying under a tree. When she saw it the milk rose in her breasts and she gave it suck. Then a Raja passed by and pitying her took her home with him and supported her and her child.

By and by the boy grew up. One night the Raja in a dream saw the most beautiful woman he had ever seen in his life. In the morning he called his courtiers and said :—

"Whoever finds this woman for me shall receive my kingdom." All the courtiers searched for the woman, but failed to find her. At last the prince went in search of her. He came to the city of a Raja who offered him service.

"What pay do you required ?" the Raja asked.

"A lakh of pice daily," answered the prince.

"What work can you do ?"

"I will do what no one else can do."

So he was appointed, and one night in the month of Bhadon the Raja heard a bitter cry outside his palace walls. The prince went out to see what was the matter. He came to a burning-ground south of the palace, where he saw a woman standing naked with a drawn sword in her hand. The prince asked the cause of her grief.

"I am a witch (*Dain*)," she answered, "and I am weeping because your Raja will die to-morrow."

"Is there any means of escape ?" the prince enquired.

"Yes ; if any servant of his offer his head to me, the Raja will live for twenty years."

When he heard this the prince at once cut off his head with a sword. Then the witch ceased from her lamenting. Next morning when the Raja heard of the death of the prince he was much grieved. He went to the temple of the Devi to pray. The goddess was appeased, and offered him any boon he chose to ask. He asked for the life of the prince. When he revived he tried to cut off his head a second time, but the goddess held his hand and said :—

"I am pleased with thy devotion. Ask for anything thou choosest."

The prince asked for the woman of the dream. The goddess granted her to him. He took her to the Raja, who conferred his kingdom on the prince, and he reigned happily for many years.

35

THE RAJA AND THE PHYSICIAN

There was once a Raja who was much oppressed by increasing fatness, so that he began to despair of his life. He called many physicians, but there was none who could give him relief. Now in a distant city there was a poor physician who was sore pressed to make a living by his profession, and at last he determined to go elsewhere in search of employment. By chance he came to the city where the Raja lived and as he was walking about he heard a herald going about proclaiming : "Whoever can cure the Raja his fee shall be a lakh of rupees ; but if he fail he shall be put to death with the most extreme tortures."

When the physician heard this notice he began to reflect that his future state could not be worse than it was then. So he went to the Raja and accepted his conditions, but first he demanded a lakh of rupees as an advance for the preparation of the necessary medicine which he said it would take six months to prepare. When he got the money he at once sent it home, so that in case he came to an untimely end, the support of his family might be assured.

When six months passed he was no nearer having the medicine ready than he was at the beginning, and his heart sank within him when he began to think what the Raja would do to him when he failed to perform his engagement. So he made a plan and at night he began to wail and cry and dashed himself so violently against the walls of his room that his whole body was a mass of bruises. When the messengers of the Raja came, he said :

"I am so wounded that I cannot appear, before the Raja unless you bring a conveyance."

So they brought a palanquin and brought him before the Raja, who demanded his medicine and threatened that if it was not ready the physician would be delivered over to the executioner. When he heard this the physician began to weep and said :

"Last night, your Majesty, I was compounding the drugs for you when 'Azrail," the angel of death, appeared and asked me why I was preparing a potion for a Raja who would die within a week. When I remonstrated with him he fell upon me and beat me sorely, as you see me now. Even now 'Azrail' is hovering over your Majesty's palace, waiting to carry you off. What then avail the drugs of your servant ?"

When he heard the words of the physician the Raja was overcome with fear and lay on his couch and wept and thus he continued for the space of a week, until by reason of his fears and neglect of food his fatness left him and he regained his original form.

When the week had passed he sent again for the physician and said :

"You see that 'Azrail' has spared me so far and lo ! my fatness has disappeared."

"This is the result of my strategem" replied the physician. "You have to thank me for your recovery."

The Raja admitted the truth of his words and dismissed the physician with a handsome present.

36

THE RAJA AND THE BEAR

One day a Raja went out hunting and going in pursuit of a deer lost his way in the jungle. The deer went out of sight and then the Raja saw a bear being hunted by a tiger. The Raja in fear climbed up a tree and the bear followed him. The Raja was frightened when he saw the bear following him. But the bear said : "Do not fear me ; the tiger is the enemy of both of us. You help me and I will help you." The Raja agreed and when it was night the bear said : "I will take the first watch and you can sleep." When the Raja went on watch the tiger said from below : "Throw down the bear and I will devour him." The Raja gave the bear a shove and tried to throw him down, but the bear had his claws well fixed in the tree and woke when he was touched. "You are a false friend," said he, "but I will forgive you this time."

Next morning the bear took the Raja on his back and brought him to his palace. When he got to his gate the Raja called his dogs and set them at the bear. Then the bear ran at him and bit him to death. As he was going away he spoke in this verse :—

Marante ko mariye, ka Raja ka Rao.

"When a man attacks you kill him whether he be king or prince."

37

HOW THE RAJA GOT HIS DESERTS

There lived once a Raja and a Rani : the Rani was so pious that she never left her bed in the morning without feeding five Brahmans. But the Raja was an enemy of Brahmans and insulted them when he got the chance. One day Bhagwan, in the guise of a Brahman, came to the Raja's palace and asked for alms. The Raja was in his stable, and when he saw Bhagwan he, as was his wont, said : "Here is dung in plenty : eat this if you will." By and by the Raja and the Rani died

and their souls went to Swarga. There the Rani received all
she needed, but the Raja began to starve. At last he went to
the Rani and said : "You are my wife. You are enjoying all
the comforts of life while I am starving. Out of your abundance
give me to eat." The Rani answered : "I disown you, sinner.
Why should I give you food. Go to Bhagwan and ask him
for what you need." So the Raja in his distress went to
Bhagwan and begged for food. Bhagwan took him to a
storehouse where was collected all the dung the Raja had
offered in his life to Brahmans multiplied tenfold. Then
Bhagwan said : "In Swarga everybody lives on the alms he
has given on earth, and all he gives is multiplied tenfold."
The Raja wept bitterly, and just then Raja Indra was passing
by and heard him. When he heard his trouble Raja Indra said :
"Take all this filth and burn it into lime : then you may bring
some pan leaves from my garden : prepare them and give them
to the gods to chew. Perchance Bhagwan will pardon you and
give you food."

The Raja did so, and Bhagwan took pity upon him and
gave him food as long as he remained in Swarga.

38

THE RAJA AND THE HANSAS

Once upon a time a famine raged at Manasarowar for fourteen years and a pair of Hansas who lived there had to go
elsewhere to find sustenance. When they had gone a long
distance they came to a beautiful tank full of fresh water and
inhabited by all kinds of birds. The female Hansa said to her
mate : "Let us stay here till the famine ends." Her mate
answered : "The tank is good but we cannot stay there until

we obtain the owner's leave." When the Hansas heard that the tank belonged to the Raja of the place, they went to him and asked his leave to stay there until times improved. He gave them leave and they settled there.

They had lived there only a few months when one day the Rani came to bathe in the tank and when she saw the Hansa's young ones she longed to have them. So she told the Raja and he sent a man to summon the Hansas to his Durbar. When he delivered the message they asked him why they were called and he told them what the Rani had said. They answered : "My friend, to-day all the birds will meet at our house and we cannot attend the Raja to-day ; but to-morrow, if Parameshwar spares our lives, we will be there."

Next morning the Hansas appeared before the Raja and saluted him. He invited them to sit down and then he asked : "It is true that birds hold meetings like men?" They answered : "Maharaja, it is true that we have our disputes and quarrels like men have and yesterday we had a meeting to decide a matter in dispute between us." "What was the question ?" he asked. "The question was, whether there were more men or women in the world." "And what decision did you come to ?" "The number of women is greater than that of men, because we count those men women who do not keep their word." The Raja was ashamed, and said : "I called you only to see you as I had not seen you for a long time." As they were going away they said : "Maharaja, listen to the words of the poet :

Bhanu uday udayachal ten chali ke puni purab panu dharai nahin ;
Jyou sar neh sati chharhi ke puni dham ki or nigak karai nahin ;
Haril ki pran hai lakri kadali puni dajo bar pharai nahin ;
Taise Zaban bare jan ki mukh ten nikali puni pichhun tarai nahin.

"The sun rises from behind Udaychal and then sets out on his course, but he does not turn his feet again towards the east.

So when Sati puts the arrow to her bow she looks not back again to home.

The green pigeon sits on wood and the plantain does not
fruit a second time.

So when a great man makes a promise he does not break
it."

The Rajah was ashamed and thenceforth he protected the
Hansas.

39

HOW THE RAJA
WENT TO THE
HEAVEN OF
BHAGWAN

There was once a Raja who thought himself the lord of the
whole world. One day his son, who was blessed with great
wisdom, asked him what he was always thinking about. The
Raja said that he was always thinking of conquering the whole
world. His son said : "That is well, but there are four duties
of a King—devotion, protection of his subjects, justice, and the
increase of his [kingdom. Out of [the four you practise only
one." The Raja said : "You are right. I have done the
first three, but I have never thought of the last. I am now an
old man and I intend to pass the remainder of my days in
devotion." So saying the Raja seated his son on his throne
and began to wander about the world as a Sadhu.

Wandering through many lands, at length he came to a
forest ; and when any one asked him where he was going, he

used to say : "I am going in search of Bhagwan." They laughed at him, and said : "You cannot find Bhagwan unless you keep the company of ascetics." So he set out in search of ascetics, and at last he came to the Himalaya, where he found a Sannyasi sitting absorbed in devotion. The Raja sat long before him, but the Saint paid no heed to him. He used daily to clean the place where the Sannyasi lay. After many days the Saint opened his eyes and asked the Raja what he desired. The Raja said : "I am seeking for Bhagwan." The Sannyasi answered : "For many years I have been concentrating my thoughts on the Creator (*Karta*) of all things, and have failed to find Him. How can you find Him in a single day ? But I will give you a *mantra* which you must repeat morn and evening, and, if possible, at all times. Perchance some day you may find Him."

After he recited the *mantra* the Sannyasi, again became absorbed in his meditations, and the Raja went on repeating the *mantra* constantly. Many days passed, and the Sannyasi again came to his senses and, finding the Raja still there, was much pleased. Then the Sannyasi said : "I give you this cup. Whenever you ask it for anything it will give it. Now go away, repeat the *mantra* for twelve years and then return to me."

The Raja taking the cup went to a city and sat beside a well. He went on constantly repeating the *mantra* and earned his living by sewing. But he never asked the cup for anything. One day it so happened that the Raja when returning from hunting came to the place where his father lay. When he knew him he fell on [his face before him and said : "Father, return with me to your palace. The life of an ascetic is very hard. How can you, who have always been giving orders to others, beg your bread ?" The Raja answered : "My son, I am more happy than you are. You may give an order which is not obeyed, but even the fish of the water and the birds of the air are ready to do my bidding. If you do not believe me, follow me to the bank of this tank." Then he led his son to the water's edge and throwing his needle in asked his son to bring it out. The Prince searched for it, but in vain. Then the Raja called a fish and ordered it to

bring it out. The fish at once obeyed his order and laid the
needle before him. Seeing this the Prince said : "Father, I
will accompany you." The Raja reasoned long with him, and
induced him to return home.

The Raja went into a forest and met another Sannyasi.
He was then absorbed in devotion, and the Raja remained
standing before him. When the Sannyasi opened his eyes he
asked the Raja what he wished. The Raja said : I wish to
see Bhagwan." The Sannyasi said : "Go and sit under that
tree. Perchance you may see Him there sooner than elsewhere."
The Raja went and sat under the tree and began to recite the
mantra, which the first Sannyasi had taught him. One day he
saw an enormous tiger running towards the tree. The Raja
went to the Sannyasi and told him what he had seen. The
Sannyasi said : "You fool ! the tiger from which you
foolishly tried to escape was Bhagwan whom you were
seeking."

When twelve years passed the Raja and the Sannyasi went
to the Saint whose dwelling was on the Himalaya. He was
glad to see them, and said : "Let us now ascend to heaven."
Then a heavenly chariot appeared, and the three took their
seats on it. When they had gone some distance the Raja saw
his own palace and thought to himself : "Why did I not enjoy
the pleasure of living there some time longer ?" No sooner
did this thought come into his mind than he fell down from the
chariot and was reborn in the family of a boatman (*Mallah*).
When he came to be fourteen years of age he thought of the
mantra which he used to recite, and he began to repeat it.
When he had repeated it for twelve years a voice came from
heaven : "Fool ! thou didst all but gain thy desires and lost it
again through love of this world. You have won it again by
your devotion. The chariot will again appear. Beware ! lest
you lose the fruit of your piety by low desires." The chariot
appeared and on it the Raja ascended to heaven.

40

THE METAMORPHOSIS OF RAJA VIKRAMADITYA

Once upon a time Raja Vikramaditya was reading with a Pandit the *Pinda Pravesha Vidya*, or the science by which a man acquires the power of entering the body of another person or beast. His servant, who was sitting outside the door, was listening and heard as much as the Raja. When the Raja was returning home the servant asked the Raja what he had been learning from the Pandit. The Raja answered : "If you bring me the body of an animal 1 will show you." The servant killed a parrot and brought the body to the Raja who immediately repeated the *mantras* and entered into it. When the servant saw this he cut his own body into pieces and tried to kill the parrot too, but it flew away. Then he went to the capital and giving himself out to be the Raja sat upon his throne. He issued orders that every parrot in the kingdom should be killed and offered a large reward for every one that was brought to him. One day it so happened that the parrot whose body the real Raja was occupying was caught in a snare and he at once asked the fowler what he intended to do with him. The fowler said that he was going to take him to the Raja and claim the reward. The parrot answered : "If you take me to the Raja you will get only a small reward. If you take me to the father-in-law of Raja Vikramaditya I will get you five hundred rupees." The fowler agreed and took the Raja in his parrot form to Raja Vikramaditya's father-in-law. The old Raja asked him what he had brought and he showed the parrot. The old Raja asked the price and he said : "Ask the parrot and he will fix the price." The parrot when he was asked, said : "My price is five hundred rupees." "What can you

do that you fix your price at so large a sum ?" he enquired. The
parrot answered : "O Maharaja ! I can decide disputes and
interpret the Shastras." So the old Raja bought the parrot and
hung it up in a cage in his court and the parrot used to read
Sanskrit and help the old Raja in deciding cases that came
before him. The old Raja was much pleased with him and
thought that he had got him very cheap.

Meanwhile the servant in the form of Vikramaditya went
into the royal apartments and talked with the Rani. She was
surprised to hear his rude and unpolished conversation. She
thought he was out of his senses and sending for the jailer had
him shut up as a madman. It so happened that there lived in
that kingdom a Brahman and his wife. They lived by begging, but they got so little that they were almost starving and
one day the Brahman said to his wife : "We cannot live in
this way. I am going into the Tarai on a begging excursion."
His wife agreed and he started. No sooner he had left the
village than a *Deo* who lived in a grove close by assumed the
form of the Brahman and went into his house. His wife was
very much surprised to see a man whom she believed to be her
husband returning so soon and he said : "What is written in
my fate for me to get I shall get here as well as abroad. I am
not going to the Tarai after all." She answered : "You have
done well. Stay at home". So the *Deo* lived in the Brahman's
house and after some time when the Brahman came home he
was astonished to see a man just like himself sitting there.
When the *Deo* saw the Brahman he rushed at him with a club
and the Brahman began to fight him. The woman could not
make out to what was the matter when she saw two men of
exactly similar appearance fighting about her. The villagers
came up and asked what the quarrel was about. The *Deo* said :
"Help me brethren ! Do you not see that this shameless ruffian
has forced his way into my house ?" The Brahman said : "Don't
you recognise me, neighbours ?" The villagers said : "In
appearance you are both exactly the same. We cannot judge
between you." The parties then went to thirty-five villages,
but they could find no one to decide their case. At last they
went to father-in-law of Vikramaditya. He asked the woman
which of the men was her husband. She pointed to the *Deo*

and said that he was her husband, that the other man was some impostor or other. The Raja then gave her over to the *Deo*. As he was going away the Brahman called out : "O Bhagwan ! Are you asleep and has justice perished out of the earth ?" Then Vikramaditya in the form of the parrot called out : "You have decided the case wrongly. Call them back and I will decide the matter myself." The Raja did so, and then the parrot called for an earthen-ware vessel with a spout (*karua*) and a piece of yellow cloth and a thread. He put these things in the middle of the court and said : "Whichever of you two will enter this vessel by the spout and come back the same way he shall be deemed the owner of the woman." The Brahman said : "I would rather lose her altogether than undergo this ordeal." But the *Deo* agreed to make the attempt and when he entered the vessel the parrot shouted to the Raja's men to cover the vessel with the yellow cloth and to tie round it a thread of raw cotton. Then he said : "This is an evilminded *Deo* ; bury him in the earth that he may never arise again to trouble the land."

All were amazed at the wisdom of the parrot ; and a few days after the wife of Vikramaditya heard of the case and sent for the Brahman to find out how it was decided. When she heard the story, as she was learned in the sciences, she at once came to the conclusion that the parrot could be no other than her husband Vikramaditya. So she determined to go to her father's house, and when she met him he told her to ask any boon she pleased. She asked for the parrot, but he was too fond of him to give him away and he refused her request. But she sat *dharna* at the palace gates, and when he found that her life was in danger he sent for her. She asked him to whom he had married her. "To Vikramaditya, of course," he answered. "And where is Vikramaditya ?" she asked. "In this kingdom, of course," he replied. "You had better ask your parrot," she said. When the case was brought down the parrot said : "I am Raja Vikramaditya." Then he told them the whole story and the old Raja gave the parrot to his daughter and she took him back to the palace.

She asked him what he had been studying for so long a time with the Pandit and he told her what he had learnt. She sent for the false Raja and addressing him affectionately, said :

"What did your Majesty learn from the Pandit?" He said : "Bring me the body of a lamb and I will show you." When the lamb was brought, the false Raja at once transferred his soul into it. The Rani opened the cage at once and Vikramaditya came out, dropped his parrot form and entered his own body. Immediately he cut the lamb in pieces and the false servant died too. After this Vikramaditya and his Rani lived for many years in the utmost happiness.

41

THE RAJA AND HIS KAMKAR SERVANT

Once upon a time a beggar went into a city and called out :

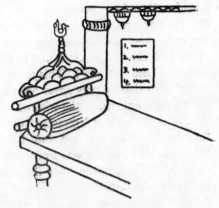

"I will sell four pieces of good advice for hundred rupees."

No one would accept his terms, until at last the Raja heard him and called him in. The Raja offered to buy his good advice.

"I must have cash down," said the beggar. When he was paid, he said :

"My maxims are—

"Never be rude to a self-made man of low birth.

"Control your anger at the beginning.

"Never dismiss an old servant for his first fault.

"Never publish a man's sin if you can help it."

The Raja had these maxims engraved on a copperplate which he hung near his bed. By and by the Raja lost his wealth and all his servants left him. One of them, a Kamkar by caste, went to a nighbouring city in search of service. Just then the King of that place had died without issue. So, as was the

custom, the people put "the garland of victory" in the trunk
of one of the royal elephants and let her loose, agreeing that
on whosoever she hung the garland he should be their King.

By chance the elephant met the Kamkar, hung the garland
on him and he became King.

Meanwhile the Raja, his master, came to beg in that city,
and, seeing the new King passing by in procession on an elephant
he remembered him ; but he followed the advice of the beggar
and saluted him respectfully. The King answered his salute and
next day the Raja went to court : he was roughly treated by
the guards. But he again followed the beggar's advice and kept
back in anger. At last the King made him gate-keeper on five
rupees a month.

Soon after he discovered that the Queen was in love with
her groom. He saw them together, but said nothing. The
Queen knowing she was found out went to the King and said :
"The door-keeper is a villain. He tried to dishonour me."

So the king called him and gave him a letter to the Chief of
the police.
"Let the bearer be put to death."

As he was taking the letter he met the groom, who said :
"Why do you trouble yourself, Jamadar Sahib? Let me take
the letter."

When the groom took the letter to the Chief of Police, he
was hanged at once.

When the King saw the Raja at the gate as usual, he was
astonished and asked him what had happened. The Raja told
him the whole story, and how the Queen was false to him.
When the Kamkar recognised his master and heard the tale,
he said :
"Take my kingdom and let me as before thy servant."

Thus the Raja retrieved his fortune by following the
beggar's advice.

May Paramesar restore all of us as he restored the Raja !

42

THE TROUBLES OF THE
ƒPIOUS RAJA

There was once a Raja who had two
sons. He was very charitable, and one
day a beggar came to his gate who gave
him his blessing. The beggar said : "I have got a daughter to
marry. If you give me money I can make her hands yellow
(get her married)."

The Raja at once called his treasurer, but the beggar said :
"This is the hour for charity : a man's mind is not always the
same : confer now on me what you please."

So the Raja put water on his hands and over in he laid
his sacred cord and recited the formula of bestowal (*sankalap-
ka-mantra*). Then the beggar said : "O Maharaja ! You have
given me much, because in this thread is tied the key of your
treasury, and with it you have given me all that you possess.
Now abdicate your throne and let me reign in your stead."

The Raja in his charity did as he said, and, taking his Rani
with him, set out to seek his fortune. On the way he put up
at an inn where a merchant was staying who at once fell in
love with the Rani. Then he went to the Raja and said : "My
wife is in the pains of labour : there is no one to tend her : of
your charity let your wife come to her for an hour or two : you
will thereby earn the merit of saving a life." The Raja fixing
his mind upon Bhagwan let the Rani go with the merchant.
As soon as the merchant got the Rani into his camp he ordered his tents to be struck and took her away with him. The
Raja waited for her till next day, and when she did not return
he took his two boys with him and set out in search of her. As
he went on he came to a river, and making one of the boys sit
down on the bank he put the other on his back and waded
into the water. When he was half way across the boy
who was sitting on the bank was carried away by a wolf.

And his foot just then slipped and the other boy was swept away by the current.

The Raja fell senseless on the side of the river, and when he came to himself he could find no trace of the boys. So he set out for a neighbouring city where the Raja had just died. Now it was the custom there that when the Raja died the nobels of the kingdom used to take their seats at the gate of city, and the first man who appeared before them, him they made their Raja. The Raja, in sorrow for the loss of his sons, was the first man to arrive at the city gate, and they gave him the throne.

Meanwhile as the wolf was carrying away the boy a hunter saw him and rescued the boy, and as he was childless he adopted the child as his own. And the second boy as he was swept away by the current was caught in the net of a fisherman who saved him and reared him as his own. The Raja was always mourning the loss of his children, and the thought came into his mind that he would adopt two boys in their stead. By chance his servants brought him these very boys, and thought he did not recognise them as his own, he felt a deep affection for them, and always kept them near him.

It so happened that the merchant in his travels came to that same city, and as he and the former Raja were great friends, he paid a visit to his successor. The Raja was pleased to listen to his conversation, and asked him to stay with him for the night. But the merchant excused himself, and said : "My wife is in trouble and is always weeping, and I cannot leave her alone. She says that she has lost her husband and that if within seven years she does not find him she will marry me : and I cannot trust my servants to take care of her." So the Raja sent his own two sons to the camp of the merchant to take care of the lady. As the boys were sitting at night outside her tent they began to talk over their adventures, and she recognised them for her sons. She ran out and fell on their necks and wept. Some of the Raja's people who were there came and told him what had happened, and he sent for the lady, whom he knew to be his Rani. The merchant he hanged, and he and the Rani and his sons lived in the utmost happiness.

43

THE KING'S SON AND HIS FAIRY BRIDE

Once upon a time there was a King who had seven sons, all of whom got married, except the youngest. So all his brothers and his sisters-in-law used to worry him to marry. At last he said :—"Well ! if I marry, it will be one of King Indra's Fairies." So he rode off. On the road he saw a well, and as heavy rain was falling, he sat down under a tree close by. Soon after a Chamar's daughter came to the well for water, and the Prince saw that, though heavy rain was falling, she and her clothes remained dry. He said to himself :—"This must be one of Indra's Fairies." Then he went to her father and asked his daughter in marriage. But he said :—"How can a Chamar marry a King's son ?" However, the Prince insisted, and at last the marriage was arranged. Then the Prince came and told his father that he was to marry a Fairy, so his father started with a grand equipage. They went a long distance, but they saw no grand house, and the King sent a camel-rider ahead to see where the bride's mansion was. The camel-man came back and said:—
"I see no mansion, but there is a hamlet of Chamars, where marriage preparations are going on, and they are saying :— 'Hurry up ! Hurry up !' the King will be here in a minute." Thus the King was wroth, and told his son to come home at once ; but he would not obey, and married the Chamar's daughter.

After they were married the bride said :—"We are married, it is true, but I will not recognize you as my husband unless you cross the seven oceans and get my ring from the faqir who lives there." So the Prince crossed the seven oceans with the utmost difficulty and found the faqir. Now this faqir used to sleep half the year and wake the other half. This time he was asleep, and the earth had fallen on him, and grass was growing on his body. So the Prince cleaned him. When the faqir woke he was about to kill the Prince but he was appeased, and gave him the ring ; at the same time he warned him not to give the ring to his bride the day he returned. When he came home and his bride asked him about the ring, he put her off and went to sleep. But in his sleep she searched for the ring, and when she found it, disappeared.

In despair the Prince returned to this faqir who was again asleep. He cleaned him, and when he woke the faqir said :— "What brings you here again ?" He said :—"I have been very careless. While I was asleep my bride secured the ring and now she has disappeared." The faqir answered :—"To find her now is very difficult. She is now among the Fairies in the Court of Indra." "Well," said the Prince, "unless you help me I shall never find her." The faqir said :—"Well ! I will tell you a plan. There is a certain stream in which the Fairies come to bathe. Sit near the place, and when they are swimming in water, seize their clothes and run to me. They will come to me and complain, and I will say to them :—'Well ! give him what is his.' And they will say :—'If he can recognize her thrice, let him have her.' Then the first time seize hold of the hand of the oldest of them all : and as you hold her they will all clap their hands and say 'he has forgotten ! he has forgotten !' But do not let her go. The next time seize the smallest of them all, and they will again mock you. But do not let her go. The third time seize her who is a leper, and do not let her go. Then they will give you up your wife and go away."

And it all happened as the faqir predicted. So when the Prince had recovered his bride she said to him :—"If Raja Indra hears that you and I are married he will kill us both. Now I will give you a flute, and whenever you want me you have only to blow it and I will come to you." The Prince, with the advice of the faqir, took the flute, then the Fairy flew off, and the Prince went home. As he was on the road he came to a wrestling-ring (*akhara*) where a number of Gusains were wrestling. The Prince sat down and blew his flute. Then his Fairy bride came and asked what he wanted. "I want to see a Fairy dance," said he. So she went away and soon come back

with a number of other Fairies and musicians, and the Prince
showed the dance to the Gusains. When the Fairies went away
the Gusains said to the Prince :—"We thought that our stick
had most excellent'qualities, but your flute beats it." He asked :—
"What are the qualities of your stick ?" And they told
him :—"You have only to tell this stick to strike any one, and
it does so at once." The Prince said :—"Let us make an
exchange." So he gave them the flute and went off with the
stick.

He then sent back his stick and told it to beat the Gusains
until they gave up his flute, which they did when the stick beat
them within an inch of their lives. Going on further, he saw a
crowd of people looking at a cooking-pot (*deghchi*) which used
to produce any kind of food required. This he acquired in the
same way as he had done with the stick : and similarly he
obtained a goat whose dung was gold. So he went home with
his treasures. One day as he was going out hunting he forgot
to bring his flute with him. And while he was away his eldest
sister-in-law saw it and blew it. On this the Fairy appeared,
and seeing it in her hand, began to scratch and tear her, whereupon she dropped the flute which the Fairy carried off. When
the Prince returned from hunting and missed his flute, and
learnt what had happened, he began to lament. He went off
again to the faqir who, when he saw him coming, knew for
certain that the Prince had lost the flute. So he told the faqir
the whole story, who said :—"Well ! it is a very difficult
business to recover it now, because the Fairies have given up
bathing in this world, and I do not know where they do bathe
now." But the Prince implored the faqir to help him once
more. Then the faqir said :—"I will give you one more chance,
and if you lose the flute now, you will never get it back. The
plan is this :—"The Fairies' washerman (*dhobi*) comes here to
wash their clothes and then carries them back in his carriage
(*rath*) : so when he is starting you cling on to the wheel, and
when you get to Fairyland (*Paristan*) you will recover your
bride. So next day the Prince hid near the washing-ghat and
clung to the carriage wheel till he got to Fairyland. When the
washerman saw him he was confounded : finally, the Prince
induced him to take pity on him and keep him in his house.

One day while he was there he met his wife. Said she :—
"You have not given up following me ?" Then she took pity on
him and said :—Well ! I will come with you. But you must do
one thing. To-night there will be a great dance in Raja Indra's
palace. You must come, and when a dance is over you must
shout out :—"The dancing is good enough, but the drumming
is atrocious. Then the drummer will go off in a huff, and you
must take the drum and play, and we will all dance our best.
Then the Raja will be delighted and give you anything you
ask." And so it happened as she said. And the King said :—
"Ask your guerdon." The Prince made him swear three times
that he would give him anything he asked. Then he said :—
"Marry me to this Fairy." The King agreed, and married them
forthwith, and the Prince took his bride home, and they lived
happily ever after.

44

THE NIGHTINGALE
WITH THE
THOUSAND NOTES

There was once a king who had seven queens, the youngest of
whom he loved the best; but he had no offspring. So he
consulted a noted faqir, who gave him out of his bag three
fruits, which he advised him to give to the queen he loved the
best. So he gave the fruits to the young queen, and she was
delivered of two lovely boys and a girl. The other queens, in
their jealousy when she was taken ill, told her that it was the
custom to have the eyes of the ladies tied up during delivery.
So when the children were born they put a stone in their place,

and placing the babies in a box, threw it into the kiln of a potter. The potter found it there and adopted the children.

One day a water-woman of the palace saw them playing, and told the queens how lovely they were. The queens gave her poisoned sweetmeats for the children, but they took them home, and their foster-mother tested them on a dog, and finding them poisoned, kept the children at home.

When the children were nearly grown up their foster-parents died, and the children, in great distress, wandered into the jungle, where they met the faqir, who recognised them at once, and gave them a stick, a kettle, and a quilt of rags. They asked him what was the use of these things. He replied : "The quality of the stick is this, that wherever it is planted in the ground a palace will be formed. When you shake the quilt gold-mohurs and rupees will fall from it. As for the kettle, you have only to wash it and put it on fire, and any food you please, will be cooked in it.

So the children planted the stick in the jungle, and lo, a palace grew up where they stayed. The kettle used to give them any food they liked, and when they wanted money they used to shake the quilt.

One day their father came to hunt in the jungle and seeing the palace was amazed; he asked the servants where the boys were. He told them to announce his arrival. The boys came out and insisted on the king coming to dinner.

When king returned home he told the story to his queens. They suspected that these must be the children of the young queen. So they sent an emissary to persuade the little princess that in a certain jungle was a nightingale that sang a thousand notes, and could speak like a man : that if she could get it she would be much delighted. So the princess asked her brothers to get her the bird. One brother went off to the faqir and asked him how the nightingale was to be found. The faqir said that the bird was in a certain jungle, but that every one who had gone in search of it was turned into stone. When any one searches for it, it calls at night out of its nest : "Who are you ?" If any one replies he becomes stone. "If you go, no matter how much it calls you, make no answer, and take it in the morning and bring it."

The prince went to the jungle, and it all happened as the faqir had told him. When the bird called to him at night he made no reply, and remained silent till the morning. In the morning he carried off the bird and came to the faqir. The faqir said to the bird : "O nightingale, see, these are my children. Never illtreat any of them." So the prince went off with the bird. He shut it up in a cage which he gave to his sister. She was delighted.

Meanwhile the king, her father, came out again to hunt. When he saw the nightingale with the thousand notes he was much pleased. When he came home he told the queens about the bird, and they were confounded. So they said : "These people have often entertained you. You should invite them to your palace, and ask them to bring the nightingale for us to see."

The king agreed and invited them to come to his palace and bring the nightingale. So the princess and the princes came to the palace with the nightingale. When they came to eat, poisoned food was placed before them; but the king was served with harmless dishes. As the children were going to eat the nightingale said : "Do not touch the food. Throw it before the dogs." When the dogs ate it they died at once. The king asked the bird to explain matters.

The nightingale told him that the queens had poisoned the food of the children, but that his dishes were harmless. Then the bird told him the whole story; and that the young queen, who had been sent by him in his rage to scare the crows, was their mother : and how the envious queens had attempted their life : and how they had been protected by the faqir.

The king was amazed, and asked the bird how she came to know this. She said : "God has given me the art of learning secrets. You may test me as you like." So he asked her many secret facts and she knew them all. So he believed and had the queens buried up to the waist and shot at with arrows and their corpses eaten by the dogs. Then he called the young queen, restored her to her royal station, and she lived happy ever after.

45

THE STORY OF SIT
AND BASANT

There were once a king and a queen, who had two sons, Sit
and Basant. One day as they were sitting together, they
noticed that a pair of sparrows had made their nest in the
roof, and had two young ones. The hen-sparrow died and the
cock took to himself another partner, who at once flung the
young ones out of the nest. The queen said to the king : "If
I die, don't marry again or my sons will fair like these young
sparrows." The king gave her his promise.

By ill-luck the queen died, and some years after the king,
at the request of his children, married another queen. When
he brought her to the palace he kept his sons in an upper
chamber, and the queen lived below. One day the boys were
playing ball, and their ball fell down into the queen's room.
Then Sit said to Basant : "Go and fetch it." Basant said :
"You fetch it yourself." Sit replied : "Well, tie a cloth over
your face and go and fetch it." Basant did so.

When the king returned in the evening he came in and
found the queen lying on her bed. He asked her what was the
matter. She answered : "Did you marry me for your own
sake or for your sons' sake ?" He said : "For my own sake,
of course." "Well" said she, "your sons have been very
impertinent to me, and I won't eat a morsel while they are in
the palace."

So the king had to post up a notice on the gate for their
expulsion, and when they read it they got on horseback and
went off to the forest. They slept under a tree and were very
hungry. In the morning Sit said to Basant : "You stay here
and I will go and see if I can get anything to eat." Soon
after some men came and seized Sit, for it was a custom in
that land, when the king died they used to go into the forest,
and the first man they met, they used to make him king in
his room.

Meanwhile Basant remained under the tree, hoping his brother would bring some food. He remained there all night. Now in the morning a parrot and a *maina* were sitting on the tree over his head, and were saying : "Such and such a king has turned out his two sons; both came under this tree. The elder went off in search of food and the younger is here still, but the elder has been made king of the land."

Basant heard this and was much distressed. He went off to the city where a grain-parcher took him in, and all day he used to tend the oven and get scraps of food. When Sit ascended the throne he proclaimed a vast reward for any one who could tell the tale of Sit and Basant. Basant told the grain-parcher that he knew the story. The grain-parcher told the king that there was a lad with him who knew the story. The king sent for him at once, but his brother was so changed from misery that he did not recognize him. When Basant told about his father and mother and the sparrows, his brother knew him, fell on his neck and they lived together in happiness.

46

THE KING AND THE FAIRY

There was once a king who had no son. Many plans he tried, but none was of any avail. Now Raja Indra had a fairy with whom a Deo was enamoured ; he wished o marry her, but she would have nothing to say to him. Then the Deo went to Raja Indra, told lies about her, and had her turned out off Indrasan.

The fairy then came and was re-born in the family of this king. When she grew up she was one day sitting in her bower (*mahal*) when an enormous monkey appeared and ran at her. She screamed and escaped into the palace ; but she did not tell her father and mother what had happened. Now this monkey was the same Deo who wished to marry her, and had got her turned out of Indrasan, and he had become a monkey intending to find her and kill her. When he found out where she was, he put up near the palace, and was always looking out for a chance of catching her and devouring her. She was so much afraid of him that she never left her room, and day by day she got so weak and thin that her father and mother were very anxious about her. Finally they agreed that if they could get her married she would perhaps recover ; so they married her to the prince of a neighbouring land.

When she started for home with her husband the Deo followed her, and when they reached a jungle he rushed up and began to devour the retinue of the prince. When she saw him eating her men she was afraid and ran away. At length in the jungle she saw a house, and in it was a room with a single door. Into this she ran and bolted the door so tight that she could not open it again. She heard people talking at the other side of the wall, but they did not hear her cries at last she found a nail, and with this she scraped a hole in the wall, and the people of the house heard her voice and took her out. The man who lived there was a Chamar, and as she was very hungry he gave her food to eat. When she had eaten she said to the Chamar :— "Make me such a robe that my whole body may be hidden. If you do this for me I will give you my golden bangle." So the Chamar made her a leathern dress, which she put on and rubbed all over with treacle and covered herself with a dirty sheet and went her way. On account of the treacle multitudes of flies settled upon her, and wherever she went on account of the flies no one would allow her to stay. At last an old woman, who lived by parching grain, took pity on her and gave her shelter. She used to make the girl do all her work, and gave her a cake or two at night. One day the old woman said to her "Go to the river and bathe." So she went to a retired place, and there she took off her leathern dress, and when she had bathed she put it on again. As she was bathing one of the golden hairs fell from her head, and she laid it on a leaf and left it float down the stream.

By chance the hair floated down past the palace of a king, and the king's son took it out, and when he saw it he went to his father and mother and said :—"Marry me to the girl whose hair this is." The king was much grieved, and next day he made a feast to all the people of the land, hoping that the girl whose hair this was would come to the feast. Great crowds assembled and the girl came too, but as she was covered with flies she had to sit apart.

Now in this land it was the custom that whenever kings were about to be married a trained elephant was let loose, and whatever girl it raised three times she was married to the king. When the elephant was loosed it went searching all round the company, and finally raised this girl three times. When the king and queen saw that the elephant had selected such a dirty girl, they supposed that there was some mistake ; so they sent for a second elephant, but the result was the same. And with a third elephant the same thing happened. So they had to marry her to the prince.

When he went home that night, and it was time for him to retire with his bride, he went to his mother and told her with tears that he could never live with such a person ; that he wished to marry the owner of the golden hair, and would never touch a creature who was so foul that no one would let her sit near them. "Well," said his mother, "I will have her put to sleep to-night in the elephant shed, and one of them is sure to trample her to death." So she was sent there, but in the night four other fairies came to her, took off her robe of leather, bathed and perfumed her, and when the watchmen saw her they were surprised at her beauty. They went and told the prince, and he ran there, and when he saw her he was delighted. He sat there, on the watch, and when the four fairies left her and she was about to put on her leathern-robe again, he ran and seized her. But she cried—"If I do not put this on I shall die." "Who is there who can harm you ?" he asked. Then she told him her whole story,

and when he asked her if she could think of any plan for
killing the Deo she said :—"There is only one way to kill him.
Take this leathern robe of mine, fill it with honey and place it
on a finely-decorated couch on the roof of the palace. When
the Deo comes he will seize it and think that he is sucking my
blood. Then you can lay in wait and kill him."

He did as she advised, and when the Deo came in the form
of a monkey and began to suck the honey the prince cut off
his head with his sword. Then he went and told his wife that
the Deo would trouble her no more, and they two lived together
for many years in the greatest happiness.

47

THE FATE OF THE RAJA OF CHANDRAPUR

The Raja of Chandrapur
was once sitting in his
palace when he heard a
noise outside ; he called the
guards and asked them the
cause of the noise, but no
one dared to go and en-
quire. Just then a man
named Birbal came to the
palace and was brought
before the Raja who asked
him his business. He
said :—"I want to serve your Majesty." "What pay do you
require ?" asked the Raja. "My pay," said Birbal, "is a
thousand *tolas* of gold a day." "And how many men are in
your force ?" enquired the Raja. "My force," said Birbal,

"consists of myself for one, my wife for two, my son for three, and my daughter for four." "Your pay is large," said the Raja, "But I will appoint you, and I shall need service from you to correspond with it."

Next night the cry was heard again outside the palace walls, and the Raja sent for Birbal and sent him to investigate the matter. Birbal took his sword and went out, and there he saw a woman lamenting bitterly. He asked her the cause of her grief, and meanwhile the Raja, who was desirous of testing the fidelity of his servant, came from the palace and hid himself close by. The woman said :—"I am weeping because the Raja of this land, who is famed for his deeds of piety, will die within a month." Birbal asked her "is there any means whereby his life could be saved ?" The woman answered :— "The Raja can live for a hundred years more if any one will sacrifice his only son to the goddess Jyoti Bara."

Birbal went at once to his wife and told her what the woman had said. She replied :—"Act as you please in this matter. I will make no objection to whatever you do." Then he went to his child's bed and woke him, and told him what the woman had said. The boy answered :—"I am ready to give my life for this virtuous king, and I shall give my life before no mean godling but before the mighty Jyoti Bara."

So the whole family went to the temple of the goddess. There Birbal laid his son before the altar and severed his head with a single blow. Seeing this the mother cut off her own head with a single blow of the sword. And immediately her daughter did the same. Then Birbal thought "what is the use of life ? It were well for me to join my family in Heaven." So he too cut off his head.

The Raja saw all this and was so grieved that he too determined to die. As he raised the sword the goddess appeared and said :—"O Raja ! I am pleased with thy devotion. Ask what boon you desire." "If thou art appeased," he said, "I desired that all these may be restored to life." The goddess granted his prayer, and they all revived. Then the Raja took Birbal home and rewarded him with half his dominions.

48

THE RAJA AND THE MUSAHAR GIRL

A Raja once went hunting in the jungle. He was very thirsty, and wandering about could find no water till he came to the hut of a Musahar. The Musahar was not at home, but his daughter, who was a very handsome girl, was there. The Raja asked her for water, but she said :— "How can you drink from my hands ?" He answered :— "I am dying of thirst ; give me to drink." He sat there for some time to rest, and when her father came back the Raja said :— "Give me your daughter to wife." He replied :— "I am a low caste man and you are a Raja. How can this be ?" But the Raja would not heed, and said :— "I will come shortly to take my bride ; see that she is ready."

In a few days the Raja came with a large party, and the Musahar was obliged to marry his daughter to him. When the Raja brought his bride home, and it became known that he had married a Musahar girl, all the people were very angry, and his father, the old Raja, called the executioners and ordered them to take the young Rani into the jungle and bury her there. They had no sooner carried out these orders than in the place where she had been buried a golden tank and a golden temple of Mahadeva were formed. The Raja, who was mourning for his Rani, went to see her grave, and when he saw the tank and the temple he was astonished, and commenced to sit there and mourn.

After many days a pair of birds, named Bahengwa and Bahengiya, came and set on the roof of the temple beneath which the Raja lay. One said to the other :— "Husband, this Raja has been long mourning here. Is there any means whereby he may recover the Musahar girl for whom he is mourning?"

The other said :—"She is not the daughter of a Musahar. she is a Fairy. If he wishes to get her he must watch till she comes to bathe at this tank, and then he must steal her garment." The Raja understood these words and did as the birds said. When he took her robe he said to her :— "I have been long awaiting you. Now take pity and come home with me." But she said :— "Why should I return with you when my father-in-law had me buried ? Give me my robe, else I will curse you." The Raja feared her words and gave back the robe and she disappeared from his sight.

He went on mourning at the temple as before, and again he heard the birds talking. One asked :— "Husband, did the Raja recover the Fairy ?" "He got her back, but he did not know the right words to say to her, and so she went away." "What should he do when she comes again, so that she may never leave him ?" "He should swear to her that he will never leave her, and that when she dies he will have himself buried with her."

When the Fairy came again the Raja followed the advice of the birds, and as she was bathing he seized her clothes and ran into the temple. The Fairy came to him and said :— "I cannot live with you now because your father had me buried." He answered :— "Pardon me this once. I swear that I will never leave you, and when you die I will be buried with you." She was appeased and came into the temple. Then he said :— "I will never return to my father. Have a palace built here and we will live together." From the fold of her robe she took out the picture of a demon (*deo*) and ordered him instantly to perform the wishes of the Raja. Within a single night he built a palace of gold. When it was done the demon immediately became a picture again. The Raja and the Fairy lived there many years in happiness.

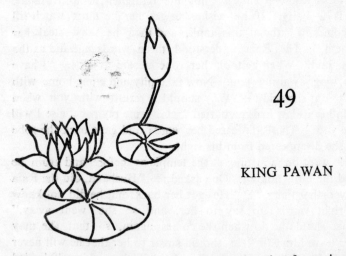

49

KING PAWAN

King Pawan (the Wind) is said to have reigned as far as Amraoti
in Berar and Bhandak in Chanda ; and there is a fable that it
was his daily custom to bathe at Pauni, to break his fast at
Bhandak, and sleep at Amraoti. His wife also had miraculous
powers. She is stated to have had the power of walking over the
tanks as on dry land, and of drawing water in unbaked pots
by means of a string that had never been twined. Both she and
Pawan himself, though they possessed wealth untold, wore
simple white garments and laboured with their own hands.
One account says that they were content with the possession of
the philosopher's stone, so that they could, if they so wished,
turn their subjects' tribute of iron ore and such like things into
silver and gold. But there came a day when Pawan's wife,
known as Kamalpati, "queen of the water lily," saw the rest of
the women going out to celebrate the Pola festival, clad in
garments of many colours and with ornaments of gold and
silver about their persons. She, too, must own such things,
and before the next Pola feast came round, by constant importu-
nity she had induced her lord to let her dress and adorn herself
as other women did. She joined the festival no longer distin-
guished by the simplicity of her apparel : her eyes were now
opened, and she found that her virtue was departed from her.
No longer would her untwined string and unbaked pot perform

their office ; no longer would the leaf of the lotus support her steps. The end of it was an earthquake which overthrew the town of Pauni.

50

THE DEITY OF THE STONE

Two Brahmans agreed that if they had a son and a daughter, respectively, they were to be given in marriage to each other. When the time came and the father of the daughter went to demand the fulfilment of the promise, the other met him on the way and refused : thereupon he appealed to the Raja of Kalinga, who was the paramount sovereign, for redress : the Raja naturally demanded witness ; the man said he could produce none, as no one was present when the compact was made near a stone. The Raja refusing to entertain his plaint without evidence, the man came to the stone where the promise had been made, and earnestly prayed to the deity of the stone to help him : the deity told him to go back to the Raja and that he would follow, but said the stone deity, "if you look back I will not go."

The man arose and departed, and he could hear the footsteps of the god following him, till at the spot where the palace of the Raja stands, the ground being covered with soft grass, the footsteps of the god were no longer audible, the Brahman turned back to ascertain if he were being followed, and that very instant the stone stood still and has remained immoveable ever since.

The Raja finally ordered the other man to fulfil his promise on the evidence of the stone.

51

SHAIKH CHILLI AND THE ROBBER

One day Shaikh Chilli was going on a journey, and his wife cooked some cakes for his support on the road. As he was eating, a robber came up and said : "I am hungry." So the Shaikh gave him a share, and they went on together. They came to an inn, and the robber managed to get a room. But Shaikh Chilli had to sleep in the verandah at the door of a room in which were four blind beggars. After a while the Shaikh heard one of the blind man say, "I have an *ashrafi* in may cap." "I don't believe you," said the second. "Show it to me." As the first blind man passed the *ashrafi* to the second, the Shaikh put in his hand and took it. When he did not find the coin, the second blind man said : "I knew you were a liar. But I have an *ashrafi* in my bludgeon." "I don't believe you," said a third. As the coin was passed to him, the Shaikh seized it too. "I know you were a liar," said the third. "But I have an *ashrafi* in my rags." When he passed this to the fourth, the Shaikh put in his hand and snatched it away. The fourth said,

"I have an *ashrafi* in my shoe." When he passed it over to the first the Shaikh got it too. The four blind man began to fight until they were all dead.

Then the Shaikh thought to himself— "If am found near these corpses I shall get into trouble." So he called the robber and bringing out one of the corpse, propped it up against the wall. When the robber came out the Shaikh said : "My servant has died. Take his body and throw it away and I will give you a rupee and a quarter." So he gave the robber a rupee, and said "Take the corpse away, and when you come back I will give you four annas."

The robber took the corpse and threw it a long distance away. In the meantime the Shaikh brought out the second corpse and put it up against the wall. When the robber returned he said : "See. He has came back. You must take him away again." Thus the Shaikh did with the third body. When it come to the fourth, the robber said : "I am half dead carrying your servant's body all night." But the Shaikh said, "Try it once more. Perhaps he won't return this time."

So the robber tied the fourth body neck and heels and took it away on his back. He came to a tank and had just thrown it into the water when a Brahman who was washing himself near seeing this awful sight cried out and ran away. The robber thought that this was the corpse which had come out of the water. So he ran after him shouting : "You have deceived me three times already and I will take care you do not do so again." At last the robber caught the Brahman and dragged him to the Shaikh. The Brahman cried, "My lord, save me from this Rakshasa. My loin cloth and six rupees are at the bank of the tank. Take them all and let me go." So the Shaikh gave the robber the loin cloth and kept the rupees himself. Then he left his friend and went home.

52

SHEIKH CHILLI AND
HIS TURBAN

One day Shaikh Chilli was going to
see his wife at the house of her
father and when he had gone a
long way he was tired and sat
down by a well to rest. He felt sleepy, but not wishing to
dissarrange his turban he lay down on the platform of the well
with his head over the mouth and fell asleep. As he slept his
turban fell into the well and when he woke he thought nothing
of his bare head and went so on to the house of his father-
in-law.

Now among his people to go about bareheaded was a sign
of mourning and when his relatives saw him thus they began to
wail and beat their breasts and called out—

"Which of our dear relations is dead ?"

"What do you mean ?" he replied. "No one that I know
of is dead."

"Then why do you go about bareheaded ?" they angrily
asked.

"Is it a fact" said he, putting his hand to his head, "that I
am without a turban ?"

But they were so enraged at being taken in that they fell on
him and beat him out of the village. So he lost his wife in the
bargain.

53

SHEIKH CHILLI AND
HIS HANDSEL

Once upon a time his father sent
Sheikh Chilli into the market with a
rupee to buy *ghi*, and said : "Mind,
you get the handsel."

Sheikh Chilli bought the *ghi*, and then he said to the Guala :
"Give me the handsel."

"In what will you take it ?" he asked.

So the Sheikh turned over the vessel, and spilling all the *ghi*,
said : "I will take it in the bottom."

When he came home he shouted to his father :

"Aba ! aba ! see, I did not forget the handsel."

"But where is the *ghi* ?"

"How could I bring both ?" he grumbled.

"Well, you *are* a fool," said his father, and this was the last
commission he gave him.

54

HOW SHEIKH CHILLI
WENT TO MARKET

Once upon a time Sheikh Chilli said to his mother :

"I have not eaten meat for many days. Give me money, and I will go the market for meat, onions and turmeric."

When he got the money, he went off to the butcher's shop and bought some meat. As he was carrying it along, a kite swooped down and carried off a piece. When he saw this, Sheikh Chilli threw the rest on the road and said :—"O kite ! sister of my mother ! take the rest of the meat to my mother. Tell her to wash it, and say I will be back in a moment with the onions and spice." In a moment the kite carried it all off.

Sheikh Chilli came home, and his mother asked to see what he had bought.

"Here are the onions and spice all right. The meat I gave your sister, the kite, to take home."

His mother said :—"You are a fool."

And this was the last time the Sheikh was trusted to go marketing.

55

SHEIKH CHILLI
IN LOVE

One time Sheikh Chilli was hotly in love with a girl, and he said to his mother :—"What is the best way of making a girl fond of one ?" Said his mother :—"The best plan is to sit by the well, and when she comes to draw water, just throw a pebble at her and smile."

The Sheikh went to the well, and when the girl appeared, he flung a big stone at her and broke her head. All the people turned out and were going to murder him, but when he explained matters, they agreed that he was the biggest fool in the world.

56

PRINCESS
POMEGRANATE

A certain King had four sons. Three were married and one was a bachelor. His sisters-in-law used to chaff him, and said :—"Are you waiting to marry the Pomegranate Princess ?"

(*Anar Shahzadi*). He asked about her, and found it was hard
to find her, as she lived in a pomegranate, and was guarded by
lakhs of Deos (Demons). At last the young Prince said :—"If
I can't marry Princess Pomegranate, I will never show my
face again."

So off he went and met a Deo in the jungle. The Prince
addressed him as "Uncle" (*Mamu Sahib, salam* !). The Deo
said :—"Well ! you have come at last." The Prince stayed
some time with the Deo and told him his mission. One day
the Deo wrote something on a bit of a tile (*thikri*) and gave it
to the Prince. As he went on he met another Deo. He gave
him the tile and said :—"*Mamu Sahib, salam* !" The Deo read
what was written on the tile, and asked the Prince what he
wanted. "All right," said the Deo, "I will turn you into a
crow and you must break one pomegranate from the tree :
but don't take more than one. The Deoni (Demoness) who is
there will try to make you take more, but don't mind what she
says, and come back." The Prince did so. As he was going
the Deoni said :—"You may as well have another." The Prince
gave way, and the Deoni wrung his neck at once, and took the
pomegranate.

The Deo knew that he had been destroyed by his greediness,
so he went and brought back his corpse and revived him.
"You are a great fool," said he. "You did not take my advice,
and this is the result." The Prince admitted his fault. "Well,"
said the Deo, "now it is hard to get the Pomegranate Princess :
but I will give you another chance. I will turn you into a
parrot, and you must obey my order." So the Prince, in
the form of a parrot, brought the pomegranate. The Deoni
tried to make him take a second, but he refused. She followed
him to the Deo's house. When the Deo saw her he turned
him into a fly. The Deoni came and said :—"Where is the
parrot who brought the pomegranate ?" "Search for him,"
said the Deo. Of course, she could not find him and went
away. Then the Deo restored the Prince to his original form
and sent him off with the pomegranate.

On the way he hid the pomegranate and went home to
arrange his marriage procession. As he went along pomegranate burst, and a lovely Princess came out of it. By chance a

sweeper woman (mehtarani) came up and saw the Princess. She said to the Princess :—"Give me your jewels which I will put on, and we can then look down a well to see by our reflections in the water who is the lovelier." So the mehtarani pushed the Princess into the well, and sat down in place of the Princess.

When the Princess fell into the well she turned into a Lotus flower. When the Prince came he saw the mehtarani and said :—"Why ! you are not half so pretty as I thought you would be." However, he put her into a litter and brought her home. When her sisters-in-law saw her they said :—"This is not Princess Pomegranate at all." Some days after the Prince went to hunt, and one of his horsemen came to draw water from the well. As he put the *lota* into the well this flower used to come into the vessel and then jump out again. They called the Prince to see this wonder, and when he put in the *lota* the flower came into it and he pulled it out. He took the flower home with him.

When the mehtarani saw it she knew it must be the Princess. So she pulled it into pieces while the Prince slept. He was much distressed when, where the pieces of the flower were thrown, a pomegranate tree grew and produced a single flower. The mehtarani knew that this must be the Princess. She had the tree dug up and thrown away, and sent the flower to her gardener's wife (*malin*), and told her to keep it for seed. The malin put it into a pot, and when the pomegranate burst, out came a lovely Princess. She stayed with the malin as her daughter. One day one of Prince's men saw her and told him. Then the Prince said :—"Marry me to the malin's daughter or I will die."

The mehtarani knew that this must be the Princess. So she pretended to be ill, and said :—"I must have this girl's liver or I shall die." The King sent for the malin and told her to give up her daughter. She refused at first, but finally the girl was given to the executioner, and her liver was brought to the mehtarani. She thought the Princess must be dead at last.

But by the will of the Almighty a house suddenly appeared where the Princess was killed. Two peacocks were there as sentries, and the Princess was inside. The Prince asked for an audience. The peacocks said :—"You have so worried the Princess that now you cannot see her." But finally he persuaded them to let him in. Finally they were persuaded, and the Prince came in to the Princess. He got her to forgive him and took her home as his bride. All his sisters-in-law said :—"This is Princess Pomegranate at last." So they were married, and the wicked mehtarani was burried up to the waist in the ground, and the soldiers shot arrows at her till she died.

57

THE STORY OF FIROZ AND THE PRINCESS

Once upon a time a merchant died leaving large wealth to his only son Firoz. The boy was soon influenced by vile associates, who plundered him and deserted him when he was reduced to poverty. One day his wife reproached him with his extravagance, and he promised to make a fresh start if he had some capital. His wife gave him one of a pair of gold bangles, the last of her ornaments, which he sold for a hundred rupees. As he was coming home he saw a crowd, and out of curiosity went to see what was going on. On enquiry he found that the dead man owed a hundred rupees and his creditor would not allow the corpse to be buried until his debt was paid. Firoz took pity upon him and, paying the debt, released the corpse.

Firoz went home and told his wife, who gave him the second bangle. This he sold, and was coming home when a respectable-looking man met him and asked him what he was about. Firoz told him he had just raised a hundred rupees, which he intended to invest in some profitable business. "I am glad to hear this," said the stranger. "Suppose I throw in a hundred gold *mohars* and become your partner ?" Firoz replied : "I agree. Let us go home and arrange the matter." So they agreed to buy rice and glass bangles (*churi*) and take them to a certain island where such things were in demand. Accordingly they bought their stock, hired a ship and started on their voyage.

It happened, however, that the way to this island by the shorter route was dangerous, and that at a certain point a beautiful hand used to emerge out of the sea and drag down and sink ships. The sailors therefore refused to go this way. The friend of Firoz however assured him that he was prepared to meet this danger. The sailors yielded to his assurances and set sail.

In due time they reached the place of danger, and saw a beautiful hand rise out of the sea. The friend of Firoz drew his sword and with one blow cut the hand off, which flew up into the air. As the ship moved forward the hand fell on deck. The partner took up the hand and locked it in a box. They went on, arrived at their destination and disposed of their goods with profit.

One day a person went round asking if any one could cure a patient whose hand had been cut off, and restore the missing portion. The partner of Firoz volunteered to cure the injury. The stranger, who was a *jinn* in human shape, asked him to follow. They went towards the sea and walked straight into the water. The *jinn* asked his companion to close his eyes and not to open them till he got leave. He consented to do so, and at once found himself standing before a splendid palace in the midst of a beautiful garden.

"Now, my friend," said the *jinn*, "you must have guessed by this time what I am. Your patient is the daughter of our king, and if you succeed in curing her father will give you any-thing you wish. As a friend, however, I would advise you to ask for the princess box." Saying this he led him into the palace and presented him to the king.

"May it please your majesty," said the *jinn*, "I have brought a physician who undertakes to effect a cure." "Take him to the princess's room." ordered the king. So he was taken to the princess, who was a lady of exquisite beauty, but short of one hand. Her visitor drew from his pocket the missing hand and, joining it to the stump, applied the ointment of King Solomon, by which the wound was instantly cured. The king hearing of the wonderful cure sent for the physician and directed him to ask his reward. "Please, your majesty," he answered, "I want nothing but the princess's box." The king persuaded his daughter to give up the box, which she did very unwillingly. He also exacted a promise from the princess never to amuse herself again by destroying ships. Then he asked her to send him home, and in her gratitude she offered to escort him.

So she brought him back to the island in the same way as the *jinn* had brought him. There his partner introduced the princess to Firoz, with whom she fell in love at once. At her request Firoz and his partner accompanied her home. By this time Firoz also was in love with her. On hearing of their love her father agreed that they should be married at once, and she consented to come with her husband to his home.

Then his partner took leave of Firoz, and as he was going away he said : "Know, Firoz, I am the man whose debt you paid when you thought me dead. I shall ever be grateful to you. Take this box. The princess will tell you what it contains;" saying this he disappeared ; and what was in the box no one has ever been able to find out from that day to this.

58

THE FOUR FRIENDS AND
THE PRINCESS

There were once four youths, one the son of a Banya, the second of a Patwa, the third of a Pathan and the fourth of a Mina, who were excellent friends and used to spend all their time amusing themselves. At last their fathers remonstrated with them for their idleness and they started with some money for the city of Delhi.

The Patwa bought some gold thread and made a splendid necklace, which he took round the city to sell. As he stood at the Lal Darwaza, the princess saw him and fell in love with him. She called him in and after asking the price of the necklace told him to come next day. That night she began to think of him and determined to go and see him. So she put on a disguise and came to the room in the inn where he was staying. She went in and found that he was not there ; so she put on the necklace which was hanging to a peg and lay down on the bed. As she moved in the dark a sword that was hanging on the wall fell on her and she died.

When the Patwa came back and found the girl lying dead in his room he was overcome with grief and fear. So he took a large earthen jar and putting the body into it threw it into a ravine close by. Next morning some one found it there and when enquiries were made it was found to be the corpse of the Princess. So the Emperor called the Kumhars and asked them to identify the pot. One man said that he had made four of that pattern, which he had sold to four friends. The four youths were arrested and three of them were able to produce their jars ; but the Patwa's jar was recognised and he was ordered for execution.

After the order was passed, the Emperor was desirous of finding the true facts of the case ; so he went in disguise to the cell in which the Patwa lay and asked him if he would care to see his friends before he died. He went first to the Banya who said :

"You need not be frightened. I will spend all I have to get you released."

When they came to the Mina he said :

"Fear not, I will give my life sooner than that you should be executed."

When they went to the Pathan boy he said :

"Do not be afraid. I have a relative in the Emperor's

service. We are arranging to get the Emperor blown from a gun
sooner than that you should lose your life."

When the Emperor saw the devotion of the three friends he
was much pleased and when he investigated the matter and
found that the Patwa was innocent of the murder, he made the
Banya his Treasurer, the Pathan his Commander-in-chief, the
Mina his Brigadier and to the Patwa he gave ten villages.

59

THE PRINCESS AND THE THIEVES

There was once a Raja who
was losing daily a bag of
gold from his treasury.
The guards became aware
of this, and as they feared
dismissal they thought it better to resign their posts. The
Raja asked the reason, and they told him. He allowed them to
go, and appointed other men in their places, and from that day
he used to watch the treasury himself.

The princess, hearing of this, also took her station in the
room with a sword in her hand. At midnight the thieves came,
but suspecting that something was wrong, they agreed that one
man should go alone through the hole in the wall. When he
put his head in the princess cut off his head. A second man
went in to his assistance, and she cut off his head also. In this
way she beheaded all the thieves except one, who had only one
ye, and was too cunning to risk his life by going in. But he

who saw her through the hole and said : "It is you, who have killed my companions. Some day I will roast and eat you".

When he went away the princess tied up all the heads in a sheet and next day laid them before the Raja. When he saw the heads he asked who had killed them, and one after another the soldiers claimed the credit of it. But at last the princess told how she had killed them, and the Raja was much pleased and said : "You are the true daughter of a Raja."

The same night the one-eyed thief broke into the private room of the princess with some of his companions, and taking up her bed as she slept carried her off into the jungle. She was much terrified, but as they passed under a spreading fig tree she caught hold of a branch and swung herself up. When they had gone some distance the one-eyed thief said : "How is this ? The bed seems lighter than it was before." And when they looked they could not find the princess. So they came back to the tree, and seeing her perched in the branches told her to come down. She said : "It is the rule with us women that when a man is fond of us he kisses us." So the one-eyed thief climbed up the tree, and when he put out his tongue to kiss her she cut it off with a knife and in the confusion ran off to the palace.

That night she waited for them again, and when they broke through the wall and one thief put in his head she cut off his nose. He called for help and a second put in his head, and she dealt likewise with him, and so with all of them in succession. They were all much ashamed at their misfortune, and agreed to meet at a garden near the city. The princess heard this, and next morning got herself up as a physician and went to the place where they were staying. She took with her a full ser of pounded glass, and coming into the garden cried out, "Vaid ! Vaid !" ("A physician. Who wants a doctor ?") They asked her if she knew the treatment for noses, and she said that she knew it well. "But," said she, "my medicine is so powerful that whoever takes a dose remains senseless for four hours." "Never mind that," said they, "provided you cure us." Then she put some pounded glass into the nose of each of them, and they all immediately expired. She took all their property, which she divided among the poor, and then returned to the palace.

60

THE DISCARDED PRINCESS

There was once a Raja to whom a daughter was born, and when he heard of it he sent for the astrologers and asked them if the girl would bring him luck or not. Though all the omens were favourable, they told him that if he kept her in his house the family would be ruined. So he had her shut up in a box and putting some pieces of gold in it, ordered his people to throw her into the river. The box floated down to a *ghat* where a dhobi was washing clothes. He took the money himself and gave the child to a potter. One day when the girl grew up, the potter was going to fire his kiln, when she said : "Father, let me fire it this time." She did so and some time after when he opened it he found that all his bricks had turned into ingots of gold.

One day the potter asked her what kind of robe she would like to wear. She said : "Let me have a sheet of bright chintz (*chira*)." He gave her what she asked and when she had worn it for some time she gave it to a dhobi to wash. He washed it at the *ghat* and laid it out to dry, when just then the Raja, her father, happened to pass by. He stopped to smoke and seeing the bright robe and thinking it to be fire he sent his servant to get a light from it. The dhobi said : "This is not fire, but cloth." The Raja was surprised and asked to whom the robe belonged. When he learnt who the owner was, he went to the potter's house and finding the girl to be beautiful, he proposed at once to marry her. The potter agreed and made her over to the Raja. He took her home and called for the Pandits to perform the marriage ceremony. When the pair began to walk round the fire, the girl said :

Pahli bhanwari phirun ; Raja pujai man ki as
Janam ki pothi bicharo Pandit ; pujai man ki as.

"I am making the first round ; your desire is being realised ; but beware; let the Pandit again consult his books." Hearing this the Raja stopped, but the Pandits again urged him to go on. Thus he performed the seven rounds ; but as he was about to complete the ceremony by putting vermilion on the parting of her hair, the girl told him the whole story. The Raja expelled the Pandits from his kingdom and taking the girl to his palace, recognised her as his daughter.

61

THE SADHU AND
THE PRINCESS

Once upon a time a Sadhu was on his travels and saw on a pipal tree the following words written :—

Himmat karai tain ;
Lai pahunchaun main ;
Ji ke na darai ;
Jo chahai so karai.
"Keep a stout heart ;
I will provide ;
Fear not for life ;
And you may do as you please."
When he came to the next city he went and stood in the

court of the king. At that time the princess was sitting on the balcony, with her head uncovered. The Sadhu fell in love with her and remained there with his eyes fixed upon her. This was told to the king who came out and thus addressed him : "O Shahji what do you want ?" He answered : "O Baba, I have fallen in love with your daughter." When he heard this the King had him driven out of the palace. Next day the Sadhu came again and as before fixed his eyes on the princess. When the king heard of it he went to his daughter and said : "Do something to kill this man." His daughter said : "I will use some stratagem to destroy him."

When he came next day as usual, the princess called out to him : "If you want me you must bring me unpierced pearls." The Sadhu started off at once for the banks of the ocean and began to throw handfuls of water over his shoulders. In the evening the ocean (*Samundar*) was moved by his devotion and assuming the form of a Brahman came and asked him what he wanted. He said that he wanted some unpierced pearls. The ocean said : "Stand out of the water and you shall receive them." Then a great wave came up and a pile of pearls lay on the shore. The Sadhu tied up as many as he could in his blanket and took them to the princess. When the king saw the pearls he was amazed and remained silent. Then the princess said to the Sadhu : "If you want me you must cut off your hands and give them to me." The Sadhu at once cut off his hands and laid them before her. Next day she called him again and said : "If you want me you must cut off your head." He answered : "As I have no hands I cannot cut off my head : but if you wish you may cut it off yourself." She did so and when the king heard of it he was pleased and had the corpse thrown away.

A butcher who used to supply meat to the king saw it and took it home. That day he was short of meat ; so he sent some of the flesh of the Sadhu to the palace. When the dish was laid before the king he complained that the supply was short, when immediately the meat spoke and said : "O foolish man, why do you say so ? Can the flesh of a man in love even run short ?" When the king heard these words he was much astonished and said : "Is it possible for you to be restored to human shape ?"

The flesh replied : "Lay me on a couch and let the princess come and say "If you love me, arise." Then I shall revive. It all happened as he said, and the king gave him his daughter in marriage and made over the kingdom to him as her dowry.

62

THE MONKEY PRINCESS

A king had seven sons, but none of them were yet married. One day the king said : "Let all my sons shoot, and wherever their arrows fall, they shall there be married to princesses of that land." So the seven sons let fly their arrows, and the arrows of six of the sons fell into the land of six different kings, but the youngest son's arrow fell into a jungle. Accordingly the six sons were married to the six princesses of the countries where their arrows had fallen, and the youngest one's arrow was found in a pipal tree, and an old woman lived near this tree. The folk said to the old woman : "The king has given an order that where his arrow should fall, there his son take a wife, and now the arrow has fallen here, and so here must he be married." The old woman said : "I have a she monkey : let him marry it : everything can be got ready here for the marriage, except that there is no means for washing up the dirty plates, and the food will be served in gold and silver dishes. Every one who partakes of food then, will be allowed to take away his plate with him." Accordingly the king being pleased, agreed to this, and led the marriage procession to the old woman's house. When the marriage procession arrived there, they saw that the old woman had prepared a right noble assembly for them. In short, when the procession arrived at the door, a splendid nautch descended from heaven and commenced their dance. After this they came and banqueted off golden and silver plates : after all had eaten, the old woman bade each take the plate that was before him. After that. the procession took its leave, and the old woman took farewell of the monkey. The young prince was much grieved that he was married to a monkey. Accordingly, on arriving at his house, the prince found that his sisters-in-law had adorned the couch. & c, and then they put him to sleep with the monkey. When the night had passed, the monkey laid aside its monkey's skin and body, and took the form of a beauteous maiden of twelve years of age. The prince seeing her was much pleased, and began to be very fond of her. Some days passed in this fashion ; then the prince's sisters-in-law and mother said to each other : "At first the prince was much grieved at thinking he was married to a monkey, but now the prince is very happy. The reason of this is not clear." Accordingly one day the prince's sisters-in-law concealed themselves and saw the monkey take off its skin and turn into a lovely maiden. So going to the prince's mother, they told her how the monkey had turned into a woman. Then the prince's mother and sisters-in-law urged him, saying "When the monkey casts off its skin, you immediately burn it, and so she will always remain a woman and will sit with us." The prince told this to the monkey-princess. She said : "Mind, you never do this : if you do this, you will never get me, and you will repent it." The prince said : "Very well ! can I get you in any way ?" She said : "If you go to such and such a place, there lives an old faqir, who sleeps half the year and wakes half the year ; there you must wait on him, and then perhaps I shall become yours at last." In short, one day the monkey-princess, having taken off her monkey skin, went to the bath : the prince at once burnt the skin : and after that, the monkey disappeared. When the prince, after waiting long, saw that the princess did not reappear, he repented of what he had done, and went out of the house to look for her. As he went, a Deo met him and was about to eat him, but the prince said : "I salute you, uncle ?" and cajoled him greatly. Then the Deo, in spite of himself, grew pleased and said : "Suppose you were my nephew, what would you desire of me ?" The prince said : "I am looking for a monkey-princess." In short, that Deo ga v him a [letter and said : "Go to such and such a place there a faqir will help you." So the prince journeyed on and came to where the faqir lived. He saw the faqir was sleeping, and all the grass, soil, &c., had collected on the top of him and all his house was completely overgrown with grass and weeds. He cleaned up the faqir's house and his body as well. At the end of six months, he thought "Now the faqir will get up," so he made the bed nice and clean and filled up a pipe of hamp, and himself withdrew. When the faqir woke up and had finished smoking his pipe, &c., he said : "Brother, where is the person who has done me all this kindness. If he comes, I will give him whatever he asks." The prince hearing this came forward and gave the faqir the [letter, and having made the faqir repeat his promise three times, said : "I want a monkey-princess." The faqir said : "You ask me a very hard thing, but as you have my promise, so stop." In six months' time a number of birds will come to bathe in the tank that is in this grove : among them will be found the monkey-princess. I will transform you into a parrot and cause you to fly. Do you repair to that spot, and when all the birds come down to bathe, take their clothes in your beak and fly away and bring them to me : but be careful, although they all cry out after you, 'Take away the monkey-princess' mind you do not look back." In short, when that day arrived, then the faqir, [turning the prince into a parrot, caused him to fly. The prince went to the spot and perched on a tree. When all the birds began to bathe, then the prince flew away with all their clothes. They all cried out : "Take away the monkey-princess with [you." The prince looked back, and immediately became turned to dust. When the faqir saw that the prince tarried in returning, he thought that the prince has certainly been deceived. Thinking this, the faqir, taking his waterpot, got up, and went to the place, and saw that there were some ashes lying on a spot near there. The faqir thought that this was very mysterious looking ash. In short, he took up the ashes, and making it into an image, breathed life into it. The prince said : "I have slept very soundly." The faqir said : "May such a sleep not fall even on your enemies." Then the prince knew what had happened and said : "This time I was tricked : now think of some other plan." The faqir said : "Wait

another six months ; when the fairies come again to bathe, then
go again in the same way." In short, after another six months
the birds came again to bathe. Then the faqir turned the
prince into a parrot and sent him to the spot. He went and
brought back the fairies clothing. Then all the fairies surround-
ed the faqir's cell and said : "The thief has come here." The
faqir said : "No." At length, the fairies agreed that they would
give him whatever he asked, provided he gave them their
clothes. Then the faqir, having made them repeat their promise
thrice, restored them their clothes. Then the prince said :
"Give me the monkey-princess." The fairies, being bound by
their agreement, said : "Very [well, we will come again to-
morrow." On saying this, the fairies flew away. The faqir said
to the prince : "Many lovely fairies will come, but among them
will be an old one of eighty years of age ; do you seize her."
In short, at dawn many fairies assembled : each one of them
was more beautiful than the other : but the prince seized the
old one, and that was the monkey-princess. The fairies called
out : "You have made a mistake," but the prince paid no
heed to them. Then the old fairy was transformed into a
beauteous fairy and gave the prince a flute and said : "Whenever you play this, I shall appear, and there will be a very fine
nautch." In short, the prince took the flute and bade good-
bye to the faqir, and went off. When he arrived at his house,
he played on the flute and displayed the nautch before his
brothers and parents. They all exclaimed : "Why, we see
to-day the same nautch, that we saw at your wedding." In
short, the prince always kept the flute by him. One day he
happened to go out hunting and forgot the flute. The prince's
sisters-in-law stole the flute and played on it and immediately
the fairies appeared and danced, and then seizing the flute, went
off with it. When the prince came and could not find his flute,
and heard what had happened, then he went out of the house in
search of it, and going to the same faqir, told him all his story.
The faqir said : "You made a mistake : well, stop here and go
at the time the fairies come to bathe." When the fairies' time
came for bathing, then the faqir sent him off, and the prince
went and met the monkey-princess. The princess said : "I will
not come now." But when the prince besought her earnestly,

then the princess said : "Well, do you come with me," and so saying, took him with her, and in the evening, when they went to dance in Indra's Court, then they took the prince with them as their drummer-boy. In short, when Indra grew pleased with their dancing, then Indra said to the monkey-princess : "Ask now whatever you want." The princess made Indra repeat his promise three times, and said : "Give the drummer-boy instead, whatever he may ask." Indra asked the drummer-boy what he would like and he replied : "The Monkey-princess." Then the king was compelled to do so, for what could he do, he had passed his word, so he married the princess to the prince. Then the princess took leave of Indra and went to the faqir, and having made a flying bed there, took leave of the faqir and came to his own kingdom, [and there lived [happily ever afterwards.

63

THE PRINCESS AND HER RIVAL SUITORS

Once upon a time there were a Raja and a Rani, who had an only daughter, when she had grown up she was still unmarried. The Rani, the Wazir, and the brother of the princess, were all distressed at this, and unknown to each other sent out Brahmans and barbers to arrange a match for her. One day the Raja himself saw her and thought to himself that it was time she was married. So he too despatched his envoys; and the four parties of envoys each selected a bridegroom and all fixed the same day for the marriage.

When the Raja called the bridegroom to go through the ceremony, four appeared, and all began to quarrel which of them should wed the princess.

When she heard the dispute, determined to end it : so she jumped into the fire and was burnt to death.

One suitor then went with her bones to Gaya to perform the funeral worship ; the second, i n despair, burnt himself ; the third, thinking it useless to fret, went home ; while the fourth, remained sitting near the pyre.

Soon after the princess and the man who had burnt himself, appeared again out of the ashes, and hearing this, the rivals came and the same dispute arose as to who should marry her.

Then her mother, the Rani, said : "You had all better go to some Raja and get him to decide the case."

So they went to Raja Bhoj and explained the matter.

At last he gave his decision, as follows :

"The man who burnt himself with her cannot marry her, as he stands to her in the relation of brother, because they were re-born from the same source.

"The man who performed her *Sraddha* cannot marry her, because that is a son's duty and she may be considered his mother.

"The man who sat by the fire lamenting her cannot be her husband, as that is the duty of a father, and she is so his daughter.

"The man who cared nothing about her, and did not take the trouble to mourn her, was the bridegroom at last."

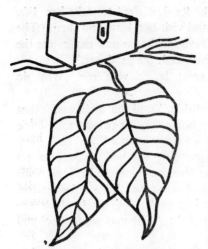

64

PRINCESS BRINJAL

There was once a gardener who was very poor. One day he asked a Koiri for alms, and he gave him a brinjal. The gardener put it in a pot and laid it on the fire, when presently he heard a sort of rattling inside, and when he opened the pot he saw inside a heavenly mansion and a fairy sitting in it. When he asked her name, she said : "I am Princess Brinjal."

He put the pot down and looked round his house, and lo ! it had become a grand palace filled with everything found in royal houses. Princess Brinjal went into the palace and sat on a cot ; and there she lived happily for many years with the gardener. One day the wife of an Ahir came with some milk and curds for Princess Brinjal. She gave her in return a pearl. The Ahirin thought :

"How can a gardener's wife afford to give me a pearl for a little curds and milk ? If I go to the Raja he will give me much more."

So she went next day to the Raja and when he took her milk he told his servants to give her some wheat husks as a reward. She went away grumbling and as she was going out she said to the gatekeeper.

"The gardener's wife gave me a pearl for my milk and I got only wheat husks from the Raja."

He went to the Rani and told her this. She thought to herself : "If the Raja hears of Princess Brinjal he will make her his Rani and turn me out. It were well to poison her before the Raja knows her."

Then she went to see Princess Brinjal, who received her

kindly though she knew that the Rani desired to take her life.
The Rani asked her to come and visit her now and then. The
Princess answered : "I never leave this house and never see the
face of a man but that of my husband, the gardener."

The Rani said : "Many great ladies visit me. Why do
you refuse ?"

"I will go there on this condition," said the Princess, "that
you have a road made from my home to your palace and hang
curtains on both sides, that no one may see me."

The Rani agreed, and next morning she had all the arrangements made and sent a maid to give notice to the Princess. She
bathed and prayed to Khuda and went to the Rani's palace.
The Rani had put some poison in a packet of betel which she
offered to the Princess, but she said : "I have come to see you
and not to eat betel."

Then she made some sherbet and put poison in it too, but
the Princess would not touch it.

Then she told her servants to cook food, and when it was
ready put poison in the Princess's plate. But the Princess
refused to taste it.

At last the Rani said to the Princess : "What are you
always thinking of ?"

"In the plain beyond the palace," said she, "is a *pipal* tree,
and in its branches is a box. In the box is a necklace of
rubies. I am always thinking of that necklace, because if any
one should break it I would die."

The Rani answered : "May I die in your stead ! I will take
care of the necklace."

Then she bade farewell to Princess Brinjal, and throwing
herself on her bed cried : "If I cannot get this necklace I
must die !"

So the Raja sent his horsemen and got the necklace at once,
and gave it to the Rani. She broke it at once and at once
Princess Brinjal died. As she was dying she said to the
gardener : "Do not bury me in the earth, but lay me on a cot
and place me in a tomb." He did as she ordered and people used
to come and see her in the tomb, so lovely she appeared. The
Raja too heard of this wonder and went to see it. He was so
enamoured of her that he seated himself beside her. One day

he was thirsty and broke a pomegranate, half of which he ate
and half he laid on the tomb. At night when Princess Brinjal
came to life she ate the pomegranate and drank water. The
Raja saw her and loved her, and in due time she was in child.
By and by her baby was born, and then the Raja learnt that if
the necklace were returned unbroken to her she would come
to life.

So he took the necklace from the Rani, had it mended and
gave it to the Princess. When she put it on she came to life,
and the Raja made her his wife, and her son became his heir,
but the old Rani was given over to execution.

65

THE PRINCESS WHO GOT THE GIFT
OF PATIENCE

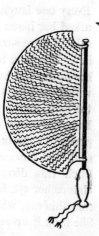

There was once a king who had seven
daughters. One day he called and asked :—
"In whom have you confidence ?" Six
answered "in you," but the seventh said "in myself". The king
was displeased with her and directed that she should be taken
to a jungle and left there. This was done. She went wandering about and came on a house, but the door was locked. She
rapped, but no one answered. Looking down she saw a key
hanging on a nail in the corner, with this she opened the door
and went in. She found the house full of furniture and food ;
so she stayed there. Some time after the king was going on a
journey and asked his daughters what they wished him to
bring them : one said a *dhoti*, another a dol, and so on. Then

he remembered the little princess, and sent a servant to the jungle to see if she were alive, and if so, to ask her what she wished her father to bring for her. The servant came to the house and found her bathing. He gave her the king's message. She called out "I am bathing. Have patience (*sabar*)." He thought she wanted this, so he came and told the king that she wanted patience. As the king was returning from his travels he brought the presents for all the princesses, but forgot the little princess. When he went on board the ship it somehow or other would not move. The captain said to the passengers :—"Think, if you have not forgotten something". All of them began to think, and the king suddenly remembered that he had forgotten the present for the little princess. He went on shore and asked a shopkeeper "do you sell patience ?" Every one laughed at him. Then he met an old women, and asked her if she knew where "Patience" was to be bought. She said "I have some. But tell me who you are and who wants it." The king told his story to the old woman ; she went into her house and brought out something wrapped in a dirty rag which the king took and went on board. When he embarked the ship started of its own accord. When the king reached home, he gave all the things to the princesses and sent her present to the little princess. When she saw the dirty rag, she said "the servant did not give me time to tell him what I wanted. Pitch this dirty rag away." They did so. Years after by chance her eye fell on the rag, and she thought "it is queer that this rag, which I threw away an age ago, has not decayed." She took it up and began to open it, and found in it a lovely fan. She was delighted, and, as it was hot, began to fan himself with it. Then she laid it upside down, and lo ! a prince stood beside her, and said :—"Why did you call me ?" She said :— "I don't know who you are, and I never called you." He replied :—"When you put the fan upside down I had to come to you ; I am the king of a distant land." So they began to chat, and after a while, as they looked at each other, they fell violently in love ; and soon after agreed to be married. They lived together many days, and whenever the prince wanted to go home the princess used to lay the fan straight, and whenever she wanted him she used to turn it upside down.

Long after the princesses said to the king :—"If you allow us, we will go and visit our little sister." He gave them leave, and just as they came to the house of the little princess the prince happened to come up. When they saw him her sisters were filled with envy. The prince used to stay all night with the princess and go home every day. Next day the princesses said to the little princess :—Let us make the prince's bed to-day." She said :—"Do so." They took off all their glass bangles (*churi*), and grinding them up, sprinkled it on his mattress and spread a fine sheet over it. When the prince got into bed the broken glass ran into his flesh. He called out :— "I am in horrible pain. Quick put the fan straight and let me go home." The princess wondered, but she put the fan straight and off he went. Next day the princesses went away, and in the evening the little princess put the fan upside down, but the prince never came. She went on turning the fan up and down, but to no purpose. She was in great grief, and suspected that her sisters had been up to some trick. Next day she put on man's clothes, shut up her house, and went off to the prince's palace. On the road night came on and she slept under a tree. On the tree sat a parrot and a *maina*. At midnight the parrot said to the *maina* :—"Tell me something which may make the night pass." The *maina* said :—"Well ; there is a princess whose father turned her out into the jungle. There she fell in with a prince. When her sisters saw how happy she was, they put broken glass into the prince's bed. He was in such pain, he had to go home, and now though many physicians have treated him, he does not recover," The parrot asked :—"Well, and what is the way to cure him ?" The *maina* replied :—"If any one were to take some of our dung, boil it well in oil and rub it on him, all the pieces of glass would come out." The princess heard all this and collected some dung and started off. When she came to the palace she shouted : —"Physician ho !" (*vaid, vaid*). The sentry announced her arrival. The king called her in and said :—"My son is very ill. If you can cure him I will give you a great reward." She said :—Light a fire and give me some oil, and I will put him right at once." She followed the *maina's* advice, and the prince recovered at once. But she took as her reward only the clothes the prince was wearing. These she took home, turned the fan upside down, and the prince appeared. The whole matter was cleared up, and they lived happily. Thus "Patience" stood the princess in good stead.

66

HOW THE PRINCESS REGAINED THE PRINCE'S LOVE

Once upon a time there was a king who had an only son. His parents determined to marry him to the only daughter of another king. So they had a picture of him drawn and sent servants with copies of it into various lands to try if they could find a king's only daughter to be his wife. On the road they met the servants of a king with an only daughter who had sent them in the same way to find a husband for her. So the servants exchanged pictures, and having settled the marriage went home. When the prince and princess each saw the picture of the other, they were pleased, and all was going well. Now it so happened that there was a jungle where the prince used to go, and in it lived a woman with whom he had struck up a flirtation. So he showed her the picture of the princess, and said "see ! how lovely she is, and I am going to marry her". At this her rival was fiercely enraged, and reflected that now the prince would cease to visit, and that his presents would stop, so she made a plan and asked the prince to give her the picture for a short time as she wanted to look at it through a glass. Then she took it inside, put some black on the eyes, and bringing it out said, "your princess has one fault. She is certainly handsome, but she is blind ; look how her eyes are closed." When the prince saw it he was greatly distressed, and said "what am I to do ? I am to be married immediately to a blind woman." So his mistress said, "don't distress yourself. Don't look at your wife at all, and when you go to her room wear a bandage over your eyes." So when he was married the prince used to stay all day with his mistress, and when he visited his wife at night he used to bandage his eyes, and call out "O eyes ! O eyes !" and then he used to kick his wife out of bed, and she had to sleep on the floor. His wife then was assured that he was carrying on an intrigue, and that her rival has planned this revenge on her.

So one day she asked her father-in-law to get her a basket, an earthen jar, some curds, and the dress of an Ahirin to amuse herself with. When she saw her husband off to meet his mistress, she dressed herself in disguise and followed him. When she came to the house, she cried "curds for sale ! curds for sale !" and was asked in. There she saw her husband, who was much struck with her beauty. They chatted for some time, and at his request she promised to meet him next day at the Lal Bazar. There he went to meet her with a bottle of perfume. As she was smelling it the bottle broke and she cut her lip and fingers. That night when he came to her room her husband cried out as usual "O ! the eyes ! O ! the eyes !" and kicked her out of bed. As she lay on the floor she began to cry violently until he asked her what was the matter. "I am in such pain," she cried. "I hurt my finger and lip to-day in the Lal Bazar." Then her husband identified her voice with that of the pretty Ahirin. So he got up, opened the bandage over his eyes, and saw that not only was his wife not blind, but exceedingly beautiful. So the mistake was cleared up : he abandoned his mistress, and he and his wife lived with the greatest affection ever after.

67

THE MERCHANT, THE PRINCESS AND THE GRATEFUL ANIMALS

Once upon a time there was a merchant who died, leaving a widow and an only son. After his father's death, the young man squandered all the family property ; at last at the request of his mother, he agreed to go on a voyage to earn his living.

Now, in his will, his father directed him always, if he could, to save the life of an animal by buying it. On the way he met some boys trying to kill a rat. He purchased it from them and took it home. Next day he met a bird-catcher with a parrot, and this he also bought for a couple of gold-mohurs. The third day he saw a man beating a cat, and this he also bought and took home. The fourth day he met some people carrying two corpses and behind them a man was holding a jar (*ghara*). The young man asked what was in the jar.

They said :—"In this jar is a snake who has bitten these two people, and now we are going to kill it at their grave."

The young man bought the snake, and then and there he determined to release it. When he opened the jar the snake flew out, kissed him on the face and disappeared. When he went a little further he met a man on horseback with his face concealed.

"Who are you ?" said the young man.

"Don't you know me ?" he replied. "I am your slave whom you purchased to-day for Rs. 500 ; and now I have come to invite you to a feast on behalf of my father."

"I will come," said the young merchant.

As they were going the horseman said :—

"My father is deeply obliged to you for saving my life, and he will ask you to take any gift you please. If you follow my advice don't take anything but the ring he wears on his finger."

"I will follow your advice," replied the merchant.

Then they came to a big cave in the hill, and left their horses outside. When they entered they found themselves in a splendid palace in a lovely garden. The horseman introduced his friend to his father, who was an old man like a king. After dinner the old man thanked the merchant for saving the life of his son.

"Take any gift you like," said he.

"If you please, I would like to have the ring you wear."

The old man smiled. "My son must have told you this. But here, take it."

So saying he took off the ring and gave it to the merchant, who put it on his finger. The moment he put on the ring four demons (*deo*) appeared to him. They saluted him, and he asked "who are you ?"

"We are at the command of him who wears the ring."

So he returned home and prepared to start on his voyage.

Now one of the demons was one-eyed (*kana*) : he brought the merchant a plant, and the merchant said to his mother :—

"Plant this in the house, and if ever you see the leaves wither, be sure I am in trouble, and when it dies, be sure I am dead."

So saying he left her, and ordered his four demons to assume human shape and accompany him. After a long voyage they reached a city. The king of the land had a daughter so lovely that the light of her countenance illuminated the city, and there was no need to light lamps there. She had vowed not to marry until she met a man who fulfilled certain conditions. The merchant desired to win her, and inquired of the Wazir what her conditions were.

"Appear as a suitor and you will be told," he answered.

So the merchant proclaimed his suit, and the Wazir took him to the palace and showed him a row of human heads. "That will be your fate if you fail," said he.

Then the Wazir took him to a garden outside the city, and showed him a mountain of mustard seed.

"The condition is that you spread the mustard all over the

garden in a single watch (*pahar*) : then you must collect it all together in a watch : then you must press all the oil out of it in a watch ; and the fourth condition is, that with the first arrow you must shoot the white crane which sits on the roof of the palace of the princess."

When the Wazir departed the four demons appeared. First they blew at the heap of mustard and spread it all evenly over the garden. Then they ran and called the Wazir and said :—

"Come back and let our master out."

"I am glad," said the Wazir, "to hear that he has given up the competition."

But when he came in he was thunderstruck to see that the mustard was spread all over the garden.

"I merely called you", said the merchant, "to satisfy you that I had fulfilled the first condition."

So the Wazir had to admit the fact, and again he went away.

Then the demons at once blew the mustard into a heap again, and then called the Wazir again.

"I don't know what to think of it," he said, "but I must admit that the second condition is satisfied."

Then he showed the merchant an oil-press (*kolhu*) and departed. The demons commenced to grind the mustard, but were surprised to find that no oil came out of it. At last the one-eyed demon examined the press, and lo ! he found a white demon concealed inside who was drinking all the oil. So he dragged him out and asked who he was.

"I am the white demon," he answered, "and am in love with the princess. It is I who imposed these conditions, and I wish no one to win her by accomplishing them. I am the white crane who sits watching her on her palace roof."

So the four demons thought it best to kill the white demon, and they did so and burned his body. Then they hurried off in search of the Wazir, who was confounded when he saw that the third condition was fulfilled.

"Now show me the white crane," said the merchant, "as I want to finish this business to-day."

Then the Wazir took him to the princess and told her the story. The princess said :—

"Take him and show him where the white crane always sits."

But when they went there, lo ! the white crane had disappeared. They searched for him in vain, and then the merchant told how he had disposed of him.

So the wedding day was fixed ; the merchant married the princess, and they went to live in a palace of their own on the bank of the river. One day the princess was sitting near the water and one of her shoes fell in which a fish immediately swallowed. Some way down the river was the kingdom of another king. The fishermen were fishing and caught a big fish which they took to the king's steward. When the cook opened the fish he found in its stomach a beautiful shoe. Expecting a present, he took it to the king. The king said at once :—

"The wearer of the shoe must be my queen."

So he sent for all the old women of the city, and at last one of them undertook to find the lady.

She prepared a boat and sailed up the river in the direction from which the fish had come. By and by she came to the palace of the merchant and anchored the boat close by, and going below the palace, began to weep. The princess was looking out of the window and called her in. When she saw the princess, she began to weep even more violently than before. At last she said :—

"I had a lovely daughter, just like you, and she was drowned in this river the other day. I weep because you remind me of her."

So the princess entertained the wily old woman. She amused the princess in every way and soon gained her favour. At last the princess told her how her husband had fulfilled all the conditions by means of his magic ring. The old woman said :—

"You should keep such a precious ring very carefully, and never allow your husband to wear it when he goes abroad, lest he may lose it."

When the merchant again went to hunt, the princess warned him about the ring.

"Don't be anxious," he said, "I take the greatest care of it."

"You must leave it with me," she replied. "I will lock it up carefully and send the demons to guard you."

So the merchant left the ring with the princess, and when he had gone the old woman took her to walk on the river bank. The princess showed her the ring which she wore on her finger. The old woman asked to see it, and when she had got it she summoned the demons, put the princess into her boat and carried her off.

When the king got the ring he called the demons, and told them to go and throw the merchant into a well. They went to do so, and found the merchant lamenting his lost princess. As they were fond of the young man, all they did was to throw him into a dry well, and they returned and reported to the king that he was dead.

Then the king told the princess that she was in his power, that her husband was dead, and she must marry him. She at first refused, but finally was obliged to promise to marry him in six months.

Now at this time the leaves of the tree which the merchant's son had planted near his house began to wither. His mother began to feel anxious, and the parrot, the cat and the rat all decided to go and help him. It was settled that the parrot should go first and find out where their master was. The parrot flew night and day, and finally alighted on a tree over the dry well in which the merchant was dying of hunger and thirst. So the parrot flew all over the jungle and collected every kind of fruit which he gave his master, and then took his leave, promising to devise some means for his rescue. On reaching home he told everything to his companions, who started to the city of the wicked king. There they learnt that the king kept the ring on his finger during the day and in his mouth during the night, and that he had four ferocious dogs posted on watch near his bed. So the rat made a hole on the roof and the cat came into the room. The dogs pursued the cat and the rat put his tail up the king's nose, so that he sneezed violently, and blew the ring out of his mouth. The rat seized it and ran away, and going at once to his mistress gave it to her, at the same time explaining how he had succeeded in recovering it. So the demons at once appeared

before the lady, who directed them to seize the old woman who
had caused all the trouble, and transport the whole party home.
Thus the princess recovered her husband, and they lived happily
ever after, and the parrot, the cat, and the rat, were well cared
for as long as they lived.

68

THE PRINCESS
OF KARNALPUR

Once upon a time a ship, came sailing over the ocean, and
the mariners cast anchor close to a city. The son of the Raja
of that city happened to be close by, and seeing a princess on
the ship fell in love with her. She made a sign to him by
rubbing her ears and eyes, and immediately the sailors weighed
anchor and departed.

The prince went home, and calling all his father's courtiers
asked them to explain the meaning of the signs of the princess.
No one could interpret them except a poor shepherd, who
said :

"When she rubbed her ears it meant that she comes from
the city of Karnalpur, and by rubbing her eyes she meant that
the Raja of that city is named Sunetra Sinha." Then the prince
asked the shepherd to lead him there ; they started and after
many days reached Karnalpur. There they put up with a
gardener's wife. The old woman asked their business, and when
they told her said : "You must conceal yourselves, and represent
yourselves as my son-in-law and the shepherd as your servant.
If you do this I think you will meet the princess some day or
other."

The gardener's wife used daily to take garlands to the

princess. One day the prince asked her to allow him to twine a garland. He made a lovely wreath and put a letter inside for the princess.

The princess when she saw the wreath asked who had made it. The gardener's wife said that it was made by her daughter, who had come to pay her a visit.

The princess gave her a present, and as she was going away struck her with an orange branch. When the prince heard this he asked the shepherd what it meant. He said :

"It means that you are to meet her to-night in the garden of oranges."

The prince went there, but fell asleep, and do all she could the princess could not wake him. When she had gone away and he woke in the morning he cursed his folly and consulted the gardener's wife what he should do. She said :

"Make another wreath." The prince made another wreath, which so pleased the princess that she gave the gardener's wife a gold coin, and as she was going away struck her with a lime branch.

When the prince heard this he asked the shepherd what it meant.

"It means that you will meet her in the lime garden."

The prince went there and fell asleep, and again the princess failed to wake him, and went away.

When he told the gardener's wife, she said :—"There is no helping you. But you shall have another chance."

The prince made a third wreath, and the princess was so pleased that she gave a gold coin to the old woman and said :

"Bring your daughter to see me to-morrow and you will be well rewarded."

The old woman dressed the prince in woman's clothes and took him to the princess. The princess asked him to sit with her, but he was afraid and sat on the ground. The princess gave him betel and asked the old woman to go home and leave her daughter with her. The prince then stayed with the prin-cess, and none of the people of the palace suspected what was going on.

But the Raja, the father of the princess, used to weigh her

daily against a flower, and this day she weighed down the flower, and he knew she had a lover.

He proclaimed a reward for any one who would catch him; but no one attempted the task but a wise old woman.

She made a hole in the floor of the princess's room and put some red dye in it, so that the prince when he paid his usual visit fell into it, and his clothes were stained. He went off at once to the old woman's house, and she called a washerman and made him promise to wash the clothes before the morning. But he went off next day dressed in the clothes of the prince to a marriage, and the wise old woman recognised him and had him arrested.

He was taken to the Raja and explained how he got the clothes. He was released and the old woman made a mark on the door of the gardener's house so that she might recognize it again. But when the prince noticed the marks he made similar signs on all the houses near, and so the wise woman could not identify the house. Soon after the prince and princess met again in the palace garden, where there was a shrine of Mahadeva. One of the watchmen saw them, and locked them up in the temple, intending to betray them next day to the Raja.

The shepherd missed the prince, and learning where he was determined to save him. So he dressed himself up as a Banya woman and taking an offering of flowers, cakes, and sweetmeats went to the temple and said to the watchmen : "Kindly open the temple, as I desire to worship in pursuance of a vow I made that I would worship if my husband returned safe and sound."

The watchmen with some difficulty let the shepherd in, when he at once changed clothes with the princess, and she escaped in the guise of the Banya's wife. When the Raja came in the morning and saw only two men inside he was wroth and threatened to hang the watchmen.

But they protested that the princess had been in the temple and had escaped in the disguise of the Banya woman, and said to the Raja.

"Let all the men and women of the city pass through the fire and prove their innocence."

The King agreed and all the people assembled. The prince and the shepherd were also present in the guise of ascetics. The Raja ordered that the princess should first undergo the ordeal. Just as she was going into the fire the prince came up to her and caught her hand and said :

"Princess, before you pass into the fire give me an alms."

She did so and called out :

"If I have touched any man but this ascetic may the fire consume me !"

Then she passed through the fire unharmed.

The Raja said : "My daughter is pure and has been falsely accused."

Next day the Raja weighed his daughter again, and again she was heavier than the flower. He knew that something was wrong, so he gave notice that if his daughter's lover would appear of his own accord he would marry him to the princess and give them half his kingdom.

The prince then came forward and told him the whole story and explained how he owed it all to the cleverness of the shepherd. The Raja rewarded the shepherd. The lovers were married, after some time the prince took his bride home, and they lived happily.

May Paramesar do to all of us He did to them !

69

THE PRINCESS AND THE DEMON LOVER

There was a certain king who was devoted to the chase. By chance one day, with some attendants, he went out hunting.

Suddenly he saw a deer bounding along, after which he spurred
his horse. Towards the evening the deer all at once disappeared. The king, confounded at this, went wandering about the
forest and saw a very high tree in the midst of a plain. Close
to the tree he heard some one weeping. Wondering who could
be lamenting in such a desolate place, when he came up he
saw a lovely maiden sitting there. Convinced that this was a
trap of the evil one, he struck her on the back with his spear,.
and said "wretch, why do you frighten men ? Come forward
and speak." Then the woman looked on the king and he on
her, and he at once became enamoured of her. So he dismounted from his horse and said, "who are you that sit alone in this
jungle and weep ?" The woman replied, "enquire not of me.
I only desire that you should sever my head from my body with
one blow of your sword." He answered, "tell me your story."
This woman replied, "meddle not with my affairs." He said,
"what matters it ?" Then she said, "I am a princess and a
daughter of the Fairies (*parizad*). One day I was walking in
my garden when suddenly a high wind began to'blow, and from
the midst of the wind a form so terrible that one dares not
look at it even by daylight, appeared. I was afeared, and he
approached and said, "princess, I have come for thy sake from
a long distance. Come along with me." I trembled and could
make no answer : so he carried me by my hair and 'flew away
with me, and dropped me in a garden, and then disappeared.
When he left me I began to walk through the garden, and soon
I saw several lovely ladies walking about. I asked them who
they were, and they all began to weep, and said, "what can we
say ?" Then one said, "I am a princess," and another said,.
"I am a Wazir's daughter," and a third, "I am a Jeweller's
daughter." Then I enquired how they had come here, and they
said "just as you did." Then they began to walk about again
and asked each other, "when will that tyrant come ?" As they
spoke a cold breeze blew, and out of it a beardless youth
appeared, armed with all five weapons, and a wallet hanging
from his neck. He seized me by the hand, and said, "Dear !
come along with me." I asked the others who this was, and
they replied, "this is he who brought you hither." Then he
led me away, incapable of resistance, seated me on a couch,.

and tying my hands, stood before me. I asked, "who are you ?" He replied, "I am of the race of the gods (*deozad*), and I have been seven years in love with you, but was unable to secure you : to-day Lat Manat has conferred you on me. The whole happiness of my life depends on you, and I forswear every woman but yourself." I could make no answer, and soon after these ladies whom I had seen in the garden, appeared one with a table cloth, another with a tray, another with vessels. They laid the cloth and washed out hands with water from a *lota*, and one whispered to me, "princess ! eat nothing." Then my abductor invited me to eat, but I said I did not feel well. Presently he embraced me, but I drew back and said, "you tyrant ! I have always heard that a lover obeys his mistress and does not annoy her. If you are really in love with me, do what I tell you. Appear in your real form." He said, "look now." Then he rolled on the ground and suddenly appeared like a palm tree. I trembled, and he at once became a young man. He asked, "did you see me ?" All night long he continued to persuade me but in vain, and when morning came in a passion he caught me up and threw me into the jungle, where for three years I have sat under this tree, eating the fruit which falls from its branches. Each night a watch before the dawn this ruffian comes and implores me to accept him. When I refuse he lets loose a demon on me so that I loss my senses and beat my head against the tree. Then he puts a spell upon me and I come to my senses, and he again entreats me, and when I refuse he flogs me on the back. O prince, do strike me with thy sword that I may escape from this persecution." He refused, and they began talking until the time for the monster's appearance came. Then by the advice of the princess the king climbed up the tree and saw all happen as the princess had described. But when the monster began to flog her the king could stand it no longer. He jumped down, cut off the monster's head, carried off the princess, and they lived happily together ever after.

70

THE TALE OF THE FOUR PORTERS

Once upon a time there was a King who had four sons. He lost his kingdom, and died, and his sons became so poor that they went to the court of another Raja and took service as porters at his gate, where they kept watch and ward by turns. One night, when the youngest of the brothers was on duty, he saw a snake creeping into the Rani's room. He followed it, and just as it was about to bite the Rani, he fired at it with his bow and arrow, and wounded it so that it retreated into a hole in the floor. But a drop of its blood fell on the Rani's garment, and he, fearing that the blood would injure her, wiped it off, and as he was doing this the Rani woke, and was wrath. Next morning she complained to the Raja that the porter had intruded into her chamber. The Raja called the eldest of the brothers and said :

"What is fit punishment for a thief ?

"Protector of the world ! you may put him to death. But take care lest you grieve not afterwards, as the Raja did who killed the hawk."

"Tell me about it," said the Raja.

Then the porter said :

"Once upon a time a Raja went into the forest to hunt, and finding no water was athirst. He sat down under a tree from which he saw that water was dropping. He collected some of it in his *lota*, and was just about to drink it when a hawk flew by, struck it with its claw, and upset it. This happened three times, and at last the Raja was so angry that he killed the hawk. Then he thought he would draw water from the source from which it was flowing. So he climbed the tree, and what did he see ? A large snake lay on a branch, and out of its mouth water was dropping. The Raja knew at once that the hawk had saved his life, so he died then and there of remorse.

O King ! never do an act hastily which you may repent by and by."

The Raja dismissed him, and calling the second porter put the same question to him.

He answered :

"You may justly punish the thief with death, but beware lest you rue it, as the King did who slew the parrot Hiraman."

"How was this ?" asked the Raja.

The porter answered :

"Once upon a time there was a King who possessed the parrot Hiraman and loved him greatly. One day another parrot came to see Hiraman and asked him to attend a general meeting of all the parrots. Hiraman got leave from the King, who as he was going said :

"Be sure to bring back with you a fruit such as is not found in my garden."

Hiraman went to the meeting of the parrots, and returned with a fruit which if an old man ate he became young again. The King gave it to his gardener and ordered him to sow its seed. After some time the tree grew and bore fruits. One night a fruit fell from it which a snake smelt. The gardener next morning took the fruit to the King, who consulted his courtiers.

"Things brought by animals should not be eaten," was their advice. "It should be tried first on a dog."

When it was given to a dog, he died at once, and the King in his anger slew the parrot Hiraman. The news spread, and next year the tree bore many fruits. An old man quarrelled with his wife, and hearing of the poison tree, went and ate one, so that he might die. But when he ate it his youth came back to him, and the King when he heard it, ate a fruit, and he also became young. He then remembered Hiraman, and in his grief died himself soon after.

The porter said :

"O King ! it is not wise to do an act which you may rue hereafter."

Then the King called the third porter and said :
"What is the punishment fitted for a thief ?"

"You may kill him," he answered, "but beware lest you repent, as the goldsmith did who put his son's wife to death."

"Tell me how this happened" said the King.

"There was once a goldsmith whose son's wife knew all the languages of the world. One day she heard a female jackal say to her mate :

" 'A corpse is floating down the river and in its thigh are two precious rubies. If any one would take the jewels we could eat the flesh."

"The woman understood them and went and recovered the jewels from the corpse. As she was going out at night her father-in-law followed her, and saw what she did. Next morning the goldsmith called his son and said :

" 'Take your wife back to her father. She is a Rakshasi and eats the flesh of men.'

"The goldsmith's son started for his father-in-law's house with his wife. On the way they reached a tree where a cow and her calf were sitting.

"The calf said to its mother :

" 'Sit behind me mother ! There are two jars full of rupees buried here and I feel it warm.'

" 'Yes', said the cow, 'and where I sit there are three jars full of rupees buried in the ground.'

"The woman understood this and said to her husband :

" 'Take may necklace to the town, sell it, and buy a spade.'

"He returned with the spade and by his wife's advice dug up the money. She came back to her father-in-law, leaving her husband behind to bring on the treasure. When her father-in-law saw her coming back alone, he concluded that she had devoured her husband. He straightway killed her, but when his son returned and he heard the truth both of them were plunged in such grief that they soon after died. This is a warning, O King ! never to do anything in passion."

Then the King sent for the youngest of the porters and asked him :

"What is the fitting punishment of a thief ?"

"Give me some navvies," he answered, "and you shall see for yourself."

So they went into the Queen's chamber and dug up the floor, and there the snake which had caused all this trouble was found wounded to death. The king then learned the truth, put his deceitful wife to death, and dividing his kingdom among the four porters, went into the jungle and became a Sanyasi.

71

THE PRINCE AND THE ANGEL OF DEATH

There was once a king who reached old age and was never blessed with a son. At last when he was well stricken in years Khuda blessed him with an heir. He was much pleased and, summoning the astrologers, required them to calculate the fortune of the prince. They consulted their books and after much consideration said :—"The prince will be very fortunate but he will die on the seventh day after his marriage."

At this the king was sore troubled and passed his days in care until his son grew up, and fearing calamity, he never married him. At last the prince grew up and asked his father to find a wife for him. Then the king told him the sentence of the astrologers. The prince said :—"All astrologers are liars. Trust not to them. No one but Khuda knows what a man's fate is." So the king found a wife for him, but when he was married the prince feared for his life and leaving his bride rode off to escape his fate.

On the road he saw some men digging a grave and asked them whose it was.

"This is the grave of the prince who has run away to escape his fate," they answered.

In great fear he rode on and found a grave being dug and received the same answer. This happened again a third time. At this his soul nearly left his body, but seeing at a distance a mosque he thought to himself :

"If I am to die, better would it be to die in the house of Khuda."

So he bathed, changed his garments and entered the mosque. There some followers of Islam were praying and when they saw him overcome with grief they asked the reason and he told them his story.

"Pray for me," he implored, "that I may be saved from the Angel of Death."

They consoled him and began to offer up prayers on his behalf. By and by the Angel of Death peeped through the door of the mosque.

"Friends" said he, "you have in your midst one whom Khuda is calling from your world, I have come for him. Make him over to me".

The believers asked :—"Art thou the Angel of Death !" "I am" he answered.

"We pity" said they, "the fate of this youth. Is there no means by which his life may be spared ?"

The Angel answered :—"If each of you give a portion of his span of life to him he may escape."

They agreed and prayed to Khuda to save him; and Khuda spared him. Then he started for home and on the road he found all the graves filled up. He recovered his bride, told the whole story to his father who prayed to Khuda with the prince and they all lived happily for many years.

72

THE PIOUS PRINCE

There was once a Raja who had a son and a daughter. One day the Prince said to the sister : "I wish to become a Sadhu."

She replied : "Do not so. You are a Prince and the life of a Sadhu is hard."

But he would not be persuaded and started on his travels. He came to a city and asked the peo-ple where he could find a carpenter. When they pointed out his shop, he went to the carpenter and asked him to make the shape of a loaf of bread out of wood. He made it for him and then the Prince tied it to his waist-cloth and went his way. By and by he came to the palace of a Raja who asked him to come in and eat. But he pointed to the loaf which hung at his waist and said : "This is sufficient for me."

Then he came into the jungle and hung himself from a tree with his feet downwards. Soon a crow flew down and began to try and pick out his eyes. He said to the crow :

Kaga, sab tan khaiyo, chun chun khaiyo mas,
Donon nain bachaiyo, ki priya milan ki as.

"Crow, you may eat any part of my body you please, but

spare my eyes, because this is my only chance of seeing my beloved (the Creator).

Thus he became perfect (Siddhi) and Bhagwan came down himself and carried him off to his heaven.

73

THE WICKED STEP-MOTHER AND THE PRINCE

There was once a king whose queen bore him a son and a daughter. But the queen died, and the king married a second wife. Before he married he had a house built a long way off, and there he sent the princess, but he kept the little prince with him. The prince was very fond of playing ball, and his father had a golden ball made for him, with this he used to play. But his step-mother hated him. One day the ball fell near her, and the prince went to her very politely and said : "Pardon me ; had I known you were there, I would have never thrown the ball, and will never do it again." But the queen seized the ball, and said she would not give it back till his father returned. So the prince slunk away, and went to bed in sorrow.

When the king came back, what does he see ? the queen's clothes are all torn, her hair is dishevelled, there is dust on her face and she is lying on the ground. "What on earth is the matter ?" asked the king. At first she made no reply. At last she asked, "Did you marry me for the sake of your son, or for yourself ?" "For myself of course," he answered. "Your son," she said, "struck me with his ball to-day and then came to fetch it. When I would not give to him, he tore my clothes and pulled my hair, threw me on the ground and beat me." The king hearing this was sore displeased and sent for the prince at once and taking him to the shore of the sea threw him in and returning to the queen said : "Don't fret any longer. I have

drowned the boy. Now get up and wash your face and hands."
She was much pleased and did as her husband said.

When the prince was thrown into the sea he came up at last
and floated to a distant shore. But his skin and flesh were all
rotted away in the water, and when only the bones remained, he
turned into a parrot and came and perched on a tree near his
father's palace, and from there he called : "My mother got me
killed, my father drowned me, all my body rotted in the water
and my bones became a parrot." When the queen heard this
she thought : "This must be the boy whom I got killed, and
now he has become a parrot." So she sent for all the fowlers of
the land and ordered them to catch the parrot. Though she
promised large rewards and they used all their skill, they could
not catch the parrot.

At last the parrot flew away and came to the house of his
sister. There too be called out : "My mother got me killed, my
father drowned me, all my body rotted in the water and my bones
became a parrot." When his sister saw him, her heart turned
towards and she cried : "If you are my brother come and lie in
my bosom. If your are not my brother go away." No sooner
had she said this, than the parrot flew down and sat in her
bosom and she took him and put him in a cage of gold and
used to feed him daily with her own hand. One day she fell ill
and told her handmaid to go and feed the parrot. But be very
careful," she enjoined. "If this parrot flies away, I will give my
life for him."

The handmaid opened the cage with great care, but as she
was feeding him he got out and flew off and again sat on a tree
near the palace of his father. And then he again called : "My
mother got me killed, my father drowned me, all my body
rotted in the water and my bones became a parrot." When the
queen heard this she again said : "Catch this parrot and I
will give a great reward. If you again fail, I will put you to
death." So they used all their skill and by chance they caught
the parrot.

Then the queen twisted his neck and threw his body behind
the palace. Near there was a garden in which no tree or flower
would grow. But that night flowers of a thousand kinds
sprang up there and myriads of lovely trees. And a tank was

made in the midst of garden and in the middle of it grew up a
lovely flower. Next morning the King's gardener awoke and
when he saw this sight he was confounded and went and told
the king. When the queen heard it, she thought in her mind.
"Surely this is on account of the boy." The king said : "Pluck
me the flower which grows in the midst of the tank." When
the gardener went to pluck it and went into a water the flower
sunk down and disappeared. And the same happened when
any one tried to pluck the flower. So the gardener went
and told this wonder to the king. The queen said, "If your
Majesty gives me leave I will go myself and pluck it." Now
she intended when she had plucked the flower to throw it
away, and bring some other flower to show to the king.
The king replied : "I shall be much pleased if you pluck
the flower." So she went and had the tank dragged with a net,
but though she used all her skill, she could not find the flower.
And whenever the flower came to the top of the water a
voice came from it saying : "My mother got me killed, my
father drowned me, all my body rotted in the water, my bones
became a parrot. Then my mother killed me again and flung
me away, and then I became a flower."

When the king heard this he was confounded. Near him his
daughter was standing disguised in filthy rags and he knew her
not. "What," said she, "will you give if I pluck the flower ?"
"I will give you half my kingdom," said the king. "But, she
said, "I do not want your kingdom; but will you give me whatever I ask ?" "I agree," said the king. She made him promise
thus three times. "You must kill the enemy of the flower." "I
will do so," said the king. Then the girl called out : "If you
are my brother come into my bosom." So the flower come
into her bosom, and lo ! it was shaded by two leaves, one on
each side, and when the king opened leaves out came his son,
who said : "I was innocent and you slew me for no fault."
The king embraced him, and the king knew it was his daughter,
and embraced her. He had the queen killed forthwith, and the
three lived happily together ever after.

74

THE PRINCE AND HIS FAIRY BRIDE

A certain king had seven sons. All of them went out hunting. As they were returning they came to a fig tree (*gular*). The eldest said let us all shoot our arrows from under this tree, and wherever each one's arrows falls there will he be married. So the arrows of the six eldest princes fell in the palaces of Rajas, and the arrow of the youngest fell into the fig tree and stuck there. Then the six eldest married in the families of the six Rajas, but the youngest said to his father :

"Give me some money, and I will go and sit where my arrow fell."

His father gave him money, and he went and sat under the fig tree. At midnight a fairy (*pari*) came out of the tree. She said :

"Why are you sitting here weeping ?"

He told all his story to the fairy and she said :

"Don't fret. I will go with you."

When the six elder princes brought home their princesses, the young prince also brought [the fairy on his horse. His mother, the old Queen, came out to receive the young prince, but he said to his mother :

"Don't take my princess off her horse."

His mother said :

"Child, why are you angry with me ?"

He replied :

"I am not angry, but I will keep her in my own room."

So he shut the fairy up in his own room and went off to hunt. When he returned the old King said to all his sons :

"Bring me a cap worked by each of your wives."

The young prince was much disturbed and said :

"How can my wife give the cap."

But she said :

"Don't worry yourself. I will bring a lovely cap for your father."

She flew to fairyland (*Paristan*), and brought from there the cap of Raja Indra, which she gave to her father-in-law, and he was much pleased. Soon after he told each of them to give him a handkerchief worked by their own hands. Again the young prince was anxious. But the fairy said :

"Don't distress yourself. I will bring a lovely handkerchief."

She flew off to fairyland brought the handkerchief which Raja Indra used to carry in his own hand. The old King was delighted. Meanwhile the fairy became in child. Then the old king asked his daughters-in-law to bring him each a dish of ther own cooking. All of them brought him various kinds of food. One day the young prince burned the monkey skin which was the plaything of the princess. She was greatly distressed and flew off to fairyland. The prince lost his senses for love of her and wandered about the jungle, where he met a faqir. The faqir asked why he was roaming about. He told the story to the faqir. The faqir said :

"Your fairy keeps her clothes beneath those of all the other fairies. I will turn you into a parrot. So fly off and fly back with the suit which is below all the others. But take care and do not look behind you, or you will be burnt to ashes."

The prince in the form of a parrot flew off and came back with the suit which was beneath those of all the other fairies. All the fairies believing him a thief, pursued him. They said to the faqir :

"There is a thief in your hut."

He said : "What have I to do with thieves."

So he turned the prince into a man again. Then the faqir said to the fairies : "Sit down. Why are you worrying this son of Adam. Settle the matter with him. What is the use of quarrelling."

Finally the fairy said :

"The matter cannot be settled in this way. But when we go to dance before Raja Indra, let him act as our drummer (*tabalchi*) and beat the drum skilfully; when Raja Indra is pleased with his playing and asks him what boon he wishes, let him ask for me, and thus, and thus alone, can he recover me."

So the prince began to beat the drum, and so excellently did he play, that King Indra and all his Court lost their senses. Then Raja Indra said :

"Ask a boon," and he replied : "Your Majesty ! give me this fairy."

So Raja Indra gave her to him, and he brought her home with him, and they lived happily ever after.

75

HOW THE FOOLISH PRINCE FOLLOWED GOOD ADVICE

There was once a king's son who was a great fool. When his father was dying, he said :

"I give you four pieces of good advice—

"When any one comes to condole with you after my death, seat him on a higher seat than your own; wear a heavy coat when you receive him.

"Speak to him sweetly.

"Feed him on food you have never eaten in your whole life."

Soon after one of his father's old friends came to condole with him. The prince went out and made him sit on one of the highest shelves in the verandah. His friend was surprised, but took his seat as he was asked to do.

Then the prince came out with a big carpet wrapped round him. His friend was surprised but he asked :

"What disease carried off your respected father ?"

"It was the disease of bread and sugar," said the prince.

He was still more surprised, but he went on to ask : "And when did he depart the life ?"

"Sugar and bread," answered the prince.

His friend thought he was mad, but made no reply.

Then the prince thought :

"I have obeyed three of my father's precepts, and now what food can I give him which he never tasted in his life ?"

Then he thought of his favourite dog, and this he had killed and served.

"What good meat this is !" he said, when they began to eat.

"Indeed it is good," answered his friend.

But when he heard it was dog's flesh he cursed the witless prince and hastened off to purify himself from the defilement of eating such accursed food.

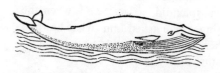

76

THE QUEST OF THE MAGIC POWDER

There was once a Raja who had seven sons; as they grew up he sent for the astrologers and asked them which of his sons was fated to succeed him. They announced that the Raj would fall to the youngest son, and that his elder brothers would become Sadhus. When the mothers of the elder sons heard this they were plunged in grief, and told the Raja that unless they got the heart of the young Prince they would commit suicide. The Raja was in perplexity and consulted his Wazir. The Wazir said : "It is better to lose one life than six." So the youngest Prince was made over to the executioners. As he was being taken away his mother wept; but he said : "Do not fret. What is written in my fate will come to pass."

His mother, as he was going, gave him some *asharfis*, and

when the executioners took him into the jungle and were about to slay him he bribed them to spare his life ; and after they released him they killed a wild animal and took the heart to the Queens, at which they were overjoyed.

The Prince wandered about for a year or two, and when his appearance was changed he came back to his father's city, and giving himself out to be a Banya took service in the bazar. Soon after the Raja sent for his sons and said : "Whoever will bring me the magic powder, the *Setu ka sapna*, he shall be my heir."

The six Princes started off in quest of it, and the young Prince, still disguised as a Banya, went with them. At last after many wanderings they came to the shore of the ocean, beyond which the *Setu ka sapna*, was to be found. As they could not get across, the elder Princes sat weeping on the shore. But the younger Prince went wandering along the beach and met a *sus* (porpoise). The *sus* asked him what his business was, and he said : "If you take me across I will bring you a golden nose-ring when I return."

The *sus* agreed and carried him across on his back. When he got to the other side he found himself in a dense jungle, and roaming about he came on a splendid palace, and when he went in he found a girl swinging. She asked him what he had come for, and when he told her, she said :

"As you have come you must marry me."

"I agree," he said, "but I must first perform the work I came to do. Then I will return and marry you."

She told him to ask for what he pleased, and he asked for the *Setu ka sapna* and a golden nose-ring. These she gave him, and he went to the shore of the sea and found the *sus* awaiting him. The *sus* took him across, and he found his brothers still weeping by the shore. He did not tell them how he had succeeded in his quest. They all went home, and when they came before the King he produced the *Setu ka sapna* and told him who he was. The moment the *Setu ka sapna* arrived all kinds of good luck came to the household, and fairies from Indrasan came to dance before the King. His father was so pleased that he made him his heir, while the other Princes became Sadhus. The Prince went back across the sea by the aid of the *sus*, recovered his bride and lived happily for many a long year.

77

THE TALE OF THE THREE PRINCES

There was once a Raja who had three sons : but trouble came upon him, and all his horses and elephants died. So the three Princes started to seek their fortunes in other lands. They came to a Raja and asked for service. But when he heard that the wages of each was a lakh of rupees a day, he refused to employ them. They went to another Raja, and the same thing happened. Then they went to Maharaja Vikramaditya, who accepted their terms and gave them service.

Soon after Vikramaditya was informed that his best garden was haunted by a witch (*dain*), seven ghosts (*bhut*) and a lakh of demons (*deo*). When all devices to expel them failed Vikramaditya ordered the three Princes to undertake the duty. So they went to the garden, and each was allotted a watch throughout the night. For the first watch the eldest son was on guard, and he soon saw the witch approaching. He asked her what she wanted. She said : "The Maharaja has had my son hung on a tree in this garden, and I come every night to devour his flesh."

The Prince took her on his shoulders and lifted her up to the branch on which the corpse of her son hung : but as she was eating the flesh the Prince cut off her right leg with his sword.

Then the second Prince came on guard. He saw seven ghosts come into the garden, and as soon as they touched the twentyone locks of the palace within it, the doors opened at once, and in the twenty-first room the daughter of the Maharaja was shut up. Her the seven ghosts used daily to roast in an oven, and, when it was cooked, used to devour her flesh. The Prince put some water on the fire-wood of the oven, and when the ghosts tried to light it, such a smoke came out that they were blinded, and the Prince killed them all.

Then came the watch of the third Prince. He saw hosts of demons coming, and challenged them to mortal combat. The leader of the demons accepted the challenge, and was defeated. Then he asked the Prince what he wanted, and he said : "I want the great tank of Indra."

The boon was granted, and the Prince got the great tank and all the fairies (*pari*) of Raja Indra. The leader of them, the Red Fairy (*Lalpari*), gave him a flute and a handkerchief, and said : "Whenever you play on this flute I will attend on you at once."

Next morning Vikramaditya sent his servants to the garden to see what had happened during the night. But when they saw Raja Indra's tank in the garden blazing like gold, they were confounded, and came and told the Maharaja. The Maharaja proposed to marry them all to Princesses of the Court. The two elder Princes agreed, but the younger refused. One day the wives of the two elder Princes went to the garden to see their brother-in-law. He was away at the time, but they found in his house the magic flute and handkerchief, and took them away. When one of them played on the flute the Red Fairy appeared from the Land of Indra (*Indralok*), consumed both of them into ashes and carried off the flute and handkerchief.

When the Prince returned and found his magic things gone, he was overcome by grief and, weeping bitterly, set out for the jungle. There he met a Sadhu, who used to sleep for six months and wake for six months at a time. The Prince, while the Sadhu was asleep, watered his garden, and when he woke the Sadhu was so pleased that he told him to ask a boon. He said : "I want the flute by which I can summon the Red Fairy."

"Go," said the Sadhu ; "this request of yours is too difficult for me."

He went on and met a second Sadhu, who treated him in

the same way. Then he met a third Sadhu, who used to sleep for a year and wake for a year. The Sadhu said : "I have been for many years in search of this flute myself : but I will help you. You must rub your eyes with black cummin (*kalanjan*, *nigella sativa*). Then you can go to Indralok and play the drum of the Red Fairy in place of her drummer (*tabalchi*) whom Raja Indra lately pitched down from heaven. This the Prince did, and Raja Indra was so pleased that he gave him the magic flute, and then he summoned the Red Fairy, but when she appeared she looked at him, and he was burnt to ashes.

Finding that the Prince did not return, in a few days the Sadhu went to Indralok and finding him only a pile of ashes, sprinkled nectar (*amrita*) over him and restored him to life. When the Prince revived he told the Sadhu all that had happened. He blackened his eyes again with cummin seed, and the Prince flew off to the bank of the river of Indralok, where all the fairies were bathing. He stole their clothes, which lay on the bank. The fairies offered anything he pleased in exchange for their clothes, and he received from them the magic flute. On his way home he halted near the hut of a Sadhu in the jungle and when he blew on his flute the Red Fairy came and danced and sung divinely. The Sadhu was delighted, and in the morning asked the Prince to exchange the flute for his stick, which had the power of killing any one its owner desired. But when he got the stick he sent it to beat the Sadhu and recovered his flute. Next he met another Sadhu, and in the same way got from him the magic cord, which binds a whole army, and from another the wishing bag, which gives anything you ask.

With these things he reached the kingdom of his father, which was beleagued by his enemies. From the bag he poured nectar (*amrita*) on his father's army and revived their powers, and with the stick and rope defeated and imprisoned the hostile army. By means of the bag he built palaces of gold and gems, and he and his relatives passed the rest of their lives in ease and happiness.

78

THE PRINCE WHO BECAME A KOL

There was once a Raja, who had an only son, whom he loved very dearly. The Prince was in the habit of going out hunting, and his father warned him never to go towards the south. For a long time he obeyed the orders of his father, but one day he determined to go in the prohibited direction. When he had gone some distance he felt thirsty, but could find no water. At last he saw a Kol felling a tree, and called to him. The Kol replied : "I was in search of you." The Prince asked him to point out where water was to be found. The Kol showed him a tank close by and said : "You can bathe here and refresh yourself."

The Prince took off his clothes and dived into the water, and no sooner had he done so then he was turned into the Kol. But he retained his senses as before. Then the Kol dived into the water and he was turned into the Prince. He put on the clothes of the Prince and went his way.

The Prince could do nothing but put on the clothes of the Kol, and just as he had done so up came the wife of the Kol. She gave him a box on the ear and said : "Why are you sitting here, you lazy rascal ?" The Prince asked her who she was.

"Are you out of your wits that you don't know your own wife, you fool ?" she answered. The Prince said : "You are not my wife. Go away ; don't trouble me." When he said this she called out "Justice, O brethren ! justice !" And at this all the other Kols came up and asked what was the matter. When they heard the case they said : "What, are you mad to-day ? Don't you know your own wife ?"

So the Prince had to put the wood which the Kol had cut on his shoulder and go home with the woman. When they got home the Kolin said : "Take off this wood and sell it in the bazar." The Prince took the wood to the town, and a man asked him what price he wanted for it. He said : "Gave what you think fair." The man gave the Prince four pice, and he took it home with him. When he showed the money to the Kolin she said : "What did you mean by taking so little for such a lot of wood ? Take me at once to the man to whom you sold it." So the Prince took the Kolin to the man to whom he had sold the wood, and the Kolin said : "Why did you give my husband only four pice for such a lot of wood ?" "I gave him," he answered, "what he asked for it." "Well, you must give me the proper price now," she said, and the man had to give her two pice more.

They went home and the Kolin prepared food. When it was ready the Prince, who could not break his caste, said : "I will not eat bread and pulse. Give me some parched grain." "What on earth is the matter with you to-day ?" she asked. "Other days you eat bread and pulse and to-day you are calling for parched grain." However, in the end she had to give him the parched grain, and in this way he lived there many days.

One day as he went to the bazar to sell his wood it so happened that a Kabuli merchant had brought some horses to the Raja for sale, and one of them was so spirited that no one dared to mount it. At last the Raja offered a reward to any one who would ride the horse. The Kol threw down his bundle and said he would try. Every one laughed and said : "What can a Kol wood-cutter know of riding ?" However, he mounted the horse and rode it all over the place. Then he took the horse to the Raja, who said : "Who are you ?" The Prince said : "Just now I am a Kol, but when the time comes I will tell you my story." Then the Raja appointed him to watch the horse and gave him a hundred rupees a month, out of which he made an allowance to the Kolin and lived in the stables of the Raja.

Meanwhile the real Kol mounted the Prince's horse and rode off ; but the horse knew the rider to be a stranger, and soon threw him off. The Raja, his father, had already sent men in search of the Prince, and they found him lying on the ground, and taking him up brought him to the palace. The Raja was surprised to find his son so rude and ignorant ; but he thought that the reason was that he had spent so much time in the jungles ; so he sent for Maulavis and Pandits, and ordered them to educate him.

One day the Sham Prince went into the bazar and met a carpenter who was selling a very beautiful bed. The Kol Prince bought it for a lakh of rupees and made a present of it to the Raja. Now the quality of the bed was this that at night the legs used to talk to each other and tell all that was going on in the four quarters of the world. When the Raja lay down that night on his new bed he heard the legs talking. One said : "This is a very wonderful Raj. The Prince is really a common Kol and the proper Prince is working as a groom in his father's stable." "That is quite true," said the second leg, "and the curious thing is that the Raja does not suspect the trick which this rascally Kol has played on him." "It is certainly remarkable," said the third leg. "But how is this wrong to be set right ?" "If the Raja," said the fourth leg, "would only make them both bathe again in the same tank they would each recover his real form."

The Raja had suspicions already in the matter, and when he heard what the legs of his bed were saying he was much pleased. Next morning he sent for the Kol and the Prince, and sent his Wazir with them to the tank. When they entered the water the Prince and Kol recovered their original shapes. The Kol was beaten and driven back to his hovel in the jungle and the Prince returned to the palace, where he lived many years in happiness.

79

THE FOUR PRINCES AND THE FOUR FAIRIES

There was once a king who had four sons. One night the king had a dream that there was a platform of silver, a tree of gold with emerald leaves, and fruit of pearls hanging on it. Soon after he saw a peacock rise from the earth and alight on the tree when it began to eat the pearls. Suddenly all these things disappeared from his view as well as the peacock. On this the king woke and found himself alone. He was confounded at this dream so that he could not attend his council. On this the king's sons said :—"Father ! what has happened to you to-day ?" He told them what he had seen in his dream, and said :—"If I see this sight once again I will live : if not I will die." They promised to arrange for him to witness the sight again if he would give them three months' time. They asked him to be consoled, and to carry on his duties as usual. The four sons then started in four different directions. The youngest son went off towards Fairyland. When the youngest son reached Fairyland he sat down at the door of a Fairy. Soon after the Fairy saw him and fell in love with him. Now these Fairies were four sisters. They all came up and saw the Prince, and asked him why he had come here. "If a demon (*deo*) chance to see you he will eat you up." He said :—"I have come to your door and now will not leave it." So the Fairies agreed to keep him as their servant. Accordingly he stayed there, and shortly after he himself fell in love with the Fairy who loved him. He told her that he had come on business. She asked him what the business was. He then told her his father's dream, and that he had come in search of the sight which had appeared to his father. So she asked him to explain what it was his father had seen. He explained it fully. The Fairy said :—

"All right ! When do you wish to go ?" He said :—"Only a fortnight remains out of the three months." The Fairy said :— "You can go tomorrow. But remember that we are four sisters. When you reach home, place four chairs in a row, and sit on one yourself and keep a drawn sword in your hand." Further, she gave him a hair and a little box, and said :—"When you burn this hair we, four sisters will appear. But take care that you do this yourself, and do not allow any one else to do it for you. If you fail we will never come. When we come we will dance. As we dance—whichever of us begins to dance and then say "Wah ! Wah !" cut off her head with the sword. By doing this the platform of silver will be produced. When the second Fairy dances and says "Wah !" Wah !" cut off her head, and out of it will be formed the golden tree. Do the same with the third, and the emerald leaves will be formed, and when you cut off the head of the fourth, the clusters of the pearls will be produced. Soon after open the box which I have given you, and out of it will come a peacock which will sit on the tree and begin to eat the pearls. Every thing will then disappear : and the four Fairies will appear sitting on the four chairs, and the peacock will return to his box." The Prince hearing this went home. As he was near home he saw his three brothers. He asked them if they had brought this wondrous spectacle with them. They said they were unable to find it. Then the three Princes asked the youngest if he had found it. "Yes," said he. The elder brothers thought it very curious that he should have succeeded when they had failed. So they made a plan to learn the secret from him, and then throw him down a well. They asked him to draw a little water for them. So he told them the secret and drew some water for them. Then they pitched him into the well. They went with the secret to the king, and proclaimed through the city that whoever wished to see the spectacle should present himself. A great crowd assembled. One of the Princes then burnt the hair and the four Fairies appeared. They saw, as they were flying through the air, that the young Prince was not there. The Princes put the hair several times on the fire, but the Fairies did not appears, but returned home. On the way back the Fairies were thirsty, and went to draw water from the well into which the little Prince had been thrown. They got a demon to let down a rope to draw water for them. The Prince caught the rope. The demon said :—"Who are you ?" He said :—"I am a man. Pull me out." The Fairies told the demon to draw him out. When the Prince came out the Fairies recognized him. When they heard his story they told him to go home and put the hair on the fire, and they would come at once. When he came home his three brothers wondered and said :—"Well, you can display the spectacle. But do not tell our father what has happened." He replied that he would say nothing. He burnt the hair, and the Fairies appeared, and all happened as they promised. The king was delighted at the sight. Then another king who was present saw the sight and wrote him to order him to present the spectable to him or stand the risk of war. The young Prince told the Fairies that the other king had demanded to get the spectable. The Fairies said :—"You may prepare to fight." The other king wondered that this inferior king should dare to resist him. When the battle came off the Fairies sent the demon to help the little Prince, and he in a moment disposed of all their enemies. Then the Fairies pardoned the three brothers, and all four married the four Princes.

80

THE MASTER THIEF

Once upon a time there was a king who was always magnifying himself, and he had an only son who was always hearing his father singing his own praises. One day as the king was eating his dinner, he said :—"On such and such a day I caught so many thieves, and

another day I caught so many, and I will catch another to-night."
His son wondered at this. "Why, he sleeps all night through
and how can be catch thieves ?" So he determined to try him,
and that night he went quietly into his father's room and stole
the bowl (*katora*) out of which he used to drink. When the
king woke and wanted a drink of water he could not find his
bowl and began to beat his servants. Then the prince came up
and said :—"Father, you are always boasting. What a hand
you are at catching thieves, and now some one has stolen your
bowl from your very bed head. This indeed is strange." Then
he produced the bowl from under his arm and gave it to his
father. The king asked :—"Who stole my bowl ?" "It was
I," said the prince, "who stole in order to try you." "I don't
believe it," said the king. The prince replied :—"Let me try
you again." The king said :—"If you can steal my tray from
my bedside to-night, then I will be certain it was you who stole
my bowl, and I will reward you and give you half my kingdom."
The prince replied :—"All right. I will steal it." So when he
went to bed the king hung his tray over his head and filled it
with water, in order that if any one touched it the water might
fall on his face, and he would wake and catch the thief. When
the prince saw that his father had gone to sleep, he took some
sand, and, going into the room, poured a handful into the tray
and when the sand had soaked up all the water he carried off the
tray. In the morning when the king opened his eyes, what did
he see that his tray had been stolen. So he called his son, and
the prince, coming with the tray, presented it to him. The king
said :—"Well done, my son. In a certain land there is a king
and he has a horse of the sea (*daryai ghora*). If you can steal
his horse, I will admit you are a clever fellow, and will give you
my whole kingdom." The prince replied :—"I will steal it."
So the prince started to steal the horse. Now the king of that
land had many astrologers (*failsuf*), who used day by day to
inform him if any enemy or suspicious character came into his
kingdom. That day, when they opened their books they gave
notice that a thief was coming to steal the horse of the sea. The
king was in great anxiety, and every day would ask the
astrologers :—"How far off is the thief now ?" When they
informed him that the thief was close by, the king ordered

that the city gates should be closed, and a guard posted to see
that no stranger was admitted, and that no person left the city.
So a guard was posted on all four sides to prevent any one
entering or leaving the city. It so happened that there was an
old woman who used to go out of the city every day and collect
fire-wood, by which she supported herself. When the guards
prevented the old woman from going out as usual, she went
forthwith to the king and began to weep and strike her head on
the ground, and implored leave to go out, saying :—"I live by
collecting wood, and this is my only means of support." She
made so great a disturbance that the king had to give her
permission to go out once and return once to the city during
the day time. So she used to go out, as usual, every day, and
meanwhile the prince arrived near the city. When he saw that
the gates were closed and no one admitted he was in great
perplexity. But next day, when he saw the old woman come
to collect wood he approached her and said :—"Old lady, if
you take me into the city I will give you many rupees." She
said :—"How can I take you in ; the guards will never admit
you." The prince answered :—"Well, let me sit in your basket,
put some wood over me and take me in ; and if any one on the
road asks you to sell the wood, don't sell it, but say :—'I won't
sell my wood today." The old woman agreed, put the prince
in her basket, put some wood over him, and brought him in.
On the road many persons wished to buy her wood, but she
answered :—"I won't sell my wood to-day." So she brought
the basket into her house, and there the prince alighted. Then
the astrologers said to the king :—"Your majesty, the thief
has arrived in the city and will certainly steal your horse."
The king was in great perplexity and issued a proclamation to
this effect :—"If any one arrests the thief, who has come to
steal my horse, I will give him half my kingdom."

Then the prince got himself up as a Pandit, went to the
palace and asked for employment. The king said :—"I must try
you first before I give you a place among my other astrologers,
come now, tell me what is going to happen." The prince
pretended to open his books, and soon after replied :—"Your
majesty has a horse of the sea, and a thief has arrived in your
kingdom with intent to steal it, and it is quite certain he

will succeed." So the king appointed him one of his astrologers. Now the king used daily to make proclamation that "whoever arrests the thief to him I will give half my kingdom" ; but no one accepted the task. At last the kotwal went to the king and said : "I will arrest the thief."

The prince heard that the kotwal was preparing to arrest the thief, so he went to the house of a poor woman, and putting on a single cloth round his loins and some grain in a basket, began to grind it, and sat up grinding till mid-night. Then he tied himself hand and foot with a rope, and just at that moment the kotwal approached on his rounds in search of the thief. When he heard the noise of the grindstone, he began to think who can be grinding at such an hour. So he looked in and saw a woman tied with a rope, going on twisting the grindstone. When the prince saw the kotwal he began to weep. The kotwal said :—"Why are you grinding at such an hour, and why are you weeping." He answered :—"A man tied me up here, gave me so much grain and went away, saying :—"I am coming back by-and-by, and if you haven't finished grinding it by the time I return, I will kill you."

The kotwal was quite certain that this person must be the thief : so he took off all his clothes and put on a loin-cloth and tied himself up with a rope, and said to himself :—"When the thief comes and unties the rope, I will arrest him." So he told the other to leave, and he went away. In the morning the king made search for the kotwal and found him tied up. So the kotwal went and said to the king :—"Your majesty, it is out of my power to catch the thief."

Now the king had in his employment three Pandits, who were brothers. They said :—"Your majesty, we will catch the thief." So the prince went to their house and said to their wives :—"To-night a devil (*shaitan*) or an evil spirit (*bhut*) will come to your house ; if you wish to escape, then light a good fire at night and sit beside it." The women believed him, and he went, and getting himself up as a barber, went to the Pandits, who were sitting on a river bank. When the Pandits saw him, they said :—"Who are you ?" He said :—"I am a barber. I thought it was daybreak and came to shave you : now what may you be doing here ?" They replied :—"We are sitting on the look-out for a thief." He said :—"If a sharp thief, like this, sees you, he will run away. Now I have a thing with me which, if you shave your heads and rub it on, you will be able to see everything yourselves, but will remain invisible to others." So they were much pleased and said :—"Come and shave us at once." As he was shaving them he cut their scalps in a number of places, and rubbed in hot lime well and said :—"Take a dip in the water." They all took a dip in the river, and as the lime was fresh, the moment the water touched it, it began to heat and burn their heads, so they ran home, screaming with pain. Their wives were quite certain that a devil had come into the house. So they took up sticks and commenced to thrash them. The Pandits kept on crying out :—"Stop, we are your husbands." But the more they cried out the more the women beat them, till at last the women lighted a lamp and saw what they had done and were filled with sorrow. Next morning the king sent for the Pandits, and when he saw them he was at first out of his mind with astonishment, and finally burst into laughter. After this no one would volunteer to catch the thief. At last the king said :—"I will catch the thief myself." So he mounted his horse of the sea, and started at night to catch the thief. The prince met him, and the king said :—"Who are you ?" He replied :—"I am your majesty's Pandit, and without your orders I have come out to catch the thief, because it is written in my books that the thief will certainly come here to-night. Now, please tie up the horse here and sit at little distance. I will watch by the horse, and when the thief comes I will straightway arrest him." The king believed his words and tethered the horse there and went and sat down a short way off. Without losing a moment the prince mounted the horse and rode off at full speed to his own land. The poor king remained wringing his hands.

When he got home his father was much pleased and seated him on the throne of his kingdom, which he ruled with the utmost wisdom and ability.

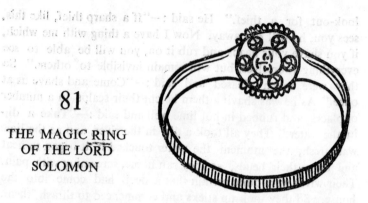

81

THE MAGIC RING
OF THE LORD
SOLOMON

There was a king who had an only son, who was worthless and did not obey his father. The king was much displeased with him. One day the prince asked his father for Rs. 300, and said he wished to travel. The king gave him the money, and the prince went to the stable and selected a horse. This he mounted and started on his travels. He came to the shore of the ocean and saw four boys diving in the water. Soon after they brought up a box out of the water. The prince offered to buy it. They asked Rs. 300 for it. He bought it and took it home. The king asked him what he had brought. He showed his father the box. The king ordered the box to be opened, and out of it came a dog. The king kept the box and the dog. Again the prince went on his travels, but before he started he gave his mother a cup of milk and said :—"Mother, as long as this milk does not become sour know that I am alive." Again he reached the same shore of the ocean, and again he saw some boys dive and bring out a box. He purchased this box also and brought it home. When he opened the box a cat came out of it. His mother said :—"You are a nice fellow ! You never learn anything, and go about buying dogs and cats." Again the prince took Rs. 300 and went to the shore of the ocean. Again the boys brought out a box. He bought it and took it home. When it was opened a snake appeared. The king was afraid at the sight and told the prince to put the box in a jungle. He did so. The prince reflected that the wretched snake was shut up in the box and would die : so he opened the box and immediately a lad came out of it. The prince said :—"Who are you ?" "I am the son of the Lord Solomon. A sorcerer turned me into a snake and put me on board his ship and shut me up in a box. He threw me into the ocean, and immediately he and his ship were submerged." Then he and the prince went to the Lord Solomon. When he saw them he was much pleased and began to distribute alms. One day the son of the Lord Solomon said to the prince :—"If my father offer you any present accept nothing but the ring he wears." Then the Lord Solomon called the prince and offered him many jewels, but he would accept none of them. The Lord Solomon asked him what he wanted, and thrice promised to give him anything he wished. Then the prince asked for the ring. The Lord Solomon with much regret was obliged to fulfil his promise. Then the prince asked the son of the Lord Solomon what were the virtues of the ring. He replied :—"Whatever you desire will be produced from the ring." As they went on they came to a certain city where a princess had made a proclamation that she would marry any one who in a single night would build a palace in the midst of the sea. The prince went to her and said he could fulfil the condition. The princess told her servants to take him to the shore of the ocean. They took him there, and having dismissed them near morning he drew out the ring and ordered it to build a palace in the sea. At once a splendid palace was built. So the prince and the princess were married and lived in the palace. One day the prince went out hunting : two or three hairs of the head of the princess, which were of gold and silver, got broken. She put the hairs on a leaf and threw them into the river. As they floated they came beneath the palace of the king of another land. The king had the hairs taken out and said :—"What must she be to whom these hairs belongs." So he called many wise women and said :—"I will give half my kingdom to any one who will bring this woman to me." One wise woman traced out the princess, and standing under her window, began to weep. The princess called her and said :—"Who are you !" She replied :—"I am your grandmother." The princess ordered her to be entertained. The old woman knew that the palace had been produced by magic. She noticed the ring with the prince, and knew that this was the magic ring. She asked the princess if the prince ever give her his ring. She said :—"He will give it

to me if I ask for it," so the prince gave the ring to the princess.
The old woman got hold of the ring and worked the spirit of
the ring and ordered him to carry the palace as it was to her
country. This was done, and the old woman obtained half the
king's kingdom, but did not give him the ring.

When the prince returned from hunting he found the palace
and the princess gone. He was plunged into grief, but finally
traced out the palace and went there. He wanted to go in, but
the servants prevented him. On this there was a quarrel, and
the king's servants killed him. When he died the cup of milk
which he had given his mother became sour. She knew he was
dead, and took out the cat and the dog which had come from
the ocean. They went off to try and restore their master to life.
The dog dived into the ocean, and taking the cat on his back,
reached the palace where the prince had been slain. They found
his corpse hung to a tree. Then the dog and cat brought their
master to life and put him in a safe place. The prince said : —
"Go and search for the ring." They went off and reached
the palace of the princess. The dog sent the cat to get the ring
from the princess. The princess told the cat that the old
woman had the ring. The cat went into her house and found
that she used to keep the ring in her mouth when she went to
sleep : so the cat made friends with a mouse, and told him to
put his tail in the old woman's nostrils when she went to sleep.
He did so : the old woman sneezed, and the ring falling from
her mouth, was seized by the mouse, who took it to the cat.
The cat took the ring to her master. He called the spirit of the
ring, who carried the palace back to its original place : so the
prince and the princess lived happily ever after.

82

HOW THE AHIR GOT THE BETTER OF THE DEMON AND ACQUIRED A WIFE

There was once an Ahir who was a great fool. One day he was ploughing his field when somebody told him that his wife had given birth to a son. He was so pleased that he gave his informant one of his pair of oxen, and going to his mother, told her that his wife had a son. She said :—"My son, how can this be when you are not married yet ?" But he insisted that it was so, and that his informant would not have told him a lie. So he took some money with him and went in search of the man and said :—"Brother can you tell me where my father-in-law lives ?" The man said :—"When you go out of the city you will see a well. The first woman that comes there dressed in yellow clothes is your wife. You have only to ask her where she lives". The Ahir was delighted, and buying a lot of presents in the bazar, went and sat by the well. Finally a woman came up, and she by chance had yellow clothes, and it so chanced that a boy had been born to her lately. The Ahir followed her with the things, and said he had brought them for the baby. She thought they must have been sent from some relation's house, so she gave him tobacco to smoke. As he was smoking the woman's husband came in and was surprised to find a stranger there. But when he went inside and saw the presents he was still more incensed from jealousy and began to thrash his wife. When the Ahir heard her cries he was greatly enraged at any one beating his wife, so he went in and beat the woman's husband soundly and turned him out. Next day he went to the landlord of the village and said :—"Give me a little land and I will cultivate it." The landlord said he had no land to spare except a field which would grow a hundred maunds of rice. "This field, said he, is empty, but in the middle of it is a *pipal* tree in which a demon (*deo*) resides; he won't let any one sow it. If you care for it you may have it." He agreed to take the field, and taking an axe with him began to cut away at the tree. When the demon saw what he was about, he roared at the Ahir and warned him to let the tree alone, but the Ahir said : "Keep quiet, or I will give you a cut with my axe". Then the demon became afraid and said :—"Well! if you spare this tree you may ask what you please". The Ahir replied :—"I was going to sow rice here and I should have got a hundred maunds of grain : I don't mind letting the tree alone for a hundred maunds of grain". This the demon agreed to give. Next day the demon's nephew (his sister's son, *bhanja*) came to pay him a visit : and the demon told him what had happened. He replied :—"Uncle ! if you only give me the order I will go and kill the Ahir." He replied : "It would be a good job." So his nephew started to kill the Ahir. The Ahir was sleeping at a well in front of his house. When the young demon saw him he got in a panic and hid in the water-tank beside the well. When the Ahir woke he put his foot by chance on the demon's head who shouted out *Bapre ! Bapre !* (O father, father). The Ahir asked :—"Who are you." He replied :—"My uncle, the demon, merely sent me to ask whether you will have your hundred maunds in husked or unhusked rice." The Ahir replied :—"Well ! I suppose I may as well have it husked." When he came back he told his uncle what a fright he had got. "All right !" said he, "it is true I only promised to give paddy, but I suppose I must give cleaned rice." So the Ahir got the best of the demon, received his tribute of rice regularly, and lived happily with the woman ever after.

83

THE WITCH AND THE BOY

One day a porter's son was wandering about and seeing a Gular tree covered with fruit he climbed up and began eating. Just then an old woman came there and said—

"Pass down some of that fruit to me."

So he bent down the branch and when he came within her reach she caught hold of him and put him in her bag. This she threw on her shoulder and went off. By and by she sat down to rest and when he got the chance he popped out of the bag and putting some stones and thorns inside he hid himself. She soon got up and raised the bag on her shoulder. She was going off when a thorn pricked her. Then she called out—

"You young rascal, you may scratch me as you like with your nails, but when I get home I will make soup of you."

When she got home and found the boy had escaped from the bag she was much disgusted, but she was on the look out for him and a few days after she found him on the same tree.

So she caught him and put him in her bag and said—

"You won't escape me this time, my boy."

So she went home and called her daughter-in-law and said—

"You cut up this boy and put him in the soup-pot. I am going to the bazar for some pepper and salt and I will be back by the time he is cooked."

When the young woman took the boy and was going to cut him up she could not help admiring him and said :

"What nice eyes you have and what a pretty round head. How did you manage to be so ?"

He answered—

"My mother arranged my eyes with a hot darning needle and she shaped my head with the rice-pounder."

"Will you make me like you ?" she asked, and when he said he would she put down her head and he put out her eyes with a hot needle and smashed her head with the rice-pounder and then put her into the soup-pot. When he saw the old woman coming back he dressed himself in the young woman's clothes and sat modestly by the fire with the corner of her sheet over his face.

When the soup was ready the old woman shared it with her family, but when she gave some of the meat to the cat the cat said—

"Spit it out ! The mother-in-law is eating her daughter-in-law."

"What is the cat saying ?" the old witch asked.

"I will be back in a moment and tell you" said the boy and with that he bolted out of the house. And it was not till the old woman looked into the pot that she found that it was her own daughter-in-law that had been made into soup. I need hardly tell you that the boy kept away from that tree in future.

84

THE STORY OF
MURDAN KHAN AND
THE DAUGHTER
OF THE JINN

There was once the son of a
soldier who fell into poverty
and said to his mother:—
"If I had Rs. 50 I would go
somewhere in search of
service." His mother gave
him the money out of her
savings. When he had gone
some distance he saw a
corpse lying near the road and a grave ready dug. A large
crowd was there, and one man would not allow the corpse
to be buried. The people remonstrated, but he would not
mind. The Sipahi enquired why he would not allow the corpse
to be buried. He was told that the dead man owed Rs. 50,
and that his creditor would not allow him to be buried till
he was repaid. No one present could afford to repay the debt.
Finally the Sipahi paid the debt with all the money he had
and buried the corpse. Then he returned home. His mother
asked him how he came to return so soon. He replied that

with this Rs. 50 he had purchased property worth many lakhs, and had now no money to pay for its carriage. He told his mother that he needed Rs. 50 more for this purpose. She gave it to him and said she had no more. The Sipahi again started with the money. When he reached the spot where he had buried the corpse, he met a Sipahi armed with sword and shield. They spoke to each other. The second Sipahi asked the other where he was going. He replied that he was a Sipahi and had left home with Rs. 50, and had got a corpse buried in that very spot by paying its debts ; and had got Rs. 50 more with which he was going in search of employment. Then the second Sipahi told him that his name was Murdan Khan, and that he also was in search of service, and that he had also Rs. 50. So they joined and went off together. When they came to a certain city, what did they see but that a river ran in the midst of it, dividing the city into two equal parts. But no one could cross from one bank to the other. They asked why this was so, and the inhabitants told them that in former times people used to cross freely, but no one had crossed for the last fifty years. If any boat put out it was sunk in the river. Then Murdan Khan proposed to his friend that if they could buy goods on this side which were not procurable on the other and take them across the profits would be great. The other agreed, but said it was impossible to convey the goods across. Murdan Khan said he would devise some plan. So they purchased goods worth Rs. 75 and tried to hire a boat, but no boatman would accept the job. Finally Murdan Khan said he would manage the boat himself, so the boatman lent him an old boat. Murdan Khan loaded the boat and the news spread in the city. All the people turned out to see the spectacle. Then Murdan Khan let his boat loose and sat on the bulwarks with his sword drawn. His friend said : —"What use is a sword on the river ?" Murdan Khan told him to watch what would happen. When the boat reached half way across, a hand appeared out of the river and caught the boat and tried to drag it under water. Murdan Khan struck at it with his sword and part of the hand fell into the boat. Then the boat got across. Then his friend asked Murdan Khan :— "What is the meaning of this?" Murdan Khan replied :—

"This was the hand of a daughter of the Jinn. She had made a vow to marry a man, so she got hold of a man to her liking. By him she bore a daughter. She also wishes to marry a man. For this reason she drags down boats that she may find some one on board to her liking." His friend, astonished, asked :— "How did you learn this?" Murdan Khan replied that he was skilled in the science by which secrets become disclosed. I saw a bracelet (*kangan*), a thumb-ring (*arsi*), and two or three rings which fairies wear on the hand, when it fell into the boat." When this bracelet was shown to the jewellers they declared it was worth the revenue of a kingdom : so they asked him whence he had stolen it. Then the jeweller informed the city kotwal. He arrested the two Sipahis and brought them before the King. He interrogated them about the bracelet. Then Murdan Khan explained how he had cut off the hand of the daughter of the Jinn and acquired the bracelet. He added that he had also a thumb-ring and two finger-rings which he got in the same way. The King was greatly pleased, and presented him with a *khilat* of immense value. Then Murdan Khan offered the fairy jewellery to the King. He presented it to his Queen. She gave it to her daughter. The Princess said :—"What is the use of a single set ? I want the pair." The King called all the jewellers and tried to get the pair of these jewels made, but no one could make them. So he sent for Murdan Khan and said :—"If you can get the pair of these jewels you may have my daughter to wife. Murdan Khan said :—"I cannot marry just now, but I am anxious to get my brother, who is with me, married. If you agree to my proposal I will do my best." The King agreed. Then Murdan Khan dived into the the river and reached the palace of the Jinn. There he announced himself to be a physician. The Jinn's daughter, who was in great pain from the loss of her hand, sent for him at once and said she would give him anything he pleased if he would cure her. Murdan Khan had the severed hand with him. He told the Jinn's daughter to shut her eyes and he could cure her at once. So she shut her eyes. Then Murdan Khan fixed the severed hand to the stump, and it became as it was before. All the Jinns were astonished at his skill. They offered him all sorts of presents. He said he wanted only the pair of the bracelet. So she gave it to him with a lot of other jewels. So he came up out of the water with the jewellery and brought them to the King, who was much pleased; and according to his promise married the Sipahi to the Princess : and the King dismissed her with her husband, accompanied by an army and valuable presents. When Murdan Khan and his friend got home all the people wondered how this poor Sipahi had gained a Princess for his bride. Soon after Murdan Khan took leave of his friend, but the Sipahi replied :—"What am I that I should take all this wealth. Stay here and we will serve you." But Murdan Khan said:—"It is not in my power to stay." "Why," asked his friend. Then Murdan Khan explained to him:—"I am the corpse which you had buried. You and I are clear, and I can stay no longer. By the order of God I had to stay with you : so now the blessing of the Almighty be on you." Then he disappeared. His friend long lamented him. Finally, he erected a splendid tomb to his memory, and appointed a Hafiz to read the Quran there, and afterwards spent his life in ease and happiness.

85

THE FOOLISH AHIR

There was once an Ahir, who was a very stupid fellow. One day an invitation came for him from the house of his father-in-law, and his mother was ashamed to allow him to accept it because he was such a very stupid fellow, and was sure to disgrace the family. But all the neighbours said that he must go; so off he started. On the way he began to think : "What shall I sing when I come to my father-in-law's house?" While he was thus thinking he saw a fox. "Ah ! I have learnt one song (*birha*) from him." Next he saw a harrow in a field and said : "I have learnt another from it." And some way on he saw some paddy-birds at a tank, and said : "I have learnt another from them."

When he reached the house where the wedding was going on, his father-in-law received him very kindly, and in the evening, when the procession was about to start, his father-in-law said to him : "We are all going to fetch the bride and there are none but women left in the house. You had better remain behind and see that nothing goes wrong." So the foolish Ahir remained behind to watch the house and the womenfolk.

Now a dacoit had plotted with some other rogues to rob the house that very night, and he came with his drum and began to play for the wedding guests, so that they should not hear his companions cutting the house wall. Then the women get hold of the foolish Ahir, and said : "You must sing us something."

So he began, and sang the song he had learnt from the fox—

Khat khut kas kihale re !

"Why are you making a sound like *khat khut* ?"

By this he meant the noise made by the fox as he scratches the ground, but the thieves thought he heard them cutting the wall. So they stopped their work for a while.

Then he began another song—

Rendariya tar senhariya.

"Your little hole is under the little castor oil tree."

He was thinking again of the fox, but the thieves thought he saw them digging under the tree which stood behind the house ; so they lay quiet.

Then he looked round and saw a box under a bed, and as he could think of nothing else to sing, he sang—

Khatariya tar pitariya.

"There is a little box under the little bed."

Now it was this very box the thieves were after; so, thinking
themselves discovered, they lay quite quiet.

Then he remembered the harrow, and sang :

Henga sa paral bate re.

"You are lying like a harrow."

The thieves were sure he saw them, so they ran away. In
the morning the dacoit came to get a share of the booty, but
when the thieves saw him they beat him well as the cause of their
failure. When the people of the house went out in the morning
and saw the hole in the wall, they said : "This fool has been the
saving of us after all." And when his father-in-law came back,
he said : "You are a very smart fellow," and when he was going
home he gave him a fine cow as a present.

86

THE SOLDIER, THE
BHUT AND THE RICH
MAN'S DAUGHTER

There was once a gallant soldier. One day he was walking
about when he saw a respectable man sitting at his door crying.
The soldier enquired the reason, and he replied :—"What can
I say ? I have one lovely daughter. One day she was sitting on
the top of the house. Suddenly she fell insensible, and her teeth
were clenched. When I heard of this I went and raised her up.
Since then she always sits naked, and beats any one who brings
her food and drink, and if no one brings it, she rushes at the
whole household with a sword. This causes me infinite distress."
The soldier replied :—"Why worry over such a petty matter ?
I will cure her at once." The merchant answered :—"Several

men have attempted the same task, but she caught them by the leg and pitched them out of the house." The soldier asked :— "What will you give me if I cure her ?" He said :—"Whatever you ask." The soldier then demanded her hand in marriage, and the merchant was so distressed that he consented, and gave a written engagement to that effect. Then he showed him the house where the girl was. The soldier began to cook some rice, and when it was ready and the fire went out, he suddenly saw a foot appear out of the girl's room and move on to his cooking-place into which it entered, and lo! there was a loin-cloth in the fire-place which began to blaze up. Then he heard a laugh and a voice saying :—"Soldier ! be off! Why let misfortune overtake you ?" He replied :—"It is not for a man to leave a business half done." Then he began to cook again, and soon after saw some earth fall from the roof, and an opening appeared, and from it a child's severed hand fell down and lay quivering on the ground, and in the same way all the other members appeared. The soldier was confounded. Then he suddenly saw a child two years old standing before him. They saluted each other, and the soldier said :—"I am he whom you desire. Brother ! two daggers cannot fit into the same scabbard." He replied : —"We must evidently fight, and may God confer her on whom He pleases." Then he began to laugh and said :— "My laugh is the signal of death. Why ruin yourself ?" Thus saying, he suddenly seized a sword and tried to escape. The soldier pursued him, but he all at once disappeared into the girl's room, and a voice of crying was heard. Soon after the girl came out dressed in splendid apparel. When the soldier saw her he fell at once in love with her; and asked :—"Who are you ?" She replied :—"I am she whom you seek. Depart ! Why should your ruin come ?" Then the soldier began to read some spells. Of course she was possessed by a bhut. Then the bhut seized the soldier by the hair and dragged him some distance, and then the soldier knew it was a bhut because its feet were turned the wrong way. However, he went on reading spells, and finally the bhut said : —"I give up all claim to the girl. For God's sake let me go." But the soldier for safety's sake then and there burnt him and took the girl back to her father, and according to the conditions her father had them married.

87

THE MERCHANT'S
DAUGHTER AND
THE JINN

Once upon a time there was a merchant, who had a daughter
eight years old and a son twelve years of age. Both used to
learn their lessons together. One day the merchant went on a
voyage with some merchandise, and charged his wife to take
care of the children in his absence. Soon after the voyage
began he was wrecked on a certain island, and he reached only
with the greatest difficulty. There he met another merchant,
to whom he related all his misfortunes; and he befriended him
and took him home with him. On his return his creditors began
to demand their money. Somehow or other he managed to pay
his debts, but he was reduced to absolute penury, and his son
was obliged to leave him in search of a living. So only the
man and his wife and daughter remained. Four years passed in
this wretched way. One day his daughter, hungry and thirsty,
was standing on the roof of the house, when she saw another
house to the back of their own, and in it three or four girls
were playing with their dolls. They asked her to join them,
and she went and joined in their play. As she was going home
after an hour or so's play the girls gave her some rupees and
food. With this she came home and gave the money to her
mother, and said :—"I was playing with the girls in the house
behind our's, and they gave me food and this money." Her
mother was confounded, and said :—"Why ! the house behind
our's is empty ! Where did these girls come from to-day ?"
Then she went herself on the roof and saw a jewelled seat
spread and a handsome young man wearing a royal crown
sitting there. When she saw him the old lady retreated, but he
got up and salaamed and addressed her as mother. She reflected, "Now that he has called me mother, why should I
hide myself from him ?" Then she came forward and blessed

him, and said :—"Child, who are you ? and where do you
live ?" He said :—"What does that matter ? I am a prince in
my own right." They continued talking, and as he was going
away he gave her a necklace of jewels of great value, and
asked her to present it to her daughter. He also gave her
money for herself, and she left him. When she came home
she gave the necklace to her daughter and the money to her
husband, to whom she told the whole story. He was a wise
man and understood it all, but told no one.

Behold the glory of God (*Khuda*) ! On this money the
family lived for some time. One day, dressed in fine clothes
and jewels, the girl was on the top of the house, when she saw
a youth, about eighteen years of age, walking about below,
with whom she straightway fell in love. But he soon disappeared. When she came down she could not help thinking of him.
By evening her eyes had got red with weeping, and she lay insensible on her couch. So it went on for some days, when
she noticed on all the shelves (*taq*) of the room a quantity of
all kinds of sweets and perfumes, and that her mother was in
distress about her. By degrees the news reached the king that
this merchant's daughter was very beautiful. He determined to
call the merchant and enquire. So he called him, and the merchant told the king the whole story. The king said :—"Do not
be uneasy. I will take measures in the matter." So he sent for his
wazir and gave him eight days' time to work out the case. With
great difficulty at last he met a wise man who promised to help
him. After he had read some spells he said :—"This is one of
the race of the Jinns and the son of a king." Then the wazir
went and informed the king and asked if he might release the
youth from his enchantment. The king said :—"I agree, and
if you succeed will give you what you please." While this was
going on the girl began to weep. The merchant went and told
the king, who said :—"Do not be anxious. Your daughter
will get well. But will you marry her to me ?" Meanwhile the
girl in a state of nature escaped from the house and went into
a forest, where she stayed on the bank of a stream. The wise
man followed her and began to read his spells. Now, behold
the glory of God ! As he was reading a boy, ten years old,
appeared and said :—"Sir, spare my life ! I have been in love

with her for five or six years. If you want a friend, take me.
Why are you murdering me at some one's instigation?" The
wise man answered not, but went on reading, and so continued for three days. On the third day behold a whirlwind
arose, and out of it appeared an army, in front of which
advanced the boy with a royal crown on his head, who challenged the wise man to do his worst. He took a cauldron of
oil and set it on the fire, and when it boiled, all the army
began to fall into it. When they were destroyed, by the power
of his knowledge, he took up the boy in a cocoanut and pitched it into the stream. On this being done, the girl at once recovered.

Now see the glory of God! Just as the procession was
going to start, the merchant's son heard that his sister was
being married to the king and arrived at the bank of the
stream. As he was bathing, he dived and found the cocoanut.
He was thinking of opening it, when the wise man ran up and
warned him to forbear. But he would open it, and a blaze as
of lightning arose from the cocoanut, which consumed the
wise man and the girl's brother. Then the Jinn went to the
king and found him sitting with his bride. He saluted the king
and said :—"You had better give up this lady." The king was
astonished, and told him to do what he pleased. So the Jinn,
with one blow, despatched the king, seized the bride and carried
her off, and she was never heard of afterwards.

88

THE WHITE WITCH

There was once upon a time a white witch who ever tried to
compass the ruin of human beings, so she one day sat

by a roadside and transformed herself into Rs. 500. Now there was also a great sage who, when he found out what she had done, went to the end of road to warn people away from the spot. He had not long to wait, however, for presently four sepoys rode past that way : so he said to them :— "Do not go by this way, sirs, for a white witch is seated by this roadside who seeks to compass people's ruin."

But the four sepoys laughed. "What," cried they, "we who have been in the heat of battle and are just returning from bloody warfare to fear a woman ?" So they went on their way. As they rode on, they presently came to where the witch was lying in the shape of Rs. 500. "Oh !" they exclaimed, "the cunning old sage did not wish us to pass this way because of this money, for he knew we would take it, and he no doubt wanted it all for himself." So they got off their horses to take it, but finding it too much to carry, they sat down beside it to watch it. But soon they began to feel hungry. "What good is the money to us if we starve by it ?" said they. "Let two of us go to the bazar and buy some food for all of us while two of us still keep guard here." To this they all agreed. So two of them went to the market to purchase some food for all of them. But as they went on, one said to the other :— "Let us poison some sweets (*laddu*) and give them to those others, then they will die, and we shall have only two to divide the money between, and consequently will have more than we would if it was divided among four." To which the other agreed. So when they reached the market, after they had feasted themselves they poisoned some sweetmeats and went back to their companions who were watching by the Rs. 500. As they sat watching they saw their comrades returning from the bazar and coming towards them, so one said to the other : — "Let us shoot those fellows as they are coming along, and then there will be only two of us to divide the money, so we shall have more than we would were it divided among four." The other agreed, so they raised their guns and shot their friends as they were coming towards them. As they fell down dead the ones that were keeping guard by the rupees said :— "Let us now go and search their bodies, and what food we find on them we will eat, for we are very hungry." So they went and searched their

bodies and found the poisoned *laddus* on them. Of these they
had a good feed, and of course died too. They were not long
dead when the sage passed by that road. When he saw their
corpses he sadly shook his head. "Alas! said he, I warned
them against their fate, but they would not listen, and the
white witch (*dain*) has compassed their ruin."

89

THE BARBER AND
THE DEMONS

There was once a barber
who was so hard up that
he determined to seek his
fortune in other lands. So
as he was going along he came to a jungle and there met a
demon (*deo*). When the demon saw the barber he danced
seven times; then the barber danced ten steps. The demon
asked the barber "why did you dance?" Then the barber
took courage and asked "why did you dance?" The demon
answered "because I intend to eat you." Then said the barber,
"I danced because I am in the habit of catching demons, and it
is now some days since I have seen one." The demon asked
"have you ever caught one?" "O! several," said the barber.
"But I have only one with me just now." Then the demon
said "let me see him." So the barber took his mirror out of
his wallet, and when the demon saw his reflection in the glass
he said "doubtless this man *does* catch demons. But don't
catch me, and I will give you anything you ask." So the barber
said "all right! Give me a thousand rupees and I will spare
you." So he got the money and went his way rejoicing. Now

the barber had a Brahman for a neighbour who, when he saw the barber's prosperity, induced him to disclose how he got the money. So he asked the barber to take him with him and see if they could not extract some more money from the demon. Accordingly, next morning they went off together, and when they reached the jungle they saw a whole lot of demons holding council (*panchayat*), so both of them in terror went up a tree ; but when it became hot the demons all came and sat down under a tree, and demon who had been swindled by the barber told his story. Then one of his friends said "had I been there I would have got in such a rage that I would have devoured the rascal." And another said "I would have strangled the scoundrel ;" and another—"I would have crushed him under my feet." When he heard these awful words the Brahman was stupefied with fear and fell down from the tree. But the barber shouted out "catch one first for me, then you can have as many as you like !" At this all the demons bolted. But the Brahman said "I have had enough of going after their money. It is well I did not lose my life." So he and the barber returned home.

90

HOW THE EMPEROR AKBAR WENT TO RUM

One day the King of Rum asked if there was of his court any one who could bring an Emperor like Akbar and a Wazir like Birbal to his court. One courtier replied : "If I receive a fitting reward I can do this." The King answered :—"I will give you a reward greater than you can ask for."

So the courtier went to his house and drew a picture of Delhi and the Jumna and its palaces full of lovely dancing-girls. He

took the picture and showed it to Akbar, who was so infatuated
by the sight, that he said to Birbal : "Let us get into this picture." Birbal advised him not to do so, but when he insisted,
he said : If you get into this picture leave a writing behind
to say that you did so against the advice of Birbal."

So Akbar and Birbal went into the picture, and in a moment of time they found themselves at the court of Rum.
Then Akbar asked Birbal : "Is there any way by which we
can return to our own land ?" "There are a thousand ways,"
answered Birbal. "Tell me only one," said Akbar. Then Birbal
said : "The easiest way is for you to dress in my clothes and
I will take yours."

So when they came before the King of Rum the King addressed Birbal as Akbar said : "You are now in my power."
Then Birbal said : "You may have what you please of my
treasure. Send your sons with my Wazir and they can bring
back what they like."

So Akbar and the sons and the Wazir of the King of Rum
came to Agra, and when he got there Akbar assumed his royal
robes and sat on his throne. When the Wazir of the King of
Rum saw this he wrote to his master that he had been deceived,
and Akbar said : "Send back Birbal safe or you and the sons
of the Rum shall die."

So Akbar got back Birbal and the Wazir and the princes
returned to the land of Rum.

91

THE WISDOM OF THE
DAUGHTER OF
BIRBAL

One day Akbar sent for Birbal and said : "Procure me masons
who will build a house neither on the ground nor in the sky."

When Birbal heard this order he was overcome with grief
and was unable to eat. But his daughter came to him

and said :—"Father, do not be distressed. Take some leave from the Emperor and I will arrange all."

So Birbal got his leave and his daughter bought some parrots and every day she used to teach them to say—

Pahunchao int gara

Tab banai Imambara.

"Bring bricks and mortar and let us build the Imambara."

When they had fully learnt their lesson one day Birbal went to the Emperor and as they were sitting together a flock of parrots flew over the palace crying :—*Pahunchao int gara, tab banai Imambara.*

When Akbar heard them he asked what this meant and Birbal replied :—"The masons are ready. If your majesty orders the materials to be brought they will build you a mosque between the earth and the sky." The Emperor laughed and said :—"You may call your masons. Who wants such a mosque to be built ?"

92

AKBAR AND BIRBAL'S DAUGHTER

When Birbal was appointed to be Prime Minister of Akbar many persons, and particularly Muhammadans, were jealous of him. One day a Muhammadan came to court and endeavoured to supplant him by a show of superior wisdom. Akbar asked him first—"Which is the best of flowers ?" He replies the *genda* or marigold, which is used in daily Hindu worship.

Next he was asked—"Whose son earns most?" His answer
was "the *banya*". Then he was asked—"Who is a greatman?"
He replied, "the King", and to the last question—which is the
sweetest thing in the world? he said : "Nothing is sweeter
than sugarcane."

When the daughter of Birbal heard of this contest of wisdom, she instructed her father how to answer. When he came
to court and was asked what was the best flower, he answered
"The cotton flower"; the son who earns most is that of the cow;
the virtuous are the great ; the sweetest thing in the world is
one's own interest.

The Muhammadan sage was worsted and left the court in
disgrace.

93

A TALE OF AKBAR
AND BIRBAL

Akbar once said to Birbal :
"If you are such a wise man,
what must your father be.
Let me see him." Now
Birbal's father was an ignorant villager, and he feared
that he would be disgraced
before the court. So he told
his father not to answer a
single question. When the
old man appeared Akbar
said : "How are you ?" But
he answerd not a word, and
though Akbar asked him many questions he made no reply.

Enraged at this Akbar said to Birbal : "How should one deal
with an idiot ?" "When a person comes before an idiot, your
majesty", was his answer, "the best way is to hold one's
tongue."

94

THE PILLARS
OF THE SKY

Once upon a time Akbar
said to Birbal : "My
palace is supported on pillars of wood and stone, but on what
does the sky rest ?"

Birbal answered : "The sky, too, is supported on columns."
"Why then do we not see them," asked the king.

Birbal replied : "Give me money and time and I will show
them to your majesty".

So the king gave Birbal a lakh of rupees and six months'
leave, and he started on his travels through the world. He
went toward the south and whenever he came to a city he used
to shout out in the streets; "Whoever will stand five hundred
blows of a shoe to him will I give five hundred rupees reward."

But no man would accept the condition. At last a man
hearing his cry came out and said : "Give me five hundred
shoe blows, and I will give you five hundred rupees." And
then and there he produced the money.

Birbal said : "You will die after one hundred blows, and
who is to bear the remainder ?"

"My wife," he answered.

"But she must be weaker than you and fifty blows will
kill her."

"Then my son will bear the rest."

"And if he die too ?"

"Then my daughter, who is all I have, will stand the rest,
for I know you come in the name of Allah and the Emperor,
and their wishes are a law unto me."

Akbar, when he heard the devotion of the man, was
astonished.

"Such, your majesty, are the pillars on which the heavens
rest."

95

THE READING OF
HEARTS

Akbar once asked
Birbal : "What is
your opinion of me ?"
Birbal replied : "I have
the same opinion of
you which you have
of me ; because hearts read hearts." Akbar said : "This is
impossible." But Birbal said, "Come for a walk in the city and
I will prove it to you." As they were going along they saw a
miserable old woman begging. Akbar said : " I *do* pity this
poor creature. Cannot you, in so great a kingdom as this,
make some provision for her by which she may pass her last
days in comfort ?" Birbal asked Akbar to stop, and going up to
the old woman said : "Old woman, do you not know that
Akbar Badshah is dead ? " When she heard this she began to

weep and said : "Alas ! alas ! how shall I now pass my days ?
It was by his virtue that I gained my daily bread, and now that
he is gone I must starve." Birbal came back to Akbar and
said : "Now your Majesty sees that the old woman loves you
because you feel for her." They went on a little further in the
bazar and saw a Sewara faqir begging, and as he beat on his
stick he was abusing a banker and extorting alms. When Akbar
saw him he said : "Birbal these wretches are the curse of the
land. Why do you not make a law to repress them ?" Birbal
asked Akbar to stop, and going up to the faqir said : "O Baba !
Do you not know that Akbar Badshah is dead ? " The faqir
cursed him and said : "May his soul rest in the lowest hell !
Did he ever give me a pice ? " Now said Birbal, "Your
Majesty sees that this man hates you because you do not feel
for him. Do not hearts read hearts ?" Akbar said : " I am
convinced."

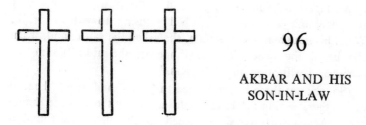

96

AKBAR AND HIS
SON-IN-LAW

One day Akbar and Birbal went out hunting, and Akbar saw a
crooked tree : so he said to Birbal : "Why is that tree crooked?"
Birbal answered : "This tree is crooked because it is the son-in-
law of all the trees of the forest." "And what else is always
crooked ?" asked Akbar. Birbal answered : "The tail of a dog
and a son-in-law are always crooked." (*Tircha* —cunning or
cranky.) Akbar asked : "Is my son-in-law also crooked ?"
"Yes, O King," replied Birbal. "Then have him crucified,"
said Akbar.

A few days after Birbal had three crosses made—one of gold,
one of silver, and one of iron. When Akbar saw them he asked
for whom they were intended, and Birbal answered : "Your

Majesty ! One of them is for your Majesty, one is for me, and one is for your Majesty's son-in-law."

"And why are we to be executed," asked Akbar.

"Because," said Birbal, "We are all the sons-in-law of some one." Akbar laughed and said : "Well, you may let my son-in-law alone for the present."

97

AKBAR AND BIRBAL

Akbar once said to his minister Birbal : "You must bring me three things—the finest jewel and the most faithful and the most faithless thing in the world." Akbar further ordered that if he failed he should lose head. Birbal went home very sorrowful and lay down on his bed refusing to eat or drink. When his daughter saw his state, she asked the cause, and, when she heard the orders of the Emperor, she said : "Do not be anxious. I will carry out his orders."

So she got three boxes, locked them up and gave them to her father, saying : "Take these and show them to the Emperor." When the boxes were opened in the first was found a lamp.

"This," said Birbal, "is the finest jewel in the world, because it illuminates the houses of the rich and poor alike." In the next box was found a dog. "This," said Birbal, "is the most faithful thing in the world, because you give it a little food and it guards your property with its life." In the third box was found the Emperor's son-in-law. "This," said Birbal, is the most faithless creature in your Majesty's dominions, for give him as much as you will he is never satisfied and you will never gain any honour through him."

Akbar was much pleased at the wit of his minister and dismissed him with a lordly present.

98

THE QUESTIONS
OF AKBAR

Akbar once said to Birbal : "Show me a ruby eight for a pice, nectar eight jars for a pice and a faithless creature worth one-eighth of a pice." Birbal went home and got an earthen lamp, some water and a dog and brought them to Akbar. "The lamp," said he, "sells at eight for a pice and gives more light than any ruby ; the water is the real nectar, and the dog is worthless and faithless because he follows any one who feeds him." Akbar was pleased with his answers and gave him a present.

99

KING AKBAR
AND
THE DONKEY

One day Akbar said to Birbal :—"Show me something new. I have seen all the sights of the world." Birbal was puzzled, and his daughter enquired the reason. When he told her, his daughter sent for a donkey and had it trained to the saddle.

She then made it known that her father was on the point of
death. When the news reached Akbar he hastened to visit his
minister ; but his daughter sent out word that if Birbal saw the
king in his last moments he would go to hell. Then she
announced that Birbal was dead, and after some time mounted
her father on the donkey, and made him ride to the house of
one of the ladies of the court. The lady was surprised to see
Birbal risen from the dead. He said :—"God has provided me
with a divine conveyance, and I am going about collecting
information for Him." She informed the king that Birbal
appeared, and he desired to see the divine conveyance. So
Birbal appeared to the king and told him the same story. The
king said he wanted, too, to go to heaven ; so Birbal made him
cover his eyes and mount on the donkey. He led the king on
the donkey to the chief market-place and left him there. After
a time the king removed the bandage from his eyes and saw
where he was. "This is something you never saw before in
your life," said Birbal, and Akbar was much pleased.

100

THE WISDOM
OF
BIRBAL

Akbar once said to Birbal :
"Is there a man in the world
wiser   than   yourself ?"
Birbal replied : "Great
king,   there   is   no man
wiser than myself." So Akbar made a proclamation throughout
is dominions that whoever would exceed Birbal in wisdom

should be richly rewarded. When the brother of Birbal heard of this he went to Akbar and said : "Oh, great king, I am wiser than Birbal." The king said : "Very well. Prove it. So he went to his brother and said : "I desire to live apart from you. Divide the ancestral property equally between us." Birbal said : "I have no objection. We will divide the property ; you can live in half the house and I will live in the other." But his brother said : "This plan will not answer at'all ; you must pull down the house and cut every brick in two." Birbal was surprised when he heard this foolish proposal ; but he said to himself : "How am I to answer this fool ? And if I do not answer him Akbar will think that my brother is wiser than I am."

On the whole he thought it best to leave the land ; so he went off to the king of Riwa and asked for employment. The king asked him who he was and he answered : "Men call me Birbal." The king then received him very kindly and asked him why he had left the court of the Emperor. He said : "I had some private reasons for going away. If you give me employment here I will stay ; if not I will go away." The king said : "My kingdom is yours ; you may stay as long as you please." So he got honourable service and stayed there.

When the buffoons of Akbar's court heard that Birbal had gone away they came to the Emperor and performed before him. When they were done Akbar was so pleased that he said : Choose what boon you please." They answered : "All we want is, leave to bathe in the royal chamber." Akbar was perplexed at this demand and thought "If I had only Birbal here to baffle these scoundrels. If I consent I am disgraced before my subject for ever." So he said :'"Give me six months' time and then I will give you an answer." Meanwhile he made great search for Birbal, but could find no trace of him. Then he sent a circular letter to all the subject Rajas saying : "I have excavated a well and a tank, and I wish to get them married. Send me all the wells and tanks in your dominions so that suitable matches may be selected." This he did, thinking that the Rajas would be perplexed to find an answer, and that only the Raja who had the benefit of Birbal's advice could get out of the difficulty.

As he expected, all the Rajas were perplexed how to give an answer to such an extraordinary letter. But when the Riwa Raja consulted Birbal he said : "Write to the Emperor and say 'My tanks and wells are all ladies, and it is the custom of my land for the bridegroom to fetch the bride ; if you send your well and tank I have no objection to the alliance.'" When the Emperor read the letter of the Riwa Raja he was quite certain that it must have been written by the advice of Birbal ; so he came himself to Riwa and brought Birbal back with him with the greatest honour to Delhi.

When Akbar got back to Delhi he sent for the buffoons and said : "Do you still desire to bathe in my private chamber ?" They said that such was their desire. He said : "You can do so." But when they came in they found Birbal standing there with a drawn sword in his hand. "Come and bathe here, my friends ; but if any one lets a drop of water fall on the floor, off goes his head." They were afraid to attempt the task, and going to the Emperor they said : "Great king ! we have received our reward. We merely wished to know if you had found in your court any man wiser than Birbal."

101

THE THIEF AND THE
CONFECTIONER

A thief went one day to the shop of a rich confectioner, and said : "Are these all the sweets you have ? I want some specially good ones to-day." "I have some better inside," he

said. While he went into the inner room to fetch them the
thief carried off his money box. When the confectioner found
that he had been robbed, he followed the thief and demanded
his money. The thief admitted having the money, but said that
it was his own. At last they were both brought before King
Akbar.

He said : "Bring some hot water and I will settle the
matter." When the water was brought he had the money placed
in it, and when some *ghi* rose to the surface, the King at once
gave the case against the thief and ordered him to be hanged.

102

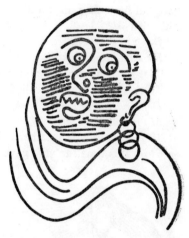

THE FATE OF
THE SHREWISH WIFE

There was once a wife who was such a shrew that every morning she used to say to her mother-in-law : "You wretched
widow ! May I see the day when your face is blackened, your
hair shaved and you led round the city mounted on an ass."
To this the old woman would say : "As long as my son is
kind to me you can do nothing. Parameswar grant that he may
never come under your influence." One day the wife began to
moan and complained of internal pain. When her husband
came and asked what he could do for her she said : "This
disease is very difficult to cure. The only remedy is that you

get your mother's head shaven, her face blackened and she led round the city on the back of an ass."

The husband went at once to his wife's mother and said : "Your daughter is sick unto death and it has been announced by the astrologers that she will never recover unless you allow your head to be shaved, your face blackened and are carried on the back of an ass around the city."

When she heard this the old woman wept sore ; but her love for her daughter was great so she allowed to be done to her as her son-in-law had said. When the procession reached the house of her daughter, her husband went in and said to his wife : "Come out and see ! We have done even as you desired." On this she pretended that the pain had left her and she came out. But when she saw that it was her own mother who had been thus disgraced she was overwhelmed with shame, and cried—

Dekh mai ki chali
Sir mundi, munh kali
"See how my mother comes —hair shaven, face blackened."
To this her husband replied —
Dekh nari pher pheri
Ma meri hai ki teri
"Look again wife whether it is my mother or thine."
From this time the wife gave up her shrewishness.

103

WOMEN RULE
THE WORLD

One day a Raja said to his courtiers :—
    "Who rules the world ?"
    They were unable to give an answer then and begged time

for consideration. The Wazir was in great distress what answer
to give, for he feared that if his answer turned out wrong, he
would lose his office. As he was going home he saw the
daughter of the Raja who was a very wise princess sitting at her
window and when she saw the anexity of the Wazir, she asked
the reason. He told her the question which the Raja had proposed to his courtiers. She said —

"When you go before my father say that it is women who
rule the world."

The Wazir trusted in her wisdom and when the Raja again
summoned him he gave this reply. Now the Raja hoped that
the Wazir would say that it was the Raja who ruled the world ;
so he was wroth and knowing that it must be some woman who
had suggested the answer, he made the Wazir tell her name.
When he heard that it was his daughter who had suggested the
answer, he sent an officer with orders to her to strip off her
dress and ornament and bring her to the court with one dirty
rag to wear.

When she came, he sent for a loathsome beggar who used to
beg about the city and he made her over to him, telling him
that he might use her as he pleased.

The princess went in great distress to his hut with the beggar ;
but before she left the palace she managed to conceal one valuable jewel in a corner of her rags. When she got to the hut
she took it out and said :—

"You must go with this to the quarter of the money changers
and sell it. You must not say a word. I will write down the
price of the jewel on a leaf and lay it and the jewel before the
merchant and he will give you the value of it."

The beggar did as he was told and when the merchant saw
that he kept silence he supposed that he was some great saint
under a vow not to speak. So he was afraid and counted out
the money as the princess had written on the leaf. This the
beggar brought home to her.

Now it so chanced that two thieves saw the beggar getting
the money from the merchant and determined to rob him. So
they waited till the beggar was out of the hut and then they
broke in. When the princess saw them she was afraid. But
she made a plan and said to them—

"You are welcome. Here I a lady of high birth have been given by my father to this filthy beggar. Will you save me from him ?"

One of them gladly agreed to marry her and she told them to go off at once and bring a litter that she would go with them as a bride. Meanwhile the beggar returned and she told him what had happened. She made him hide himself and by and by the thieves returned and brought with them a litter and bearers. Then she said to them—

"The first night I came here Devi sat on my breast and would have taken my life had I not vowed to offer to her a black goat on the eighth of every month and this is the day of the sacrifice. I dare not set out till it is done."

So one of the thieves went to get a goat and soon after she said to the other :—

"I am sorry that when I sent your brother for the goat I forgot to ask him to bring some flowers as well, for without them the sacrifice cannot be performed. So he went away to get the flowers and then she called the beggar and seating herself in it with him she told the bearers to take them to the house of the thieves. When they arrived there, they went in and bolted the door and told the bearers that the house was her's and if the thieves came up they were to beat them off.

When the thieves came and could not get into their house they made a great disturbance, but the people of the quarter who were sore afflicted by them came up and drove them out of the place. Then the thieves went and made a complaint to the Qazi.

When the princess heard that they had complained to the Qazi she went to him herself and told him that she had bought the house for two hundred rupees and if he wished he might come and see it that night at the first watch. When he saw that she was a handsome girl he readily agreed to come. Then in the same way she went to the Kotwal and asked him to come at the second watch ; the Wazir she asked for the third watch and Raja for the fourth watch of the night.

When the Qazi came she kept him talking about the thieves until the Kotwal knocked, when she told him to take off his clothes and hide behind the water-pots.

So she dealt with the Kotwal and when the Wazir knocked she told him to take off his clothes and put on a woman's old ragged petticoat and sit in a corner and grind the flour-mill.

In the same way when the Wazir came and after he had been some time with her the Raja knocked, she made him take off his clothes and hide under the granary. Meanwhile she went into another room and soon after the Raja felt thirsty and went to where the water was kept to get a drink. The Qazi was so frightened that he moved and knocked down the water-pots, and when the Raja saw him standing naked there he was sure he was a Rakshasa and began to scream for help. Then the princess came down and when she brought a light the Qazi, Kotwal and Wazir, were all discovered to the Raja ; they were all ashamed. But the girl said to her father—

"Do you not know that I am your daughter and it is women who rule the world."

So the Raja took her to the palace and had her duly married, but the thieves he made over to the Kotwal.

104

THE SOLDIER AND HIS VIRTUOUS WIFE

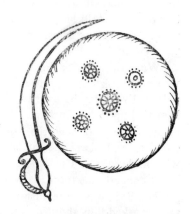

There was once upon a time a soldier who had a beautiful wife, but he was very poor. At last his wife said : "My dear husband, our wealth is gone. What is the use of our living like this any longer ? You had better go abroad and earn money for our support."

"How can I go abroad without money for the journey ?" he asked.

"It is bad," she said, "to eat the bread of charity in the
house of your father-in-law. I will get some money from there,
and then you can go abroad and seek your fortune." As he was
going away she asked him, "How shall either of us know if
the other has ceased to love ?"

"How can I provide for this ?" he asked. So she went into
the garden, and picking two buds of *chameli* came to him and
said : "Let each of us keep one of these buds, and whichever
of us loves another his or her bud will blossom."

When he was starting, she put on her finest clothes and was
taking leave of him, but he turned away from her. She fancied
that he did not like her dress, so she went and changed it for
another. But even then he turned away his face from her. She
was grieved and said :

"My dear husband, what have I done that you have lost
your love for me ?"

"Fine dress", he answered, "does not befit the wife of a
soldier." He said : "Take my sword and shield. Now give me
the shield and cut at me as hardly as you can with the sword."
She did as he told her, but he parried all her blows. Then he
said : "Keep these arms, and in time of need with them protect
your virtue."

With this advice he left her and went to a distant city,
where he took service with a Raja and guarded the gate of his
palace. Every day he used to look at the *chameli* bud which he
kept tied up in his turban. One morning the Raja was sitting
at his gate and saw the soldier looking at the bud. He was
curious, and sent one of his servants to see what the soldier
was looking at. The soldier said : "I do my duty honestly.
What concern has the Raja with my private affairs ?"

The Raja was more curious still, and going himself to the
soldier asked him about it, and the soldier told about the buds.
Soon after the Raja went on his travels and came to the city
in which the soldier lived. He was a man of dissolute habits,
so he sent for an old woman and told her to bring the most
beautiful woman in the city to see him. She went to the wife
of the soldier and proposed to her that she should visit the
Raja. She agreed to go for four lakhs of rupees, but the Raja
gave her five lakhs, of which she kept one lakh for herself and

gave four to the soldier's wife. When the Raja came she kept him in conversation for some time, and when he tried to approach her she drew her sword, fell upon him and wounded him sorely.

When he was recovered from his wounds he came back to his own city and told the soldier what had happened to him. The soldier told him that this was the work of his wife. The Raja approved of her fidelity to her husband and advanced him to honour.

105

THE CLEVER WIFE OF THE WAZIR

There was once a Wazir of a certain King who had amassed much wealth, and was very rich. He was so devoted to this that he neglected his business at Court, and finally lost his post. For some time he supported himself on his savings, but when he began to fall into want his wife advised him to go another city and try to obtain service.

They came to another city, and the Wazir took a small house, where he placed his wife and he himself began to attend the King's court and sat with the other courtiers. No one took any notice of him, till one day the Wazir of the King was passing his house and, seeing his wife, was carried away by her beauty. He asked who lived there, and when he heard the story he sent for the ex-Wazir and promised to protect him. So nex day he took him to the court and said : "This man can bring the Rangtatiya bird from the forest."

Now the King had been long seeking the Rangtatiya bird ; so he was much pleased and gave the young man a thousand rupees, and said : "I give you a month's time to fetch the bird."

The young man was afraid to protest ; so he went home and told his wife. She said : "The Wazir is sending you to get you out of the way as he wants me. Sit in the back room and do not show yourself, and I will outwit him."

When her husband was supposed to have gone in search of the bird, the Wazir used to visit her daily. At last he said : "Your husband will never return and you had better come to live with me." She answered : "Come to-morrow and I will give you an answer."

Then she gave her husband fifty rupees, and said : "Go secretly to the bazar and buy several jars of treacle and some cotton dyed in various colours."

When he brought these things home she made him dig a deep pit in the inner room and she spread a sheet and on it she laid the coloured cotton. Then she said to her husband : "Go into hiding, and when the Wazir comes make a great knocking outside."

The Wazir came in and sat down, and by and by her husband made a noise at the door. "This must be my husband," she said. "He has doubtless brought the Rangtatiya bird."

The Wazir was afraid and asked her to hide him. So she took him into the inner room, and he at once fell into the treacle. Then she signed to her husband to go out, and she pulled the Wazir out of the hole. He asked her to wipe him, and she threw over him the sheet with coloured cotton, which stuck all over him. Then she shouted to her husband : "Here is the Rangtatiya bird." When he saw him he went at once to the King, and the King sent his courtiers to fetch the bird. When he was brought into the court, the young man said : "Pour some water over him and you will see how his colour will improve."

So they poured water over him, and all the cotton fell off, and they found it was the Wazir. The King laughed, and when he heard the tale he dismissed the Wazir and appointed the young man in his place.

106

THE DEVOTED WIFE

There was once a woman who was such a good wife that she was known as Pativrata, or "the devote spouse." One day she was pounding rice and her husband came in and asked for a drink of water. She dropped the pounder in the middle of a stroke and as the blessing of the gods was upon her, it remained hanging suspended in the air as it was. A woman of the neighbourhood who happened to be there saw the miracle and was astonished. "How can this be ?" she asked. "This comes from my devotion to my husband," she answered.

Her friend came home and said to her husband: "The next time I am pounding rice you ask me for a drink of water and I will prove to you what a devoted spouse I am." He did

so, but the pounder fell on his head and broke his skull.
All the neighbours ran up and beat and abused her, and one
man made this verse :

> *Pativrata jo nari hoe,*
> *Musal akase tange soe ;*
> *Kulata chale pativrata chal ;*
> *Apne pati ke phore bhal.*

"A devoted wife can keep the grain pounder suspended in
the sky, but if a vicious woman tries to imitate her, she breaks
her husband's crown."

107

A WOMAN'S
WILES

Once upon a time a hunter went into the jungle and saw an
enormous egg. "Here is a monstrous egg," he thought to
himself, "let me see to what animal it belongs." So he
got up a tree to watch, but before he got up he burnt the
grass and cleared an open space round the egg.

Now the egg was that of a snake. When the snake saw
the smoke she hastened up, and said :

"If I only knew who tried to burn my egg, I would bite
him."

But when she saw that her egg was safe, she said :

"If I only knew who took care of my egg while I was away,
I would reward him."

The man called out from the tree :

"It was I saved your egg."

"Come down," said the snake, "and don't be afraid."

After a while he took heart to come down, and when the snake asked him what boon he desired, he said :

"Give me ears."

"This is a hard thing you ask ; but you shall have it. Henceforth you will have the power of understanding the speech of animals."

So the hunter went home and sat down to dinner. As he was eating, two ants came across the floor, and he heard one say to the other :

"Let us pick a couple of grains of rice out of his dish."

"No ! wait," said the other, "don't you see he is hungry and if we bother him now he may kill us."

When he heard the ants talking, the hunter could not help laughing.

His wife heard him and asked him what he was laughing at.

"I dare not tell you," he said.

"But you must," she answered, "or I will throw myself into the well."

He held out fur a long time, but at last he had to tell her, and the moment he told her, he died.

Then she began to bewail herself ; but when the neighbours came and heard all about it, they said :

"You evil woman ! why bewail your loss. You yourself caused your husband's death."

Such are the wiles of women and no one should tell them a secret.

108

WHAT A CLEVER
WOMAN
CAN DO

A Manjhi had a son and a daughter ;
the son was very lazy and used to
sleep half the day. Whenever his father remonstrated with
him for his laziness all he would say was—

> *Sukh se soai Horu,*
> *Jekare gaya na goru.*
> Sound sleeps Horu,
> Who has neither ox nor cow.
> (*Cantabit vacuus coram latrone viator.*)

Then the Manjhi asked his daughter what she thought of
her brother, and she said :
"I don't agree with him. He sleeps at ease who has a wife
with the lucky marks."

> *Sukh soai soi,*
> *Jekar nari sulakshan hoe.*

"Very well," said her father. "We shall see what your
lucky marks will do for you."
So he picked out a wretched orphan boy in the village and
married her to him. He used to go out every day and cut
wood in the jungle for his living. By good luck every day he
used to come across a sandal tree, and this he used to sell to
a Banya for a measure of grain. One day his wife said :
"I should like to see some of the wood you cut."
When he showed her it she said :

"Why, this is sandal wood, and this is how the Banya has been swindling us for ever so long."

So she went off to the Banya and said :

"Here you have a house full of our sandal wood which you have been robbing us of I don't know for how long. I am off to the Raja to put in a complaint against you."

Now the Banya feared the Raja, and did not care to be sued in his court ; so he said :

"I really don't know much about it. I am generally away from home and my wife does the bargaining for me. Perhaps there has been some mistake ; but I will set that right."

The end of it was that she made the Banya disgorge every penny of the money, and she bought I don't know how many *bighas* of land and how many cows and oxen—in short, she and her husband became quite rich people ; and one day her father and mother, who had become very poor, came begging about the place, and could not believe it when they told them of their daughter's prosperity. But when she saw them she fell at their feet and treated them kindly. But she said :

"He sleeps at ease who has a wife the lucky marks."

And none could gainsay her words.

109

THE LAMENT
FOR SOBHAN

There was a certain washerman who was a servant in a king's house. He had a donkey which he called Sobhan (beautiful). One day that donkey died, the washerwoman wept for its loss. At that time the queen summoned the washerwoman. The washerwoman came weeping. The queen asked—"Why are you weeping?" She said :—"My Sobhan has died" and crying

out—"alas ! my Sobhan ; alas ! my Sobhan," began to weep.
The queen, too, then began to cry out "alas ! my Sobhan !
and to weep." The queen's hand-maidens seeing the queen
was crying, began to weep too. The king hearing the queen
crying, began to weep and call out :—"Alas ! my Sobhan !"
and the king's servants also began to cry. When the king's wazir
heard all this noise of weeping, he was struck with wonder
as to what might be the cause of this noise. In fear and trem-
bling he came to the king and said :—"If I may, I would speak
a word." The king said :—"Speak on." The wazir asked :—
"Who was Sobhan?" The king said :—"I do not know, ask
the queen ; for when I saw her crying, I too began to weep."
In short, the wazir inquired of the Rani   The queen said :—
"I do not know, ask the washerwoman." In short, the
washerwoman was asked, and she said :—"It is the name of
my donkey which has just died." Then everybody felt ashamed.

110

HOW SILLY A WOMAN CAN BE

Once upon a time a man began lecturing his wife on her duties.
"A good wife," said he, "instead of wasting her time, spins
cotton, makes thread, and gets cloth made." "Oh ! all right,"
said she. "Get me a spinning wheel and some cotton, and see
what wonders I will do." The husband bought a spinning wheel
and some cotton for her. The wife began spinning, and when
the thread was made, went out in search of a weaver. On
enquiring from her neighbours, she learnt that a clever weaver

lived near a certain tank. She went there, and seeing no one, called out "O weaver ! ho !" A frog in the tank called out *"tar* !" She looked in, and being sure that the answer came from the water, she said : "Ah ! the weaver lives here," and she called out : "Look here ! I want some cloth woven. Here is the thread" : and throwing in the thread she said : "Please weave it nicely. When shall I call for it ?" The frog again happened to call out *"tar* !" so she answered "all right I will call to-morrow" (*kal*). So she went home well satisfied with what she had done.

When her husband came home she told him all about it, and next day she went to the tank and called out :—"Weaver ! here I am. Please give me the cloth." The frog called out *"tar"* again. "What ? to-morrow ! (*kal*). This will never do. I will wait another day, but I must have my cloth to-morrow. If you don't give it I will punish you by carrying off the door of your house."

Next day she came again, but the frog called out *"tar"* again. "Do you think I am going to be fooled in this way ?" But all the frog said was *"tar"*.

So in her anger she plunged into the tank in search of the weaver's door. Presently her hands fell on two heavy pieces of something. She brought them up and they looked like bricks. "I have got the door of your house at any rate," said she. "I hope this will make you more careful in future." When she came home she told the whole story to her husband. "Let me see the bricks," said he, and when he saw them he said :—"These are bricks of gold. We are now rich : take care of them." "What will you do with them," she asked. "I will buy good clothes and ornaments and slave girls," replied her husband.

Next day she thought she would save her husband trouble by buying some slave-girls and other things. So she sat at her door and began asking every pedlar who passed if he had clothes and orgnaments and slave-girls for sale. At last an old woman passed by, and when she heard her question, said to herself : "What can this foolish creature want ?" So she asked :—"My daughter ! have you any money to buy these things ?" "No," said the lady, "but I have two bricks of gold, and my husband said he would buy these things with them. You may take the gold bricks if you bring me what I want." "All right," answered the old woman "I will bring the things to-morrow."

Next day the old woman came and said : "Here, my dear ! I have brought you all you want," and she showed her a lot of shining brass ornaments and some red and green dresses of common cloth. "Oh ! how beautiful," said the lady, "and where are slave-girls ?" "Here they are," answered the old woman, and showed her half-a-dozen big dolls, all dressed up. The lady was delighted, and the old woman went away grumbling that she had been a loser by the bargain.

The lady then put on one of her new dresses and the ornaments and began to distribute work to her slave-girls. She put two of the dolls in the kitchen and said :—"Cook dinner for your master who will return soon." Two she seated at the door and said :—"You must open the door when your master come." Then she lay down for a nap, putting the two remaining dolls near the bed with orders to wake her when their master arrived.

The husband came and knocked at the door, but no one answered. He knocked again, saying "what on earth is up with this precious wife of mine ?" and so he went on knocking until at last the lady woke, opened the door, and let the husband in.

"What happened to you, my dear ?" he began, without noticing her new dress and ornaments. At last he said : "Hullo ! from where did you get these ?" "I will tell you all presently," said she, "but why did not the slave-girls open the door ? I put two of them there on the look-out for you." "Slave-girls ! What on earth do you mean," he asked. She made no answer, but seizing a stick began to thrash the dolls. He looked on in amazement, and asked his wife to explain what these dolls were there for. "Come down and have your dinner first, and I will tell you all," she replied.

Then she went to the kitchen and said :—"I hope the girls have got ready dinner and have not been lazy." But when she saw no dinner ready her anger increased. "I thought," said she, "that like a good and faithful wife I would spare you the trouble of buying ornaments and dresses and slave-girls, so I found an old pedlar woman who got me all these things." "And the money ?" asked her husband. "Oh ! I paid her the money, and she was so obliging as to take the two golden bricks."

Then her husband lost all patience. "Wretch !" said he, "you have ruined me," and he turned her out of the house in disgust.

So she wandered about in the jungle, and next morning a party of thieves arrived there, and began to examine and divide their plunder. She had been awake all night, and had just fallen asleep, and she dreamt that her husband had followed her, and was calling her to come back. She called out, "I am coming ! I am coming !" and jumped up. The thieves thinking themselves pursued, took to their heels, leaving all their plunder behind them. She came up, and seeing a lot of money and jewels, she took possession of them, and tying them up in a bundle proceeded homewards. She showed all the wealth to her husband, who was delighted and took her back.

She had no idea, however, of the value of the property, and asked her husband what they should do with it. "We will spend it," said he, "when Shabrat, Ramzan, and 'Id come," meaning the feasts.

She thought these were people to whom her husband intended to give the things. She was curious to know who they were, so next day when her husband went out she asked every one who passed if his name were Shabrat, 'Id or Ramzan. One man happened to be called Ramzan, and when he told her, she asked him in, and told him to take what her husband had left for him. Then she brought out a third part of the property, and was giving it to him when he asked the reason. "I am sure I don't know," she replied, "but there is a lot of these things, and my husband said they were intended for Ramzan, Shabrat, and 'Id. I was waiting for them. You are Ramzan, and this is your share. I wish the others would come and take their shares too." "O ! I see," he answered, beginning to understand how the land lay. "I think I can help you by sending these men, for I know them both." "O ! do please," she answered. So he went off and sent his brothers, instructing them to give the names of 'Id and Shabrat. When they came and gave their names, she said :—"I am glad you came. I have been bothered waiting for you. Wait till I bring your shares ;" and so saying, she gave them what remained of the plunder. "I suppose you can divide it ?" she asked. "That we can," they answered, and cleared off. "How pleased my husband will be at what I have done !" she thought to herself.

When her husband returned she told him all she had done. "I hope you are pleased now !" she asked in triumph. But he cursed the day when he had married such a fool, and again he turned her out.

She went again to the jungle, and it so happened that a camel, laden with the king's treasure, had lost its way. She found the camel, and seizing the nose-string, led it home and showed it to her husband. He killed the camel and buried the treasure in his house. But he was afraid his wife would blab out the whole story, so he made her go to bed, and going to the bazar bought a lot of parched rice (*khil*) and sugar sweet (*batasha*), and having scattered them in the courtyard, woke his wife and called out "run ! run ! see how it has been raining *khil* and *batasha* ; " so she came out and began collecting them in great glee.

A few days after a cryer came round, proclaiming that one of the king's treasure camels had been lost, and that any one who knew anything about it should give information on pain of death if they failed to do so. So she went to the door and called out that she knew all about it. Then up came the Kotwal, and she told him that she had found the camel and brought it home. "And to whom did you give it ?" he asked. "To my husband, of course," she answered. "Where is he ?" "He is out." "Well I will wait for him."

When he came back the Kotwal asked him where was the camel and the treasure. "What do you mean ?" the husband asked. "He means, " said his wife, "the treasure on the camel I gave you a few days ago." "Please sir," said the husband, "don't believe a word of what my unfortunate wife is saying. To tell you the truth, she is a lunatic." "What !" screamed his wife, "I am mad, am I ? I can point out the treasure this moment." "Ask her," said her husband, "what day did she bring the treasure ?" "Yes ! my good woman ! tell me that." "Why that was the day it rained *khil* and *batasha*." "There now," asked her husband, "can you doubt she is mad ?"

So the Kotwal laughed and went away, pitying the poor woman.

But her husband thought it was not safe to keep her any longer, so, like an ungrateful wretch that he was, he turned her out, and never had anything to say to her as long as he lived.

111

THE MANJHI GIRL
AND
THE BAMBOO

Once upon a time there was a Manjhi who had seven sons and a daughter. One day the girl went into the field and brought home some vegetables, and as she was preparing them for dinner, she cut her finger with the sickle and a drop of blood fell among the greens. She said nothing about it; but when her brothers tasted the dish and found it more tasty than usual, they asked her about it, and when they learnt the reason they began to think how good human flesh must be. So they determined to kill their sister. All but the youngest agreed to this, and finally his brethren forced him to kill his sister, but he would not taste her flesh. When the others had eaten, they buried the bones of the girl under a clump of bamboos, and from them sprang such a bamboo as was not to be found in the jungle for beauty.

One day a Raja came into the jungle to hunt, and when he saw the bamboo he was so pleased with it that he had it dug up carefully and planted in his garden.

Every night the girl used to come out of the bamboo and walk about the city. At last the servants watched her and saw her going back into the bamboo. They went and told the Raja,

who lay in wait for her next night, and when she came out
of the bamboo he caught her by hand. Then he took her
to his palace and married her. He summoned her brothers,
and the youngest he rewarded with five villages, but the others
he banished from his kingdom.

112

GANGA RAM
THE PARROT

There was once a fowler
who used to go every day
to snare birds in the
jungle. One day he wan-
dered about till the evening
and caught nothing, so he lay down under a tree. On the branches he saw perched a number of parrots, and he began to think
within himself that if he could catch one of them he would be
able to support himself comfortably. So he went and told his
wife, and she went with him next morning, and they laid a set of
snares. Meanwhile they heard the parrots talking among
themselves, and the leader of them, whose name was Ganga
Ram, said to the others :—"Brethren, we ought not to stay
here any longer. Let us go to some other jungle." The others
said :—"O Ganga Ram ! whenever we find a comfortable
place you are always advising us to go elsewhere. Why should
we mind your words ? We intend to stay here." Ganga Ram

answered :—"If you do not mind my advice you will rue it." "We intend to stay here all the same," they said.

The fowler heard what they were saying, and he climbed up the tree and laid bird-lime on the branches. When the parrots flew back in the evening they were all snared. Then they said to one another :—"Brother ! what Ganga Ram predicted has now come to pass." "Yes," said Ganga Ram. "By and by the fowler will come and kill us all. They cried :—"Pardon us, O Ganga Ram ! you are our leader. Now plan some device whereby we may escape from this misfortune." "Brethren," said Ganga Ram, "there is only one means of safety. When the fowler climbs up the tree we must all pretend to be dead; then he will throw us down one by one. There are seventy-four of us. You must listen carefully and count seventy-four thuds on the ground, and when you are sure that we have all come down, we can fly away in safety.

They agreed to his plan, and they did as he advised. But they counted wrong, and when only seventy-three parrot had been thrown down they all flew away, and Ganga Ram, who was the last, was caught by the fowler. When he found that he was a captive, he said to the fowler :—"Friend ! I am now at your mercy. If you kill me it will be no advantage to you. But if you save my life I will bring you large profit." The fowler spared his life, and shutting him up in a basket brought him home. When his wife saw the bird she said :—"You must take him to the King." The fowler said :—"O Ganga Ram ! may I sell you to the King ?" Ganga Ram answered :— "You may sell me, but you must take my proper price." "And what is your price ?" the fowler asked. "My price," said Ganga Ram, "is a lakh of rupees."

So the fowler took Ganga Ram to the bazar, and as he went along he called out :—"Who will buy my parrot for a lakh of rupees ?" At last a merchant bought the bird for the price he asked and put him in a cage. His wife was always talking to the parrot, and one day he said :—"I am lonely ; get me a *maina* to talk to me." So she got a *maina*, and it was hung in a cage close to Ganga Ram's, and they became great friends.

Soon after the merchant had to go abroad on business, and he told Ganga Ram to watch his affair. One day the merchant's wife went to see a dance at a neighbour's house and by accident she took away a young man's shoes and left her own there. When the young man saw the shoes in the morning, he was seized with love for the owner of them. So he employed two old women to search for them. One of them went about with the shoes, crying out :—"Who has lost a pair of shoes ?" The banker's wife came out and recognized her shoes, and the old woman, pretending to be her aunt, got into her confidence, and by and by tried to induce her to pay the young man a visit. But as she was going Ganga Ram asked her what she was about. When she told him, he explained to her the old woman's wiles, and taught her what her duty was to her husband. So her honour was saved, and when her husband returned she told him what had happened, and he was so pleased at the fidelity of Ganga Ram that he asked him to choose any boon he pleased. Ganga Ram said :—"The only boon I crave for is my liberty." So the banker let him go, and he went back to the jungle and ruled the parrots as before with wisdom and justice.

113

THE AHIR AND THE COW OF PLENTY

There was once a poor Ahir in whose herd the Cow of Plenty (*Surabhi gae*) was re-born. The cow had six calves. The wife of the Ahir was a shrew and never gave him enough to eat, and used to be constantly abusing him. So he used to save a little of his food and take it to the field to eat while he was at work.

One day the cow saw this and said to her master :—"Why do
you conceal your food in this way ? Give the scraps to my
children and I will give you as much milk and sweetmeats as
you desire." The Ahir did as the cow ordered, and she gave him
as much of the choicest food and sweetmeats as he needed.
Then she took him to the hole of a snake and said :—"Master,
whenever I give you milk and sweets you must always put a
little milk and one sweetmeat near the hole for the use of the
snake."

The Ahir obeyed her orders.

One day the little son of the Ahir come to the field and his
father gave him some of the food which he received from the
cow. The boy tied up some of it in his waist cloth. His father
said :—"Do not commit this folly. If your mother sees this
she will kill me and the cow." The boy promised that he would
not show it to his mother; but one day his mother saw some of
the sweetmeats with him and asked him where he got them.
He said :—"My father gave them to me and the Cow of Plenty
gives them to him every day." She said :—"If the cow is such
a fool I will have all her calves killed by the butcher and I am
going to him this very moment."

When the Ahir heard from his son what his wife had said
he was terrified and told the cow. She said :—"Don't be
anxious. I am going to bring my children. Go and take leave
of the snake and then we will all go to another country."

The Ahir went to the snake and told him what his wife had
done. The snake said—"Do you wish me to do anything ? I am
always at your service." The Ahir answered :—"My mother, the
cow has not told me to ask you for anything, but whatever she
advises I will ask you to do." He went to the cow and asked
her what service he should require from the snake. The cow
said :—"Ask him to give you his flute and handkerchief." The
snake gave him what he wanted. Then the cow seated the Ahir
on her back and with the help of her children carried him
off into a jungle. There she made a platform (*machan*) on a
palm tree and seated him there, and used to feed him every
day with milk and sweetmeats until as he ate this food his hair
became the colour of gold. One day the cow ordered her
children to take him to the river to bathe, but she warned them
not to lose a single one of his hairs. By chance one of his

hairs broke off and the calves put it in a leaf cup and let it float down the stream. It floated past a ghat where a princess was bathing and when she saw it, she took it to her father and said "If I cannot marry the man who owns this hair, I must die."

So the Raja sent out many messengers to trace the owner of the golden hair. One old woman came to the forest where he was staying with the cow and said she was the sister of his mother. The cow warned him against her wiles, but he would not heed, and one day the old woman induced him to go out with her in a boat and carried him off to the city of the princess.

The princess was delighted to see him and was about to marry him at once, but he blew his flute and the Cow of Plenty and her calves appeared at once and began to break down the palace of the Raja. He came out and implored the cow to take pity on him. He agreed to build a splendid house for her and she consented to live there with her calves. The Ahir then married the princess, and by reason of the Cow of Plenty, the Raja enjoyed the utmost prosperity.

114

THE OLD WOMAN
AND THE CROW

An old woman was one day frying rich cakes (*puri*) in a frying-pan, when a crow came and said : "Mother, give me a cake !" "Go and wash your bill first," she said. So the crow went to the water and said :—

Pannar, pannar, tum pannar, das !
Do panariya, dhowai mundariya,
Matkawen puri panch.

"Water, water, thou art water's slave ! Give me water and let me wash my bill. Then I'll ogle the five cakes." The water replied : "Bring an earthen pot from the potter and you can take water and wash the bill." So the crow went to the potter and said :—

Kumhar, kumhar, tum kumhar das !
Tum do handariya, khinchai panariya,
Dhowai mundariya, matkawen puri panch.

"Potter, potter, thou art the potter's slave ! Give me a pot, I will take water, wash my bill and ogle cakes five." But the potter said : "Bring earth and I will make an earthen pot for thee." So the crow went to the earth and said :—

Matar, matar, tum matar das !
Tum do matariya, banai handariya, khinchai panariya ;
Dhowai mundariya, matkawen puri panch.

The earth said : "Bring the deer's horn and dig the earth." So the crow went to the deer and said :—

Hiraniya, hiraniya, tum hiran das !
Tum do singariya, khodai matariya
Banai handariya, khinchai panariya,
Dhawai mundariya, matkawen puri panch.

But the deer said : "Go to the dog and he will fight me and break my horn ; then I will give it to thee." So the crow went to the dog and said :—

Kuttur, kuttur, tum kuttur das !
Tum laro hiraniya, tutai singariya, &c.

But the dog said : "Bring me some milk, and when I drink it I will fight the deer." So the crow went to the cow and said :—

Gaur, gaur, tum gaur das !
Tum do dudhariya, piai kutariya, larai hiraniya, &c.

But the cow said : "Bring me some grass, and when I eat it I will gave you plenty of milk." So the crow went to the grass and said :—

Ghasar, ghasar, tum ghasar das !

Deo ghasariya khawai guariya;
Dewai dudhariya, &c.

But the grass said : "Bring a spade (*khurpa*) and you may collect as much grass as you wish." So the crow went to the blacksmith and said :—

Lohar, lohar, tum lohar das !
Tum do khurpiya, khodai ghasariya;
Khawai gauria, &c.

The blacksmith said : "How will you take the spade ?" The crow said : "Put it round my neck and I will manage to carry it away." So the blacksmith heated the spade and hung it round the neck of the crow, and when he tried to fly away with it his neck was burnt and his head fell off and that was the end of him.

115

THE WEAVER AND
THE JACKAL

A weaver was once going along the road with his cotton carding bow on his shoulder. A jackal came across him unexpectedly and was much surprised to see an instrument which was quite novel to him. "I have seen a gun," he said, "and I am used to bludgeons ; but these men are always inventing some new plan for our destruction. It were well for me to be cautious. But I must stand whatever fate pleases to send. To run away is useless because even a gun would destroy me at this distance." So he came up to the weaver, who was even more frightened than the jackal was, because he had never seen such an animal in all his life. The jackal made a profound bow and said :

Hath ban sir men dhana ;
Kahan chale Dillipaty Rana ?

"With an arrow in your hand and a mighty bow on your
head where are you going Lord of Delhi ?"

The weaver was pleased and answered—

Ban ke Rao, ban hi men rehana,
Akhir bare ne bare ko pehchana.

"Lord of the jungle, the jungle is thy fitting abode. At all
events it is only the high-born who could recognise one of
equal rank with himself."

116

THE PARROT AND
THE GURU

There was once a banker who taught his parrot the speech
of men. One day it so happened that a Sadhu passed by
where the cage of the parrot was hanging and as he came
near the parrot said : "Salam Maharaj !" The Sadhu looked
round in evey direction and tried to see who had saluted him.
The parrot said : "It was I saluted you. Maharaj : you point
out to all men the way which leads from this world of sorrow
to the region of eternal peace. May it please you to explain to
me the means whereby I may escape from this cage." The
Sadhu answered : "Let me consult my Guru and then I will
reply to your question."

The Sadhu went to his Guru and explained the case of
the parrot. To his utmost surprise and terror the Guru, the

moment he heard the case, spread out his limbs and lay in a
swoon. The Sadhu poured water over him and revived him
with great difficulty.

Next day as the Sadhu was passing by the place where the
parrot's cage was hanging, the bird asked him if he had consulted the Guru about his case. The Sadhu told him the condition into which the Guru had fallen when the matter was laid
before him. The parrot answered.

"You did not perhaps understand the Guru's meaning;
but I have understood it and I am greatly obliged both to him
and to you. Salam Maharaj. Now go your way."

When the Sadhu had gone the parrot spread out his feet and
and wings and lay in a dead swoon in the bottom of his cage.
When his master came to feed him and saw his state he cried:
"Alas my parrot! He is dead!" So he opened the door
of the cage and threw the bird on the ground. Immediately
he got up and flew away.

117

THE BABBLER BIRD
AND THE ELEPHANT

Once upon a time an elephant lived in a forest, and was so
proud of his strength that he defied every rival. A babbler
bird lived there also, and one day he said to the elephant:
Certainly you are very powerful. But do not be proud.
Some day you may fall into trouble."

The elephant answered:
"Be not troubled about me. I depend on my strength."
"Well!" the bird replied:

"When you fall into misfortune, remember my words."

Soon after Bhagwan gave leave to the Shardul in a dream to descend on earth and devour the elephants. So he came down and by chace fell on this very elephant.

The babbler flew up and said :

"What do you mean by devouring my elephant?"

The Shardul answered :

"What I do, I do by orders of Bhagwan."

"What right has Bhagwan to give such an order?"

"Let us go to him."

The Shardul, the babbler, and the elephant appeared before Bhagwan.

The Shardul complained that the babbler had interfered with him, and said to Bhagwan :

"Thou didst appear to me yesterday in a dream and didst order me to devour the elephants."

Bhagwan was angry and said to the Shardul :

"Do not mind what the babbler says."

Meanwhile the babbler pretended to fall asleep and Bhagwan called him and said : "Why do you interfere with my orders?"

The babbler answered :

"Why did you wake me out of such a pleasant dream ? I was dreaming that I was married to Sita."

"How can you be married to Sita, you rascal, in a dream?" enquired Bhagwan. "Why not?" said the babbler. "If you give orders in dreams and then uphold them, why should I not marry Sita in my dreams?" Bhagwan was confounded and told the Shardul to spare that particular elephant.

Then the babbler said to the elephant : "Did I not tell you that your pride would one day bring you to ruin and that you would want my aid? Now be more careful in future."

The elephant went away sore ashamed.

118

KALI DAS
AND
HIS PARROT

There was once a foolish Raja who
kept fourteen Pandits in court. It so
happened that the celebrated Kali
Das came to the Raja's court and
the other Pandits were jealous of
him. The Raja, in order to try his
powers, put to him this question :
"My favourite cow and mare are
both about to be delivered. State when their offspring will be
born and what they will be." Kali Das naming the time said :
"The cow will have a calf and the mare a foal." In due time
the animals were delivered ; but in order to disgrace Kali Das
the Pandits had them blindfolded at the time of birth and they
put the foal beside the cow and the calf beside the mare and
each animal adopted the young of the other as its own.

When the foolish Raja was convinced that the prediction
of Kali Das was false he had him put in prison as an impostor.
Now Kali Das had a favourite parrot which he loved
exceedingly. When his master did not return, the parrot
spoke to the wife of Kali Das and asked her what had become
of her husband. She answered : "He has gone to the Raja's

court and has not returned." The parrot replied, "I suspect that some evil may have befallen him. Take some charcoal, mix it in water and blacken my wings." The lady did so and the parrot flew off and sat upon the roof of the palace and went on calling "*Radha Krishna! Radha Krishna.*" When the Raja saw the bird he said to his Pandits : "I see a bird of the shape and voice of a parrot, but his feathers are as black as those of a crow. What is the explanation of this?" The Pandits were nonplussed; at last they said "Maharaja ! You had better ask the parrot." So the Raja asked the parrot to explain his case and the parrot said : "When the ocean took fire I was flying about near it and I so pitied the miserable fish that I tried to put out the fire and my wings got blackened by the smoke." "When did anyone hear of the ocean getting on fire ?" asked the Pandits. "That was the same time," answered the parrot "when the cow was delivered of the foal and the mare of the calf."

When the Raja understood the parrot's meaning, he became conscious of his folly and, after disgracing his Pandits he released Kali Das from prison and dismissed him with a handsome present.

119

RAJA RASALU AND HIS FAITHFUL ANIMALS

Once upon a time Raja Rasalu set out from home with his four faithful animals—the hawk, the cat, the parrot and the camel. In the evening he halted near a city in a grove, and a s he found himself overcome with sleep he divided the night into four watches and distributed them among his animals.

The first watch was that of the hawk. The wise bird perched on the back of the camel, and soon after a gang of four thieves appeared and tried to steel the camel. As soon as one of the thieves touched the camel the hawk sprang upon him and plucked out his eyes. He returned and told his companions, and then the second thief made his attempt.

This time the cat was on guard, and when the thief approached the camel she spring on him, and as he was a bald-headed man she tore his scalp with her claws till he roared with pain and fled to his companions.

Then the third thief made his attempt, and this time the parrot was on guard. All he could do was to speak. So when the thief came up he addressed him from the back of the camel—

"You rascal. One of your companions has been sorely wounded and another has lost his eye. Do you wish to lose your life, for this will surely be your end."

The thief was so astonished to hear these words from above the camel that he was terrified and made his escape.

Then came the fourth thief, and this time Raja Rasalu himself was on guard. But his eyes were heavy with sleep and then the fourth thief came and carried off the camel. When the Raja awoke and found that he had been robbed he called his animals, and they protested that it was no fault of theirs, so he sent them to search for the camel.

The cat climbed over the walls and roofs and went all through the city. At last she found the camel where the thieves had hidden it near the house of an oilman. Raja Rasalu went and complained to the Raja of that city, and the thieves were caught and hanged. He was so pleased to hear of the cleverness of the animals of Raja Rasalu that he asked him : "Why do you prefer to stay outside the city ?" Rasalu said that he preferred the pure air of the jungle and that he had no fear, as he was protected by his faithful animals. The Raja said : "I have been always hearing of the might of Rasalu and his animals, but now I have seen for myself. I shall try to imitate you as far as possible."

120

HOW THE WASHERMAN'S ASS BECAME A QAZI

There was a certain schoolmaster who had a very stupid pupil. One day, when he did not know his lesson, the master called him "Ass." A fool of a washerman who was passing by, on hearing this, said :—"Mr. teacher, was this boy once a donkey ?" 'Yes," said the master, "he was a donkey, and my teaching has made a man of him." The washerman said :— "I have nothing in the world but an ass, and if you can turn him into a man, I shall be delighted to bring him to you." "All right," said the teacher. "Go and bring him." So the washerman came up, thrashing his ass to make him come quickly ; and asked the teacher :—"How long will it take to turn my ass into a man ?" "A year's time," replied the teacher. A year after he returned and asked the master where his ass was. The master replied:—"Your ass has become the Qazi of so and so city," and draws a salary of Rs. 1,000 a month, and holds a Court." By chance, when the washerman first went to the teacher, the Qazi was in the school and knew all about the master. The washerman asked the way to the Qazi's Court and went on. The Qazi did not know him and paid no attention to him. The washerman came back and said to the master :—"In truth he has become a great man, and when I went into his Court he did not even look at me." The master replied:—"Of course, he won't notice you if you approach him in this way as he is a great officer on a high salary. But take a rope and hobble and go into his Court and shake them and say:—"Have you forgotten the rope and hobble with which you used to be tied ?" He did as he was told, and then the Qazi remembered the circumstance, and he thought :—"If I don't get rid somehow of this fellow I shall become a laughing stock." So the Qazi gave the washerman a thousand rupees and dismissed him. The washerman showed the master the money, and he took half of it as the feed of the ass. The washerman went home blessing his good luck, and in this way every year he used to receive a present from the Qazi and lived a happy man for the rest of his days.

121

HOW THE NEEDLE SUCCEEDED IN KILLING THE TIGER

Once upon a time a needle set out to kill a tiger. On the road he met first a bludgeon, then a scorpion, then an insect which eats the mango-fruit, and then a piece of cowdung, all of which the needle took with him. All five came to the house of the tiger, and the needle stood up straight on the threshold, the scorpion got into the tiger's oil jar, the insect into the fire-place and the piece of cowdung spread itself on the doorstep. When the tiger came back from the jungle the needle ran into his foot as he was going in : he then put his paw into the oil jar to get some oil to rub on the wound and he was stung by the scorpion : enraged with the pain he ran to the fire-place to light a lamp to see what had happened to him, when the insect got into his eye and blinded him. "Misfortunes never come singly," said the tiger, and he rushed out : but he trod on the cowdung; slipped and broke his back, and this was the end of him.

122

HOW THE MONKEY
GOT THE BETTER
OF THE TIGER

A soldier was going in search of service : on the road he met
a monkey. They both halted at a well. The soldier wanted to
bathe. The monkey said:—"Ask the people who draw water
here to give you some." They all refused ; the monkey bit them,
and they all ran away. The soldier bathed and said to the
monkey:—"I am hungry." The monkey gave him some gram
out of his mouth. The soldier then went off with the well ropes
which the people had left behind. They next met a woman with
curds. The monkey seized one potful and drank the other. Then
they met a Dom ; the monkey robbed him of two winnowing
fans (*sup*) : next they met a washerman, whose ass the monkey
seized. At last they came into a jungle, where lived a tiger and
an old woman. The monkey said to the old woman :—"Give me
a place to stay." The old woman put him up in the upper room.
Then the monkey said:—"I want to spit." The old woman said,
"spit outside." But he spat down, and it fell on the tiger. The
tiger said :—"Where is this water coming from ?" The old
woman said:—"The birds must have spilt it." Then the monkey
said:—"I want to sing the Malar." The woman said:—"Don't :
or the tiger will kill you." The monkey jumped down and stole
a drum and began to sing. Up came the tiger. "Who are you ?"
said he. The monkey said :— "Who are you ?" "I am a
deo" (demon), said the tiger. "I am Mahadeo," said the
monkey :— "Let me see your tail," said the tiger. "I want
to see yours first." The tiger showed his tail. The monkey
tied the well rope to his, and showed it to the tiger. "Can you
spit," said the tiger. "You spit first," said the monkey. The
tiger spat, and the monkey upset the pot of curds ; the tiger
thought it was the monkey's spittle. "Show me your ear," said

the tiger. "Show me yours first." When the tiger showed his
ears the monkey tied the two winnowing fans on the sides of
his head. This was enough for the tiger, who ran off in alarm.
The monkey jumped on his back, and after going some distance, jumped up a tree. The tiger cleared off. Then the soldier
seized all the tiger's wealth, and he and the monkey lived
happily ever after.

123

THE LITTLE BIRD THAT
FOUND THE PEA

Once upon a time a little bird, on its through the woods, picked
up a pea and took it to the grain-parcher to be split : but, as
ill-luck would have it, one-half of it stuck fast in the socket of
the mill-handle, and the grain-parcher being unable to get it
out, the little bird went off to the carpenter and said : "Carpenter, carpenter, come and cut the mill-handle : my pea is in the
mill-handle; what shall I eat ? what shall I drink ? and what
shall I take to foreign countries ?" "Be off," said the carpenter.
"Is it likely that I shall come and cut the mill-handle for the
sake of a single pea ?"

Then the bird went to the king and said: "King, king, chide
the carpenter : the carpenter won't cut the mill-handle : my pea
is stuck in the mill-handle : what shall I eat? what shall I drink?
and what shall I take to foreign countries ?" "Be off with you,"
said the king. "Do you think that for the sake of a single pea
I am coming to chide the carpenter ?"

Then the little bird went to the queen and said : "Queen,
queen, speak to the king : the king won't chide the carpenter :
the carpenter won't cut the mill-handle : my pea is in the

socket of the mill-handle : what shall I eat ? what shall I drink ? and what shall I take to foreign countries ? But the queen said : "Be off with you. Do you think that for the sake of a single pea I am going to talk to the king ?"

Then the little bird went to the snake and said : "Snake, snake, bite the queen : the queen wont't talk to the king : the king won't chide the carpenter : the carpenter won't cut the mill-handle : my pea is in the socket of the mill-handle : what shall I eat ? what shall I drink ? and what shall I take to foreign countries ?" But the snake said : "Be off with you. Do you think that for the sake of a single pea I am going to bite the queen ?"

Then the little bird went to the stick and said : "Stick, stick, beat the snake : snake won't bite queen : queen won't talk to king : king won't chide carpenter : carpenter won't cut mill-handle : my pea is in the socket of the mill-handle : what shall I eat ? what shall I drink ? and what shall I take to foreign countries ?" But the stick said : "Be off with you. Do you think that for the sake of a single pea I am going to beat the snake ?"

Then the little bird went to the fire and said : "Fire, fire, burn stick : stick won't beat snake : snake won't bite queen : queen won't talk to king : king won't chide carpenter : carpenter won't cut mill-handle : what shall I eat ? what shall I drink ? and what shall I take to foreign countries ?" But the fire said : "Be off with you. Do you think that for the sake of a single pea I am going to burn stick ?"

Then the little bird went to the sea and said : "Sea, sea, quench fire : fire won't burn stick : stick won't beat snake : snake won't bite queen : queen won't speak to king : king won't chide carpenter : carpenter won't cut mill-handle : what shall I eat ? what shall I drink ? and what shall I take to foreign countries ?" But the sea said : "Be off with you Do you think that for the sake of a single pea I am going to quench the fire ?"

Then the little bird went to the elephant and said : "Elephant, elephant, dry up the sea : sea won't quench fire : fire won't burn stick : stick won't beat snake : snake won't bite queen : queen won't speak to king : king won't chide carpenter : carpenter won't cut mill-handle : my pea is in the socket of the mill-handle : what shall I eat ? what shall I drink ? and what shall I take to foreign countries ?" But the elephant said : "Be off with you. To dry up the sea would take the whole host of elephants. Do you think that for the sake of a single pea I am going to assemble all the elephants ?"

Then the little bird went to the *bhaunr* (a tangled, creeping plant) and said : "*Bhaunr, bhaunr*, snare the elephant : elephant won't drink up the sea : sea won't quench fire : fire won't burn stick : stick won't beat snake : snake won't bite queen : queen won't speak to king : king won't chide carpenter : carpenter won't cut mill-handle : my pea is in the socket of the mill-handle : what shall I eat ? what shall I drink ? and what shall I take to foreign countries ?" But the *bhaunr* said : "Be off with you. Do you think that for the sake of a single pea I am going to snare the elephant ?"

Then the little bird went to the mouse and said : "Mouse, mouse, cut the *bhaunr, bhaunr* won't snare elepnant : elephant won't drink up the sea : sea won't quench fire : fire won't burn stick : stick won't beat snake : snake won't bite queen : queen won't speak to king : king won't chide carpenter : carpenter won't cut mill-handle : my pea is in the socket of the mill-handle : what shall I eat ? what shall I drink ? and what shall I take to foreign countries ?" But the mouse said : "Be off with you : do you think that for the sake of a single pea I am going to cut the *bhaunr* ?"

Then the little bird went to the cat and said : "Cat, cat eat mouse : mouse won't cut *bhaunr* : *bhaunr* won't snare elephant : elephant won't drink up the sea : sea won't quench fire : fire won't burn stick : stick won't beat snake : snake won't bite queen : queen won't speak to king : king won't chide carpenter : carpenter won't cut mill-handle : my pea is in the socket of the mill-handle : what shall I eat ? what shall I drink ? and what shall I take to foreign countries ?" And the cat said : "By all means : the mouse is my natural prey. Why should I not eat it ?"

So the cat went to eat the mouse and the mouse went to cut the *bhaunr* saying :

> Hamko Khao ao mat koi
> Ham bhaunr ko katat loi.

"O eat, O eat me no one. I will take and cut the *bhaunr*."
And the *bhaunr* went to the snare the elephant, saying : "O
cut, cut me no one. I'll take and snare the elephant" ; and so
one with each one till it came to the carpenter, who extracted
the pea, which the bird took and went away rejoicing.

124

THE JACKAL AND
THE LODHA'S WIFE

Once upon a time there lived a jackal in a sugarcane field, and
every day the wife of the owner, a Lodha by caste, used to pass
by with her husband's food. The jackal used to stop her on
the way and say :— "Give me some of the food or I will kill
your husband because I owe him a grudge." So she through
fright used to let him eat. This went on for some time. At
last the Lodha said to his wife :—"How is it you bring me such
bad food? It looks like some one's leavings." Then she told
him what the jackal used to say to her. He said :—"To-
morrow I will dress in your clothes and bring some food by the
way you generally meet him." And so it was settled, and the
next day the Lodha came by dressed in his wife's clothes, and
the jackal came out as usual and began to eat. Then the jackal
said :—"O, scratch my back, something is biting me." So the
Lodha began to scratch him with one hand, and with the other
drew his knife and cut off the jackal's tail. On this the jackal
ran away, and there was peace for some time. To have his
revenge the jackal used to go and spoil and eat up the Lodha's
field. One day the Lodha said to his wife :—"I can't stand
this any longer. You must go into the sugarcane field and pick
up pieces of straw and wood, and while you are doing it you
must cry, and if the jackal comes out and asks you what you

are doing, you must say, O ! my husband is dead, and I have to pick sticks to cook the dinner we always give for our dead." It happened as the Lodha had said, and the jackal was pleased when he heard the news, and said he was a good riddance. And when the sticks had been picked and the jackal was going, the woman said :—"O ! do come to my husband's dinner and bring all your friends with you. It is to be to-morrow night." The jackal thanked her for the invitation. Then she came home and drove in a lot of pegs in her yard with a piece of string tied to each, and then she went into the house and drove in a very big peg with a *barat* or will-rope fixed to it. That night the jackal came with his companions. The Lodha's wife came out and caught one of the jackals, and was about to tie it up when the others began to cry out and were about to run away. But she said, "it is our custom to tie a string round the necks of our guests." Then they all submitted and had themselves tied. The jackal who had given so much trouble was the last to be tied, and the Lodha's wife tied him inside and went into the next room and pretended to cook. Meanwhile the Lodha, who was concealed inside, came out and began to beat the jackal who, in trying to escape, strangled himself and died. Then the other jackals broke their strings and went off singing this rhyme :

> *Bhitar howe mar pitai,*
> *Bahar nachti Lodha mai.*

Beating is going on inside while the Lodha's wife is dancing with joy outside.

125

THE GOAT AND
THE TIGER

There was once a he-goat and his wife, and she was about to kid. So she said to her husband :—"Let us find some quiet place where I may lie in."

By chance the goats selected the den of the tiger, and there two kids were born. A day or two after the tiger came back, and when the he-goat saw him coming he asked his wife what had better be done. She said :—"Don't be nervous. When the tiger comes near I will squeeze the kids' legs and make them squeal." Then you say to me :—"Why are the children crying ?" And I will say :—"They are crying because they want some fresh tiger-meat. I have some of it dried here, but they do not care for that."

When the tiger came they did as they had planned, and the tiger was so much frightened that he forthwith ran away. As he was still running he met the jackal, who said :—"Good morning, uncle, I have not seen you for a long time. Where are you running to ?" The tiger replied :—"I am running away because some animals have occupied my den, who eat tigers, and when I went there just now I heard them planning to eat me." "What nonsense," said the jackal. "Come with me and I will soon drive them out." So the tiger and the jackal came together to the den, and the he-goat saw them and asked his wife what it were best to do. She said :—"Leave it to me." So she began to squeeze the legs of the kids, and when she made them squeal she called out :—"I can't think what ails these children to-day. They want some tiger and jackal-meat for their breakfast, and I have plenty dry in the store-room, but they must have it fresh."

When they heard this the tiger and the jackal scampered off and never came near the place again. So the goats had the use of it as long as they pleased.

126

THE JUDGEMENT OF THE JACKAL

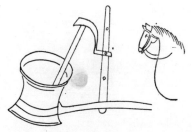

A merchant was once returning home from abroad. On his way he was belated, and put up at the house of an oilman.

He gave his horse to his host, and said :—"Brother, tie him up carefully." The oilman tied him to his mill. In the morning, very early, the merchant awoke, and was waiting for the oilman to come out. When he appeared he said :—"Friend, your horse got loose during the night, and I know not where it has gone." Just then the merchant came out, and seeing his horse tied to the mill, said :—"Why, here is my horse." "That is not yours," said the oilman. "My mill gave birth to it last night."

The merchant was very much enraged, and said :—"If you wont give up the horse let us go and get Siyar Panre the jackal to judge between us." So they went to Siyar Panre and explained the case to him. He said :—"Go back to the house of the oilman and I will come in a couple of hours."

He went off to a tank, and after wallowing in the mud for some time, came out and sat on the bank. When he did not come at the appointed time the merchant and the oilman went to look for him, and found him sitting there. They asked him why he had not come at the appointed time. He replied :—"I have been so busy that I could not come."" What were you so busya bout?" asked the oilman. "The tank took fire," he answered, "and I was hard at work in putting it out." "Are you mad?" said the oilman. "Did any one ever hear of a tank taking fire ?" "Did any one ever hear," asked the jackal, "of a mill giving birth to a horse?"

The oilman was confounded and restored the horse to its owner.

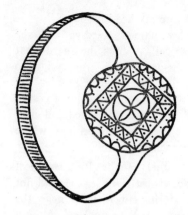

127

THE WIT OF
MUHAMMAD FAZIL

The proverb runs—*Parhe na likhe, nam Muhammad Fazil.* "He can neither read nor write and he is called The Scholar."

This is how the proverb arose.

There was once a Raja who employed a Persian teacher to instruct his sons and when he died he left a son whose name was Muhammad Fazil, who was as ignorant as his father had been learned. Him the Raja summoned and ordered him to serve in the place of his father. He had to accept the post, but as he was totally ignorant, he began to think how he could ever discharge the duties. And such a fool was he that the boys used to shout after him and call him Tadda, or Fool, until he came to be known to every one by that name.

One day the Raja sent for him and said :—"My ring has been stolen and you must from your books discover the name of the thief as your father used to do."

The teacher was in great distress and said : "Give me time to consult my books and I will give an answer to-morrow."

But the Raja was wroth and cast him into prison and threatened to hang him next morning if he did not find out the thief.

The teacher lay down, but from sorrow he could not sleep, at last he called out :

> *Ao re sukh nindiya ;*
> *Subh ko kat jae mundiya.*

"Come sweet sleep, for I shall lose my head by dawn."

Now the Raja had a female slave named Nindiya and she was listening at the door of the cell. When she heard what she supposed was her own name, she was afraid, and going to the teacher told him that the ring was concealed under the Raja's bed where she had placed it and implored him to save her life. The teacher promised to do as she asked and next morning when he was called by the Raja, he showed him where the ring was hidden and thereby gained great honour.

One day the favourite riding camel of the Raja was lost and Muhammad Fazil was ordered to trace it. He did not know what to do and went wandering in distress near the palace, when what should he see but the camel grazing in a ravine.

So he went to the Raja and said :—"Your Majesty's camel is grazing in such a ravine with his head to the North."

When they went to the place and found the camel as he had said, his renown still more increased.

Another day the Raja was walking with the teacher in the garden and finding a worm known as Tadda he concealed it in his hand and asked the teacher what he had. He was confused and cried out "Tadda, Tadda, your time is now come."

The Raja did not know that Tadda was his nickname and was astonished at his wisdom.

At last Muhammad Fazil was tired of running constant risk of his life, so one night he took a dagger and went into the room where the Raja was asleep. He was about to stab him, when he thought to himself that it would be safer to drag the Raja out into the courtyard and kill him there, where there was no chance of any one hearing the noise. Just as he dragged him out, the roof of the palace fell in and the Raja fell on his knees before him and said :—"My preserver, I owe my life to you. Share with me half my kingdom."

And this was the way the idiot Muhammad Fazil prospered.

128

THE RIVAL CASTES

Four men, a Dhuniya, a Mali, a Julaha and a Jat, once went to a Raja for employment. When he asked the Julaha who he was, he said :

"I am a Khatak Pathan."

The Dhuniya said :

"I am a Tank Pathan."

The Mali said :

"I am the arranger of melody."

When he asked the Jat what his caste was, he said :

"I am of the caste of Khuda."

"You rascal," said the Raja, "what do you mean ?"

He answered—

"This Khatak Pathan does weaving in my village. This Tank Pathan cards cotton. This arranger of melody sings at the weddings of Chamars. If they are of these noble castes then what is my caste but that of the Lord Almighty ?"

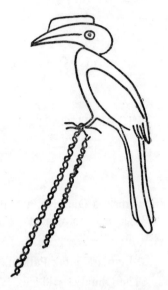

129

THE FORTUNATE
WOOD-CUTTER

There were once two boys who earned a poor living by cutting wood in the jungle. One day they went out together and agreed to meet under a large banyan tree. The younger brother finished his work first and when he came to the tree he saw a Sadhu sitting there. He bowed at his feet and the Sadhu blessed him and said : "My son, you shall be married to-day to the Rani of Singaldip."

Saying this he disappeared and when the boy went to his load of wood he saw a very pretty bird perched upon it which had an iron chain fixed to its leg so long that it trailed on the ground. The boy took hold of the chain, and the moment he did so the bird flew away with him to Singaldip, and leaving him there, disappeared. He walked along, and suddenly saw a wedding procession (*barat*) passing by. The bridegroom who was going to be married was not only lame but blind of an eye, and his father thought to himself :

"If the Raja of Singladip sees that the bridegroom is lame and blind of an eye he will never marry his daughter to him. It would be better for me to hire a boy and let him act the part of the groom at the wedding, and when it is all over he can go away and my son will have his wife." He told his plan to the clansmen who were with him and they approved. Just then they met the woodcutter and asked him who he was and where he was going. When he told them that his home was in Jambudip they were much pleased, because they thought that, being a stranger, he would keep the secret. So they told him their plan and he agreed to go with them. They dressed him in the wedding robe and brought him before the Raja. All the people assembled, and the marriage was duly performed. Then the bride and bridegroom were sent into the marriage chamber (*kohbar*). When they were together the bride was very happy, but the bridegroom was in low spirits. She asked him what was the matter and he answered : "How can I admire your beauty when I am starving ?" She said : "What do you mean ? Thousands were fed here to-day, and were you, the Raja's son-in-law, alone left to starve ?" Then he told her the whole story, which she wrote down, and then out of her box of dolls she took some sweetmeats which she gave him and they lay down to sleep. In the morning he went to bathe, and there he saw the same bird with the chain hanging to its leg.

He recognised the bird and took hold of the chain, when the bird in a moment flew away with him and brought him back to the jungle where he was before. Then it disappeared. He was overcome by grief, but putting off his wedding dress, he shut it up in an earthen pot and buried it in a dung heap behind his house, when he came back he said to his mother : "Mother I have been all night in a jungle so dense that no one ever saw it even in his dreams."

When the princess saw what it was getting late and that her husband did not return she was plunged in grief and told her mother, and her mother told the Raja. For five years the princess never ceased searching for him but in vain. At last she gave notice that she would reward any one who could tell the best stories. Many came and told her stories, but she got no trace. Finally she asked her father to allow her to travel in search of him, and she assumed the dress of a prince and started. After many days she came to Jambudip where the woodcutter lived. One day the woodcutter heard that this prince was in search of stories. He went to her and told her his own tale. Then with tears in her eyes she embraced him and said :

"You are me dear husband for whom I have been searching so many years, but I want more proof."

He went and dug up the pot which contained his wedding robe which, when she saw, she was convinced. She took her husband home with her and told her father how she had found him. He received him gladly, and after he had been there some days loaded him with wealth, horses, elephants, and sepoys and sent him home with his wife and they enjoyed many years of happiness.

May Parameswar restore the fate of all of us as he restored that of them !

130

THE WISE AND
THE FOOLISH
BROTHERS

There were once two brothers, one of whom was wise and the other foolish. They fell into poverty, and finally they agreed to go in different ways in search of employment, and whichever of them succeeded should support the other.

The fool went to a Raja and asked for service. "What can you do ?" asked the Raja. The fool was puzzled what to say. At last he said : "I can make verses and work the fan." So the Raja took him into his service on sixty rupees a month. One day the Raja said : "It is quite time we heard some of these verses of yours." The fool did not know what to do, so he went out and stood reflecting under a tree. He stood without moving, and some pigs, thinking he was a tree, came up and began to rub themselves against him. When he could stand this no longer he said,

"Tum kitno ragaro ghiso main janun tor chalaki."

"You may rub as much as you please, but I know your cunning."

This was the only verse he could think of and so he went and stood before the Raja. Just then the barber came in and prepared to shave him, and as he was getting ready the fool recited this verse. When he heard it the barber turned pale, and falling at the Raja's feet begged his forgiveness. "What have you done ?" asked the Raja. The barber said : "My razor is steeped in such deadly poison that had it touched your Majesty's beard you were dead in a moment. This is the work of the treasurer, who has induced me to attempt your life." So the Raja ordered the treasurer to be executed and appointed the fool in his room.

Some time after the Raja said to the new treasurer : "It is time we saw how you can use the fan." The fool was displeased at this order, because he thought it beneath his dignity to fan the Raja. But he had to go and when he began to fan him he knocked off the Raja's crown. The Raja was wroth, and called for the executioner ; but just then a poisonous snake came out of the crown and bit the Wazir so that he died. The Raja was so pleased that he made the preserver of his life Wazir. Then the new Wazir sent for his wise brother, who was in extreme poverty. When he came he said : "Fate rules the world, and a man's wisdom and exertions avail nothing."

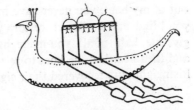

131

THE MAGIC BOAT

Once upon a time a rich man fell into poverty, and, leaving his wife and children at home, went into a foreign land to make his living. One day his wife was sitting at her door, lamenting the hardness of her fate, when a Sadhu passed by and asked her the cause of her trouble. She told him all her circumstances, and he then gave her a boat, and said : "The virtue of this boat is this. It will give you all you ask of it ; but when it gives you one rupee it will give your neighbours two." She was much pleased, and when the Sadhu went away, she began to ask the boat for large sums of money, which it always gave her ; but as much as she got, her neighbours always got double.

After a time her husband came back with a considerable sum of money which he had made. When he found all the neighbours, whom he had left in poverty, much richer than himself, he was amazed, and asked his wife how they had managed to get rich without ever leaving the village in which they were born. She was told him about the magic boat which always gave her neighbours double what it gave to her. When he heard this he was overcome by envy, and said : "This was an evil gift you received from the Sadhu." So he took the boat, plastered a piece of ground, and placed the boat within it. He then implored the boat to burn one of his houses. It did so, and at the same time burned down two houses of each of his neighbours. Then he asked the boat to make a well in his courtyard. This was done : and there were two wells in each of the courtyards of his neighbours. Then he implored the boat to deprive him of one of his eyes, and if he became one-eyed all his neighbours became totally blind and began to fall into their wells.

Then they all came and begged him to restore their sight. But he said : "All the time you were making heaps of money out of my boat, you never gave me a share. Now I have made you blind and I will not restore your sight until you promise to give me half of all you make by me." So they had to agree, and then he asked the boat to restore him his eye, whereupon all his neighbours recovered their sight.

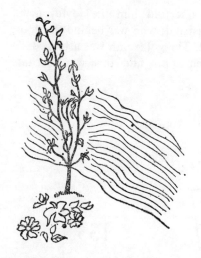

132

THE THAKUR
AND
THE GOLDSMITH

There was once a Thakur who was a very clever fellow; but his wife was unfaithful to him and loved a goldsmith. The Thakur knew this, but said nothing. One day the goldsmith paid her a visit while her husband was supposed to be asleep, but he was listening to what they said : "My dear," said the woman, "if the Thakur would only get blind, what a good time we should have." "I will tell you what to do," he replied. "Fast for the whole month of Kartik and then pray to Bhagwan to make your husband blind, and he will certainly perform your desires."

When the month of Kartik came the woman began a regular fast and planted a Tulasi tree on the bank of the river. When she went away the Thakur dug a deep pit just under the tree and hid himself there. When she came to say her prayers, she began to pray : "O Mother Tulasi ! Make my husband blind." From beneath the ground he answered in a feigned voice : "My faithful devotee, give your husband the best of food and then he will surely get blind." So the wife began to feed her husband on every delicacy she could think of and after some time he said to her : "Me dear, I really think my sight is not as good as it used to be." She was sure that the charm was working, so she went on feeding him on all kinds of excellent food. Until at last he said : "My dear, I really can hardly see at all."

Then she sent for her lover and told him the joyful news. But as he came in, her husband, who was behind the door, cut off his nose with his sword. The goldsmith was ashamed to tell any one what had happened to him and this was the last visit he paid the lady.

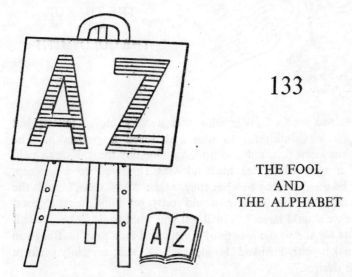

133

THE FOOL
AND
THE ALPHABET

A stupid boy was once sent to school and though he was a long time under instruction he learnt nothing. When he came home his father gave him a book to read and as he turned over the leaves he burst into tears. "What a clever boy this is !" every one said. "See how he has already begun to realise the misery of human life." But whenever he was given a book to read, he always wept. At last some one asked him why he did this, and he answered : "When I was at school the letters looked big and fat on the black board and I now weep to think how thin they have become since they got into this confounded book."

134

BANKE CHHAIL
AND HIS WIFE

There was once a Musalman whose wife was such a shrew that every morning she used to give him a sound beating with her slipper. She had a daughter and when she grew up her parents were on the lookout for a husband for her ; but the temper of her mother was so well known that no one would dare to marry into such a family. Finally one day a notorious character, who was known as Banke Chhail, or "the cunning rascal," came and proposed for the girl, and her father was so glad to settle her in life that he agreed to the match at once and they were married.

Before the ceremony took place Banke Chhail bought a parrot, a cat and a dog, and when he was taking his bride home he brought his animals with him. On the way the pair sat down at a well to rest and a number of village curs came out and began to bark at Banke Chhail's dog. His dog barked at them in return and his master, drawing his sword, cut off his head at a single stroke. "You rascal," said he, "do you dare to bark without my leave ?" This astonished his wife ; but they went on a little farther and as the morning broke the birds in the trees began to sing and when the parrot heard them it too commenced to chatter. Banke Chhail at once pulled it out of the cage and wrung its neck. "You fool," said he, "you did not remember that you belonged to Banke Chhail and you dared to open your mouth without his orders."

His wife was still more surprised, but she said nothing and they went on. They set down to rest in a garden and soon a rat appeared. Banke Chhail called to his cat and said : "Catch me that rat." The cat at once obeyed his orders and killed it. When his wife saw this she began to think to herself "What a terrible husband I have got. It would be well for me to obey him." And when they reached home she found it to be her interest to obey him in all things and became a very loving and obedient wife ; so much so that when some time after her father

came to pay him a visit, she looked out through a chink in the
door and was afraid to admit him without the leave of her husband. By and by Banke Chhail came home and said to her :
"Your respected father is waiting at the door. Why did you
not let him in ?" "How could I do so without your leave ?"
she answered.

The Banke Chhail went out brought the old man in. When
he saw how changed his daughter, was, he said to his son-in-
law : "You know what a life my wife leads me. I wish you
would tell me how you have succeeded in reducing your wife
to order. Perhaps I may be able to deal with my wife in the
same way." Said Banke Chhail : "Good, Sir, bring a brick and
some moist clay and make me a lamp saucer out of each." It
is easy quoth the old man to mould the soft clay, but when the
clay gets hard no power on earth would mould it."

"In short," said Banke Chhail, "your wife's character is
fixed and cannot be mended. I dealt with my wife in season
and you see the result." The old man went home sorrowful.

135

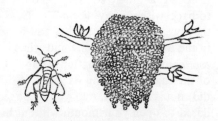

HOW THE BANYA
BAFFLED THE
ROBBERS

Once upon a time a Banya was going about on business and
fell among thieves. When he found out who his companions
were, he began to think how he could get out of their clutches.
So he climbed up a tree and began to break some of the dry
branches. They asked him what he was doing. "In my town,"
he said, "wood is so scarce that every scrap sells for two
annas." The thieves, knowing that the Banya had very little
money about him, thought that they would do better by selling

wood than by robbing him ; so they all fell to and collected a large bundle.

When they got to the town the Banya said, "Brethren, I am very sorry to hear that since I went away wood has fallen to two pice a bundle." "You rascal," said they, "we will pay you off before long." The Banya knew that they would come soon and rob him ; so one night he was awake and he heard them outside. Then he whispered to his wife so that the thieves could hear him, "Did you bring in the bag of gold which I tied on the *nim* tree in the yard ?" "No," said she, "it must be there still." "Then we are ruined," was his reply. When the thieves heard this, they at once climbed up the tree, when they touched a large wasp's nest, which they did not see in the dark. The wasps came out and stung them, so that they were hard put to make their escape.

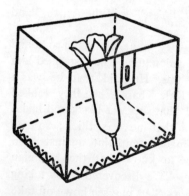

136

THE TALE OF THE FOUR DRUNKARDS

There were once four drunkards, one of whom was addicted to spirits, the second to *bhang*, the third to *charas*, and the fourth to opium. They were reduced to great poverty and at last determined to go abroad in search of employment. As they were going along they came across a horse. One of them got up on the neck, the second on the shoulders, the third on the back, while the fourth clung on to the tail. They came to a city and stopped at an inn, but their lamp had no oil ; so the first said to the second, "Go and bring oil," and the second passed the message to the third, and the third to the fourth.

At last they agreed that they should all lie down and that he that woke first should go and fetch the oil. As opium eaters do not sleep, he lay awake and in the night a dog came and tried to carry away their food. The opium eater who was awake, struck at the dog with a stick and this made him howl and run away. Hearing the noise, the others woke, and said to the opium eater, "Why don't you go for the oil ?" When the lamp was lit they said, "Let us lie down again ; but we must tie up the horse lest it be stolen." One said, "What is the use of tying the horse ? Let us each hold on to one of his legs while we sleep." So they lay down and the horse, who was hungry, soon managed to get loose. When they woke and missed the horse they made sure it had been stolen. So they said, "Let us take the omens and find out who is the thief." They filled a *chilam* and one took a pull, and said, "I am sure the thief is black." The second took a smoke, and said, "Yes, he is black and he has only one eye." "That is true," said the third, "and he has a long beard." "Yes," said the fourth, "and his name is Kale Khan."

When they had settled this, they went along the road and by and by they met a man in a palanquin. They stopped him and asked him what his name was. He said that he was a Mahajan and that his name was Kale Khan. When they looked at him more closely they found that he was black and had a long beard. Then they made sure that he was thief ; so they hauled him before the Raja and made complaint against him. The Raja enquired how they came to know that the Mahajan had stolen the horse. Said they, "We discovered it by taking the omens." "Well," said the Raja, "let me see how you take omens." So he got a pomegranate and put it in a box and said, "Now take the omens and tell me what is in this box." They were perplexed, and said, "Great king ! Have a *chilam* prepared for us." When the *chilam* was brought, one of them looked at it and said, "It looks to me rather round." "Yes," said the second, "and it is red." "That is true," said the third, "and there are grains (*dana*) in it." "True," said the fourth "and it is a *kali*." When the Raja heard this he was convinced that they had taken the omens aright and he gave judgement against the Mahajan and made him pay for the horse.

137

THE RASCALITY
OF THE JAT

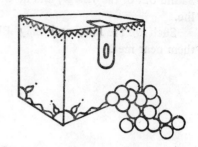

The wife of a Jat once told him to go into the jungle to cut wood. He climbed up a tree and while he was cutting a branch a Sadhu came and sat under the same tree. He bathed at a well close by, worshipped his Salagrama and then untying his tangled locks took out a small box. This he opened and taking out sixteen *ashrafis*, counted them over and put the box away in the same place. The Jat was watching him all the time and when the Sadhu went away he followed him and asked him to come and take food at his house. The Sadhu said, "How can I eat at the house of a Sudra?" "I am a Sudra no doubt," said the Jat, "but you can eat *pakki roti* (food cooked in *ghi*) at my house." So he went home with the Jat and when he went in, his host said to his wife : "I have brought home with me a Sadhu who has sixteen *ashrafis* tied up in his hair. You must go and cook *puri* cakes for him ; when you bring them to him I will go into the kitchen and rush about the place ; then you must ask me what is the matter."

She did as he ordered, and when he began to rush about the kitchen she called out and asked him what was the matter.

"Matter enough," he shouted. "Either you or this rascally Sadhu has robbed my box containing sixteen *ashrafis*. "The Jatni shook her clothes and said : "I never touched your box ; you may search me if you like." The Sadhu too began to shake his clothes, but the Jat rushed at him with his bludgeon and cut off his matted locks with his sickle, when the box fell out. "You thief," said the Jat, and raised the alarm and all his kinsmen ran out with their clubs and hunted the wretched

Sadhu out of the village, and he was hard pressed to save his life.

Such are the Jats, and may Bhagwan never bring one of them near me !

138

THE BANKER AND
HIS SERVANT

There was once a banker who used to put his servants absurd questions and when they failed to give an answer he used to cut off their noses. In this way hundreds of men lost their noses.

One day a crafty old fellow went and offered to serve the banker. He said : "You know the condition. If you fail to answer any question of mine you will lose your nose." The man agreed. "But," said he, "I must make one more condition. If you fail in asking questions you must let me cut off your nose." To this the banker assented.

Next day the banker sent out his servant to collect some money that was due him, and when he came back he asked : "What did you say when you met my creditor ?" "I asked for the money." "And then ?" "Then he paid me." "And then ?" "I gave him a receipt." "And then ?" "I started for home." "And then ?" "I came to a jungle." "And then ?" "I met a fowler who had trapped hundreds of birds in a snare." "And then ?" "A bird broke the snare and flew away." "And then ?" "A second flew away." "And then ?" "A third flew away." "And then ?" "A fourth flew away." "And then ?" "Then a fifth flew away." "Confound you and the birds," said the banker. "I am tired of asking you questions." "Then," said the servant, pulling out a knife, "I regret to say I must cut off your nose." So the banker was glad to pay him a lot of money and get rid of him.

139

THE TALE OF BALI SINH

There was once a man named Bali Sinh, who was half an idiot, and used to wander about the village like a fool. One day a barber passed through, and being hungry asked for help.

"Go," said the people in fun, "to Bali Sinh and tell him that his wife has had a child and that you are coming from his father's house with the news." The barber went to Bali Sinh and told him this story, at which he was much pleased, and called all the women to sing the birth song, and this is what they sang :

"O, younger brother of my husband ! my liver aches. Whom may I awake ?

"My mother-in-law sleeps in the upper room ; my husband's sister sleeps on the back of the elephant ; my husband sleeps at the door ! Whom can I dare to awaken ?"

As they sang, Bali Sinh had food prepared for the barber, and said to him :

"Wait for a couple of days, until I have some clothes and jewelry made, and then we will take them for the baby."

When the things were ready Bali Sinh and the barber set off together. The barber began to get uneasy lest Bali Sinh should find out the trick : but he remembered that it was a custom for women to wear yellow clothes when they had finished the ceremony after their child was born. Just then he saw a woman in yellow drawing water from a well.

"There is your wife," said the barber. "I will just go and see my family and return by and by." The barber disappeared, and, following the woman to her house, sat down at the door. The woman's husband was away and she and her mother-in-law were alone in the house. They supposed Bali Sinh to be some distant relative, and asked him in to bathe and eat.

Just as he came in the baby happened to cry. Bali Sinh gave the mother a couple of slaps, and said :

"You, wretch ! why don't you take care of the baby ? You are more occupied about cooking than about the child, which is the only cause of my having taken such a long journey."

The woman was angry at his violence, and asked her mother-in-law who he could be. They thought he must be some unknown relative. By and by the real husband came back, and when he heard what had happened, he was wrath and shouted to all his clansmen. They all rushed up with their bludgeons and beset the door, when Bali Sinh ran out and cut off the head of the unfortunate husband with his sword.

The villagers ran away in fear, and Bali Sinh took up his quarters in the house and kept the widow as his wife. He lived in idleness, and after a while all their grain was spent. At last his wife said to Bali Sinh :

"You had better go and earn something."

He went to the Raja and asked for employment.

"There is a graveyard here sixteen *bighas* in area. You may have it to till, if you please."

Bali Sinh agreed, and when he went there began to dig the freshest grave. The dead man's ghost appeared, and angrily asked :

"What do you mean by digging my grave ?"

"Why should I not dig it ?" said Bali Sinh, "and what's more, it will produce me a thousand maunds of rice."

"If you let it alone, I will give you that much rice," said the ghost.

Bali Sinh agreed, and let the grave remain undisturbed, and the ghost used to bring him a thousand maunds of rice every harvest.

After a while the ghost, in his anxiety to collect the tribute of rice, began to get weaker and weaker.

One day his sister's son came to see him, and said :
"Uncle, what is making you so thin ?"
When he heard about the rice he encouraged him—
"Don't fret ; I will go and kill Bali Sinh."
That night the young ghost came to his house and tried to
get in through the house drain. Bali Sinh heard him and, think-
ing it was a thieving cat, stood over the mouth of the drain
with his bludgeon in his hand. When the ghost put his head
inside, Bali Sinh began to whack him.
"Have pity on me !" cried the ghost.
"Well, what do you want ?"
"I only came to ask," said the ghost, "whether you would
have the tribute in paddy or husked rice."
"Well, yes !" said Bali Sinh, "I may as well have rice, as
it will save me the trouble of husking it."
So the ghost had to keep him in rice all the days of his life,
and Bali Sinh prospered.

140

THE FAQIR AND
SHER SHAH

A certain King had no sons : he ordered his ministers to distribute alms and get the people to pray that the King might have
a son. One day a Faqir entered the city, and when he learnt
what was going on, promised the King two sons, on condition
that he got one of them. The two sons were born and named
Sher Shah and Azim Shah. When they grew up the Faqir
appeared and called on the King to fulfil his promise. The
King, unwilling to give up one of his sons, was about to present him instead with a low-caste boy : but the Faqir read the
King's heart and was going to curse him, when the King, in

fear, gave over Sher Shah to him. Sher Shah went to take leave of his mother and encouraged by saying he would fix an arrow in the palace wall : as long as it stuck there she might know he was alive. Then he went with the Faqir to his hermitage (*takiya*), and the Faqir leaving him there, took a large leathern vessel (*kuppa*), and went out to beg for oil. While he was away Sher Shah saw a skull in the room which addressed him, and said :—"You will soon be like me." Sher Shah asked why was this. The skull replied :—"The Faqir has a large iron boiler, and it is his custom to boil boys in oil in it as a sacrifice." How can I escape." asked Sher Shah. The skull answered :—"When the Faqir comes back with the oil, he will ask you to go five times round the boiler and bow to it. You must pretend not to know how to do it, and ask the Faqir to show you. Then, as he is bowing to the boiler, you must seize him by his legs from behind and pitch him in. Then you must take some of the oil and sprinkle it on all the bones which lie round the hut of the Faqir. These are the remains of boys whom he has sacrificed. When the oil touches them they will revive and be your servants." Sher Shah carried out his instructions, threw the Faqir into the boiling oil, and revived the bones. They all became his servants and returned home. Then his mother told him that the arrow had shaken a little in the wall just about the time of his danger, but then became firmly fixed.

141

THE PRANKS OF HOP-O'-MY-THUMB

A man had four sons. The youngest was only a span long, and was called Bittan or "Hop-o'-my-Thumb". The elder boys

used to kill game and eat it, and leave only the bones for
Bittan. One day Bittan in his anger went out hunting and
hunted two hares, which he followed into their hole and drew
them out. He gave them to his elder brother's wife. When he
came to dinner she told him to go to the kitchen for his food,
and then he found as usual that his brothers had eaten all the
meat and left only the bones for him. Then he said :—"Give me
my share of the inheritance and let me shift for myself." So they
gave him his share of everything. He sold his share of the
cattle and gave the money to his wife. He went off in search
of service.

On the road he met an Ahir's son who had a lot of cattle.
Bittan said :—"Come with me and I will marry you to a King's
daughter." When Bittan got him on board a boat he pitched
him into the river and took all his goods. He returned and
gave the money to his wife. Then he bought a horse and
burned his house down. He loaded the ashes on the horse and
went off on his travels.

He met merchant with a heap of money. The merchant's
mother was very tired. The merchant said to Bittan :—"Give
my mother a lift on your horse." Bittan said :—"If I put
your mother on my horse all my money will turn into ashes."
He said :—"If it does I will make it up for you." So he put
the merchant's mother on his horse, and when he came to the
house Bittan put the old woman down and said :—"There you
see ! All my money has turned into ashes. Pay me up." Then
the merchant had to pay.

Bittan brought all the money home. When his brother saw
all the money they said :—"Where you did get all this ?" He
replied :—"I got it by selling ashes." So they all burnt down
their houses, loaded the ashes on their horses, and went off to
sell it. But every one laughed at them, and in the end they
fell into poverty.

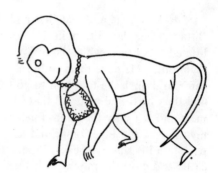

142

THE SCHOOL
OF LOVE

A merchant had educated his son in all branches of learning,
except the art of love. He employed a clever Kathak singer to
instruct his son in this department. The Kathak showed the
world to the youth for some time, and finally pronounced him
perfect. The son got a lakh of rupees from his father and went
abroad to trade. When he reached a certain city, as he was walking about, he was fascinated by a lady, whom he saw on a house
top. She marked him down as her prey, and sent her attendant
to negotiate with him. He induced the young man to believe
that she was a fairy, and came only occasionally from fairyland.
She constructed an underground passage in her house, and her
mysterious appearances caused the young man to believe her
story. Finally, though he was allowed to approach no nearer
the object of his desires, she and her friends swindled him out
of all his money. He returned and told his father, who called
the Kathak and remonstrated with him on the result of his instruction. The Kathak engaged to recover the money if the merchant would advance him another lakh of rupees. The merchant
agreed, and the Kathak procured a monkey, whom he taught to
keep a quantity of precious stones in his pouch, and to produce
them when called on. The monkey was named Arzu Beg—"the
lord of desire." When the monkey knew his business the Kathak
and the young man proceeded with the monkey to the city where
the lady lived. Number of persons visited the monkey, and to
each, under the Kathak's orders, he presented a valuable jewel.
This attracted the lady, who became exceedingly affable to the
young merchant, and the monkey constantly made her valuable
presents. Finally, she asked to get the monkey ; but the young

man referred her to the Kathak, who finally sold him to the lady for two lakhs of rupees. For some time he produced precious stones to order, but one day the lady's mother asked him for a couple of rupees to buy food, when, his supply of jewels being exhausted, he fell on her and her daughter and entreated them despitefully. By this time the Kathak and his pupil had left the place with the money, and the lady was left to lament the trick that had been played upon her.

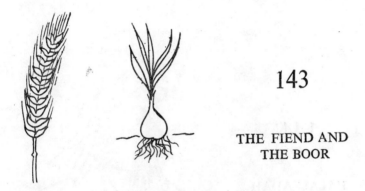

143

THE FIEND AND THE BOOR

Once upon a time a man met the fiend upon the road. Quoth the fiend : 'I have a wish to do business in partnership with you.' 'Who are you ?' said the man. 'The fiend.' 'I too have a mind to do something in partnership with you,' said the man. So they began to counsel together what business they should engage in. 'Let us cultivate some ground,' said the man. 'What shall we sow ?' quoth the fiend. 'Wheat.'

So they went and sowed wheat. When the wheat was ripe the fiend called the man to divide the crop, and said : 'What would you like best—the root or the top ?' 'I'll take the tops and you can take root,' said the man. The fiend agreed to this. So the man cut the crop and left the fiend the roots. The fiend dug up the roots and found he had been outwitted. He k ept his counsel, however, and determined to take the tops of the next crop. The next year the fiend asked the man what they should sow, and the man said : 'Onions.' When the crop was ready the fiend called the man to divide it : and, before the man had time to say aught, said, 'Last time you took the tops : this time you shall take the roots, and I the tops.' So they divided them accordingly. The fiend went home and did not trouble the man again.

It has become a proverb among the Arabs :

"You are the man with whom the devil sowed onions and was outwitted."

144

HALALZADAH
AND
HARAMZADAH

There were two brothers, Halalzadah and Haramzadah (legitimate and base born). In the same country there was a Qazi. Halalzadah went to the Qazi to ask service. The Qazi said : "If you take service with me it must be on condition that if you leave me I shall cut off your nose and ears, and if I turn you away shall do the like with me, and your daily meal shall be one leaf full."

Halalzadah agreed to this, and entered his service. The Qazi gave him his cows and his goats to graze, and gave him

a tamarind leaf (one of the smallest of leaves) full for his meal.
This did not satisfy Halalzadah. And he told the Qazi that he
could not work on an empty stomach. But the Qazi merely
replied that if he did not like it he might leave. At last Halalzadah, when he had spent all his own money and began to
starve, went and asked for his discharge. Thereupon the Qazi
took a knife and cut off his nose and ears, and he went his way.
His brother Haramzadah saw him and asked him the cause of
his pitiful condition, whereupon Halalzadah told him how the
Qazi had served him.

Haramzadah said : "Show me the Qazi's house and I will
go to him." Halalzadah told him the way and he went to the
Qazi and asked him whether he was in want of a servant. The
Qazi told him he required a servant, and he made the same conditions with him as with his brother. Then the Qazi gave him
the cows and goats to graze. Haramzadah grazed the cows and
goats and brought them home and went into the garden and got
a plantain leaf (the biggest of all), and taking it to the Qazi,
asked him for his dinner. The Qazi gave him a plantain-leaf
full, and Haramzadah took the cattle out again to graze : and
he killed one of the goats and called together his friends and
made a feast, and he brought home the rest of the cattle again.

The next day Haramzadah took out the cattle to graze again
and sold a dozen of the goats and four of the cows, and running
home to the Qazi said : "God is merciful that He saved my
life today." "How so ?" said the Qazi. "The wolves came
and carried off twelve goats and four cows, and I saved myself
only by climbing up a tree." The Qazi abused him and asked
him where he took the cattle to graze. He said, "To the west"
and the Qazi told him in future to take them to the north.

Haramzadah then went into the garden and got a plantain
leaf, and having got it filled, ate as much as he could and gave
the rest to the beggars. Then he went and took out the goats
and cows to the north to graze. This time he sold them all and
ran back to his master, and said : "Qaziji, Qaziji, a pretty
order you gave me to take the cattle to the north." "What has
happened ?" said the Qazi. "Why, when I took the cattle to
the north a herd of tigers came and carried them off, and I only
saved myself by hiding in a cave in the mountain."

Next day the Qazi told him to take out a certain horse and give it a walk. Haramzadah took out the horse and, as he was going along, he met a horse-dealer and agreed to sell it to him on condition that he should cut off the tail, so he cut off the tail and went home and stuck it in a rat-hole in the stable, and beat down the earth about it to make it tight. Then he went to the Qazi, and the Qazi asked him if he had carried out his orders. Haramzadah replied that he had walked the horse out and brought it home again and put it in the stable. Then he got his meal, a plantain-leaf full as usual. The next morning Haramzadah ran to the Qazi, beating his breast, and saying, "O Qazi, come to the stable and see what a misfortune has happened : the rats carrying off the horse, only half his tail is left out of the hole : make haste, or they will drag down the whole of it. Then the Qazi ran to the stable and tugged and tugged at the tail till it came out of the hole, but no horse with it, and Haramzadah told him the rats must have eaten the rest. In short, the Qazi is completely ruined : and, what is worse, his family are dishonoured by Haramzadah, who finally gets his discharge with his master's nose and ears.

145

THE FOUR FOOLS

Four men, one of whom was lame, the second blind of an eye, the third bald, and the fourth hump-backed, were sitting one day outside of the village, when a stranger came up and made a *salam* to them. They at once began to quarrel and disputed for which of them the salute was intended. The stranger smiled and said :—"For the biggest fool of you four." So they went to the Raja to decide who was the biggest fool.

The bald man said :—"I had a wife whom I deeply loved. One day I asked her for fire. She replied that she had just coloured her hands and feet with *lac* dye (*mahawar*) and could not dirty them. So I took her on my back and went to a neighbour's house, who gave me fire in an earthen pot (*borsi*). As I was taking it home the pot began to burn my head, but I could not take it down as I was holding my wife, and I was afraid to break it. So the end was that my crown was so burnt that all my hair fell off."

The humpback said :—"I was one day ploughing and a stranger came and told me that my wife was delivered of a son, and that I ought to go and give her the birth present (*lochana*). So I took some clothes and jewellery and went as he told me. A woman then showed me a bady and took the presents. As I was dandling the baby on the top of the house her real husband came in and knocked me down. So I have been hump-backed ever since."

Then the lame man said :—"I had two wives who loved me so much that they used to wash my feet daily and drink the foot ambrosia (*charnamrita*). One day only one wife was at home. She washed my feet and drank the water. When her co-wife returned she was so much enraged that she cut off my leg with a knife."

The one-eyed man said :—"I also had two wives, who used to sleep each on one side of me on my extended hands. One night the lamp needed trimming, so I called a maid who let the burning wick fall into my eye. I could not release my hand except by waking one of my wives. So my eye was lost."

Then the Raja said :—"The man who had neither wife nor child and still gave the birth offering was the greatest fool of all." So the others returned home in grief and mortification.

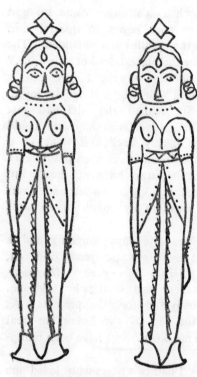

146

THE SEPOY'S SON

In the vicinity of Delhi there was a small village, and in this village a Maulvi kept a school, which was largely attended by the village boys. Every day the Maulvi used to go home at twelve for his mid-day meal, but in his absence he always told the boys to keep guard over the school by turns while he was away lest anything should be stolen.

One day when he returned from his breakfast he found one of his pupils, a sepoy's son, whose turn it was to keep guard, sleeping. "You fellow !" he exclaimed, beating him, "supposing while you slept some one had crept in and stolen the school property ? You would not have known anything about it."

The boy woke with a smile. This annoyed the Maulvi very much, and he struck him again. But the more he struck the boy the more he laughed.

"You are a strange boy to laugh when you are beaten," said the Maulvi. "Why do you laugh ?" "I do not know why I laugh," replied the boy, and all his teachers questioning him on the subject could elicit from him no other answer. It became noised abroad that there was a sepoy's son in a certain village who laughed when beaten instead of crying, and when questioned about it he always said he did not know why he laughed. At length it came to the ears of the Badshah of

Delhi, who at once sent for the lad and said to him :—"Why
did you laugh when beaten by your master ? Is a beating a
thing to laugh over or cry over ?"

"I do not know, your Majesty, why I laughed," answered
the boy.

"If you do not tell me I shall have you put into prison,"
said the Badshah.

But even this threat was not effective. The lad persisted in
saying that he did not know v hy he laughed when struck. So
the Badshah had him consigned to jail without food or water.

A few days after this the Badshah of Rum sent the Badshah
of Delhi two dolls, asking in a letter to tell him which was the
prettier and which the heavier, and which the better of the two.
So the Delhi Badshah sent for the wisest men in the land, but
none could tell which was the better one, though they weighed
them both and tried in every way to find out the superiority of
the one over the other. So the news spread everywhere that
the Badshah of Rum had sent two dolls to the Badshah of
Delhi, asking him to find out the superiority of one over
the other, and though the Delhi Badshah had sent for the
wisest men in the land, none were able to tell. At last it
reached the ears of the sepoy's son in prison, who, when he
heard it, said he thought he might be able to tell. So his jailors
told the Delhi Badshah that the boy who was imprisoned for
not telling why he laughed when beaten, said he could tell
which doll was better than the other that were sent by the
Badshah of Rum. So the Delhi Badshah sent for the lad.
When he came before His Majesty he sent for the dolls and two
bits of straw. When they were brought he put one bit of straw
into the ear of one of the dolls and it went down its stomach,
then he put the other bit of straw into the ear of the other doll
and it came out of its mouth.

"Your Majesty," said he, "the doll into whose stomach the
straw went is the better one, the prettier one, and the heavier
one; for whatever you say in her ear she will never repeat; but
as for the other doll, whatever is whispered in her ear comes
out of her mouth." The Badshah of Delhi was very muc h
pleased when he heard this, and at once had him released from
prison and gave him a grand mansion to live in with a beautiful

garden attached to it, and also wrote to the Badshah of Rum, saying, he had a boy in his court who had been able to answer his question. When the Badshah of Rum read this he sent several questions to be answered by the boy. But the lad said :—"What is he sending such childish questions to be replied to, which any boy in my village could answer : let him ask something worth answering." When the Badshah of Rum got this message he sent to ask the lad what his god was like, and if he ate and drank like human beings. When the sepoy's son heard this he said to his own Badshah that this question he would only answer at Rum in the presence of the Emperor of that country; so his Badshah sent him to Rum. When he came into the presence of the Badshah of Rum, that monarch said to him :—"Who is your god, and does he eat and sleep like people do ?"

"I will answer your question", said the boy, "if you get off your throne and place me on it, and take your crown off your head and place it on mine". "Well", thought the Badshah of Rum, "it is not much he is asking me, I might as well do as he wishes". So he got off his throne and placed the boy on it, and took off his crown and placed it on the boy's head.

Then the boy said :—"My god is so great that he has taken you off your throne and placed me on it, and has taken your crown off your head and placed it on mine."

The Badshah of Rum was so struck with the lad's reply that he at once embraced him and went to his queen's apartments and told her all about him, at the same time asking her what reward he should give him.

"Marry him to our daughter", said the queen : "for though low in birth he is high in intellect; you will never find a boy like him." The Badshah of Rum took his queen's advice and married the lad to their daughter. After a few days the boy returned to Delhi with his bride, and a letter from his father-in-law to the Delhi Badshah, telling him what a wise boy he was. When the Badshah of Delhi read the letter he went at once to his queen, and asked her what should he do for this boy who had saved the honour of his court by answering all the questions put to him by the Badshah of Rum.

"Marry him to our daughter", also said his queen : "for he

fully deserves that reward". So the Badshah of Delhi also married him to his daughter.

One day, some time after this, the fortunate youth was lying on his cot in the beautiful garden attached to his mansion, when his two wives came towards him,—the Badshah of Delhi's daughter with something for him to eat and the Badshah of Rum's daughter with something for him to drink. When he saw them he sent for one of his servants and said to him :— "Go, tell the Badshah of Delhi that when I was a school-boy and was beaten by my Maulvi for going to sleep when I should have kept guard, I laughed because I dreamt that I was lying on a cot in a beautiful garden attached to a mansion, and that the Badshah of Delhi's daughter was bringing me some food to eat and the Badshah of Rum's daughter was bringing me some water to drink, and it seemed so absurd to me that I laughed in spite of the beating I got ; but when asked about it I was afraid to tell, for your Majesty would surely have had me beheaded if I had, angry at the impudence of a poor village-boy and a sepoy's son dreaming of marrying your daughter ; but now that my dream has come true, I tell your Majesty what I feared to tell you then why I laughed though beaten."

147

THE ADVICE
OF THE SADHU

Once upon a time a Sadhu wandered about the streets of a city and called out :

"I will sell four pieces of good advice for four lakhs of rupees."

No one except a merchant would accept his offer. When he paid the money the Sadhu said :

> *Bina sang na chaliye bat :*
> *Thonk thankke baitho khat :*
> *Jagat ko pucche na koi :*
> *Krodh mari pacche phal hoe."*

"Do not travel without a companion.

Do not sit on a bed without touching it first.

No one interferes with a man as long as he is awake.

He who restrains his anger reaps the fruit of it."

Soon after, when he went on a journey, the merchant remembered the advice of the Sadhu and went in search of a companion.

The only one he could find was a khenkra or crab. They started together and came to a city, where the merchant made much wealth by trade. On their way back they came to a jungle, and the merchant lay down under a tree in which lived a crow and a snake who were sworn friends. When the merchant fell asleep the crow said to the snake :

"Go down, brother, and bite this man to death, and then I can make a meal of his eyes."

The snake crawled down at once and bit the merchant, so that he died, and the crow flew down and was just about to peck out his eyes, when the khenkra caught the crow with six of his claws and held on to the merchant's turban with the other six. The crow was afraid lest the man should revive and kill him : so he asked the khenkra to let him go. But the khenkra said :

"I will not spare you until you bring my master to life."

So the crow had to ask the snake to come down and suck out the venom, and the merchant came to life again. He said :

"What a sleep I have had !"

"May no one sleep such a sleep as yours", said the khenkra. He asked the khenkra to explain, but the khenkra said :

"First shoot the crow which is sitting on that tree."

The merchant killed the crow with his bow and arrow. When the khenkra told him the story he said :

"I have got back one lakh of my rupees."

He went on further and came to the house of a thag. His daughter sat outside, and near her was a seat hung over a concealed well on which she used to entice travellers to sit, and then pitch them in headlong. She offered the merchant water and invited him to sit down : but he remembered the advice of the Sadhu and touched the seat with his stick, when he toppled into the well. When he saw this he cried :

"I have got back my second lakh of rupees."

He went on further and came to an inn where there were seven thags, who planned to rob him, but he again remembered the advice of the Sadhu and kept awake. In the morning the thags said :

"You are the disciple of a great teacher, otherwise you would certainly have lost your wealth."

On hearing this, the merchant said : "I have got back my third lakh of rupees."

At last the merchant came home, and as he went into his house he saw a young man sitting with his wife. He suspected evil and was about to kill him when he remembered the last precept of the Sadhu and restrained his hand. Then he asked his wife who the young man was and she said :

"This is your own son born after you left home, and of course you do not recognise him."

The merchant cried :

"I have got back my four lakh of rupees."

148

THE TALE OF TISMAR KHAN

Once upon a time an old woman came to a weaver's door selling treacle ; he bought half a pice worth and applied it

to his beard. Immediately a number of flies settled on it, and
with one stroke of his hand he killed thirty. Then he said
within himself : "I will weave cloth no longer. I am Tismar
Khan, the slayer of thirty. I will go and take service with the
king."

So he went to the king and asked for employment. The
king asked him what his name was and what pay per month
he would accept. He said : "My name is Tismar Khan and
my pay is one hundred rupees a month. I can do work that
no one else can do."

He was appointed in the king's service, and one day it so
happened that a tiger missed his way and came into the city,
and killed many people. The king sent for Tismar Khan
and ordered him to kill the tiger. He was sore afraid and
thinking that it was high time for him to leave the place he
drew his arrears of pay from the treasury and started. He
went to a washerman to borrow an ass to carry his baggage.
Just then a shower of rain came on and he went into the shed
of the washerman for shelter, and found them all half dead
through fear of the tiger. But Tismar Khan said : "I don't
fear the tiger. But Tapakua (the dripping) has come, and I
am much more afraid of Tapakua than any thing else."
The tiger just then had crept into the ass shed to escape the
rain and when he heard these words he was afraid. "Who can
this terrible Tapakua be of whom they are all so frightened?"
he thought to himself, and he lay down quietly among the
asses.

When the rain was over the washerman said to Tismar
Khan : "I don't care to go out myself. But you can go and
take any of the asses you please." Tismar Khan went out into
the shed, and thinking the tiger to be an ass laid hands on
him. He tied him up with a rope and fastened him to a
post near his house. Next morning when he got up and
found the tiger tied up he was much surprised and delighted,
and when the king came and saw the tiger he was so much
pleased with the bravery of Tismar Khan that he gave him a
handsome reward.

Soon after a foreign sovereign with a great army invaded
the kingdom, and the king appointed Tismar Khan Comman-

der-in-Chief and sent him out with all his force. At first he
marched in the rear of the army, but the soldiers shouted
"Khan Sahib, come on." Unaccustomed as he was to riding
he suddenly spurred his charger, which carried him under a
t ree. He held on to a branch, but the tree come out by the
roots, and he rode on dragging it after him. When the
enemy saw him advancing in this terrible fashion they were
seized with sudden panic and immediately dispersed. Tismar
Khan returned in triumph. The king was so pleased that he
made him his Wazir and gave him his daughter in marriage.

149

THE TWO LIARS

Once upon a time a liar set
out in search of employ-
ment. He came to a city
and put up at a Banya's
house. The liar and the
Banya began to talk, and
the Banya said : "My
father was a very rich man
and kept pack-bullocks.
One day one of the bullocks

got galled, so my father left it in the forest to take care of
itself. As my father was returning with the laden bullocks he
saw this bullock and a *pipal* tree was growing out of its back.
So he at once determined to keep this bullock and sell all
the others, which he did : and now he carries all his merchandise,

no matter how much it weighs, hanging from the branches of the *pipal* tree, growing on the bullock's back." The liar replied : "I have seen this bullock of yours that has a *pipal* tree growing on his back. My father rented 200 acres of land from a Raja, and my father and I cultivated the land, and in October we sowed wheat in the fields. When the wheat began to grow my father said that there would not be any grain in the ears unless the fields were watered, and how were two men to do it ? we must have help ; so my father jumped into a tank, and went by a subterranean passage to where the clouds live, and began to beat the clouds. The clouds said : 'Why do you beat us?' My father replied : 'I have sown 200 acres of land in wheat, which wants to be watered : so go and rain in my fields.' The clouds said : 'Very well ; we will go.' My father said. 'To ensure a good crop the fields must be watered three times.' The clouds replied : 'All right ; we shall rain thrice.' They kept their word, and the crop was better than my father expected."

"Then my father went to your father and sold him all the wheat, which your father took away in sacks hung on the branches of the *pipal* tree that was growing out of the bullock's back. But your father did not pay all the money for the wheat, and he still owes my father 200 rupees, which I have come to recover." The Banya said : "Brother, forgive me, I cannot surpass you in lying."

150

HOW THE MISERLY BANYA
WAS PUNISHED

A respectable Muhammadan gentleman (*miyan*) had once occasion to make a journey, and was obliged to stop for the night at the house of a miserly Banya, who entertained him in the most wretched way. The Banya and his wife were alone in the house, and when they lay down near the Miyan on the upper storey, he began to think how he could pay them off. After a while the Banyain said to him, "Cannot you tell us a story to make the night go quickly?" "I do know a tale," answered the Miyan ; "but it is certain to make you and your husband quarrel." "Never mind," said she, "you must tell it." The Miyan pretended to be sleepy, and said nothing for a while. The Banyain called out again : "Miyan Sahib ! won't you tell us the story?" He said : "I was very busy thinking of something." "What was it?" she asked. "Well," said he, "I was in the service of a Raja for the years, and when I was leaving him I got from him two bricks of gold. As I was coming home with them I had to cross the river which runs just behind your house, and I dropped my golden bricks. Now I am thinking that I must get some boatmen to drag the place to-morrow."

The Banya was listening to all this talk, and when he heard of the bricks of gold he thought he would have a try for them himself ; so he slipped quietly out of bed and went down to the river to grope about for them. Soon after, the Banyain got up, too, on the same errand, and when she groped about to wake her husband to come with her, she found he was not in his bed ; so she asked the Miyan if he knew what had become of him. "Well," said he, "a woman came to him not long ago, and no doubt he went with her." When she heard this, the Banyain was fiercely enraged and rushed out in search of her husband, abusing him at the top of her voice, so that all the neighbours awoke and heard about his misconduct.

Meanwhile having searched in vain for the golden bricks, the Banya came home wet and miserable. When he came he missed his wife, and asked the Miyan if he knew what had become of her. He said : "Well, not long ago a man came and called her out, and I suppose she has gone away with him." When the Banya heard this terrible news, he too, rushed out of the house, swearing and abusing her until he came to the end of the street, where he met her. There each fell on

the other and they half-killed each other before matters could
be explained. But before the time for explanation came the
Miyan took good care to make himself scarce.

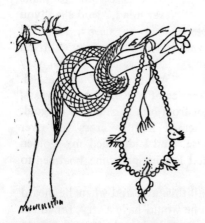

151

THE BANYA BOY
AND
FOUR WIVES

There was once a Banya, who had a very sharp son. When
he grew up his father did his best to get him married, but
several times his proposals were rejected. Finally, with great
difficulty, he made the arrangements. The night before the
marriage day his son was asleep, when he saw in a dream that a
daughter of a Badshah, of a Raja, of a Sahukar and of a Nat,
were all four attending on him. When he woke his father called
to him to come and be married, but he answered that he would
not marry until he could marry all these four. His father was
enraged that all his trouble should come to nought; so he beat
his son, who ran away to a distant land.

There it so happened that the daughter of the Badshah was
carrying on a flirtation with the son of the Wazir. Just at that
time they were walking about in the garden and were planning
to hire a servant who would keep their doings secret and would
carry letters from one to the other. At the moment in came
the Banya's son, who said that he had come from far and
wanted service. They asked his name, but he said he had forgotten it, and only knew that people called him *murkha* (fool).

They decided that he would answer, and gave him the berth. Some time after these two were chatting as usual and *murkha* was listening. At last they asked him what they had been saying. "Well," said he, "I heard you say that *murkha* had no jacket. Let us have one made for him by tomorrow." The girl replied, "Yes. This was just what we were saying;" and next day had a jacket made for him, believing that he was a utter fool. Again they were chatting, and she asked *murkha* what they were saying, and in the same way he wheedled a coat and turban from her.

Soon after the lovers planned to run away, because, as the princess said, her father would never let them marry. So she told her lover to go at midnight, that very night, to her stable and bring three horses saddled, ready, near her window. When he came he was to fling a clod at the window. The moment *murkha* heard this he went off to the Wazir and said : "Your son is planning to run off with the Badshah's daughter. You had better be careful, lest the Badshah murder you and your family." The Wazir took the hint and promptly locked his son up in a room, where he remained tearing his hair in misery. Meanwhile at midnight *murkha* took the three horses to the window, woke the Badshah's daughter, and she and her maid came down, and the three of them started off. When they had gone some way the girl called to the supposed Wazir's son : "we have gone far enough. Let us halt here as I am dead tired." But all *murkha* replied was "Humph, come along." After some time she again wanted to halt and got the same reply. At last she said : "Why are you so cruel ? You know I never rode a horse in my life and I am almost tumbling off." But he only gave her the same answer. So it went on till morning when the Badshah's daughter discovered that it was with *murkha*, not with the Wazir's son, that she had eloped. She was so horrified that she fell off the horse, and when she came to her senses, wept incessantly. Then her maid told her to harden her heart, that it was her fate to go with *murkha* and not with the son of the Wazir, and that she had better trust in Providence.

So when evening came the maid gave *murkha* a gold-mohur and told him to go to the bazar and buy some delicate food for

her mistress, and hire a comfortable house where they could
stay. He went into the bazar and could not find any food he
liked, so at last he bought some carrots which he thought would
be soft food for the lady, and he also got some *halwa* and
puris, thinking that she might eat these if she did not fancy the
carrots : and he could not find a first-rate house, so he saw a
grain-parcher's oven, and thinking that this would be warm
spot, he hired it for the night.

When he put the carrots before Badshah's daughter she
became insensible at the sight, and when she recovered, she
said : "How can I eat a thing I never saw in my life before ?"
But the maid hinted to her that *murkha* had a little sense after
all and had brought *halwa* and *puris* : so she ate some of these.
Then the maid asked him if he had hired a house, and he said :
"Yes ; I have got excellent quarters." Then he took them to
the grain-parcher's oven, and at the sight the Badshah's
daughter again lost her senses. But the maid went out and at
length found a tolerable house, where they stayed for the night.

Next morning *murkha* went into the town and saw some
jewellers testing a diamond. Up came the Raja's jeweller and
pronounced the diamond false. *Murkha* objected and said it
was genuine. Then the Raja's jeweller said : "I will make a
bet with you. What will you stake ?" The Badshah's daughter
was wearing a diamond necklace, so *murkha* went and asked
her to give it to him. She at first refused to give it, but *murkha*
threatened to kill her. So she had to give it to him. Then
murkha took it to the bazar and said : "I will stake this."
The king's jeweller answered : "If the diamond is genuine I
stake my house and wealth and my place against the necklace."
So the diamond was tested, and they put it on an anvil and
struck it with a sledge hammer. The diamond was not broken,
nay, it penetrated the iron. So *murkha* won the house, and
wealth and place of the Raja's jeweller. Then he returned to
the Badshah's daughter and said : "Come along. I have got
another house for you." So he brought her to the jeweller's
house. She had no idea how he got it, for she knew nothing
of the gamble.

Some days after her maid asked *murkha* to call a barber's
wife to give her mistress a bath. So he went off and called the

woman, who used to bathe the Raja's wife, and she did the same for the Badshah's daughter. But when she went back to the Rani, she mentioned how lovely *murkha's* wife was. The Rani told the Raja, and was anxious to see her. So he gave a general dinner in his garden and *murkha* had to bring his lady. She was wearing her diamond necklace, but oppressed by the heat, she took it off and hung it to a tree, and when she was going away forgot all about it : and only remembered it when she reached home late at night. Then she besought *murkha* to go back and fetch it. So he went back, but the glitter of the diamonds had attracted a black snake. When *murkha* touched the necklace the snake bit him and he died.

Next morning the gardener came, and seeing *murkha* dead, threw his body into the river and took the necklace. Now as the corpse of *murkha* went floating down, it so chanced that a number of Nat girls were bathing, and all of them set to tease one girl by saying : "Here comes your husband floating down." When the body came close by, this girl saw that he had died of the bite of black snake : so by a spell she knew she revived *murkha*, and tied a string round his neck by means of which he became a parrot. Then he shut him up in a cage, and every night she used to open the string, when he became a man again. Meanwhile she kept him in her hut until it so happened that the party of nats wandering about, doing their tricks, come below the Raja's palace. The Raja's daughter saw the parrot and sent word to her father to get it for her. At first the Nat girl refused to give it up, but the Raja's daughter was so pressing that she was obliged to give her the bird.

The Raja's daughter was delighted and took the parrot out of its cage. By chance she noticed the string round its neck, which, when she untied the parrot, turned at once into a man. This delighted the Raja's daughter still more, particularly as she was obliged to live alone. So she used to keep *murkha* in his parrot shape all day and turn him into a man at night. But one night the guard heard two people talking in the princess's chamber, so they climbed up on the top of the house and seeing *murkha*, tried to arrest him. *Murkha* had to escape, and running into the house of a Sahukar, implored him to save his life. He said that he did not mind helping him, but that he could think

of only one plan. "I have," said he, "an only daughter. Now if
you are ready to marry her, you may go into the room, and when
the guard comes, I will tell them that my son-in-law is the only
other man in the house." *Murkha* had to agree to save his
life : so when the guard came to search the house the Sahukar
put them off, and next day married *murkha* to his daughter.

Murkha then lived at the Sahukar's house. But one day the
maid of the Badshah's daughter with whom he first eloped,
happened to pass by and saw him. She came and told her
mistress, who would not believe her. "Why," said she, "he is
dead and the necklace is lost, and some one else must have
taken his shape." But the maid insisted that it was he. So she
made her mistress come with her, and when she saw him, sure
enough it was *murkha*. So she caught him by the arm and said :
"What are you doing here ? Come home at once." On this, up
came the Sahukar's daughter and says : "What are you doing
with my husband ?" But the Badshah's daughter said : "He is
my husband—not yours."

As they were disputing thus a policeman came up and was
carrying all three to the Raja, when on the way the Nat's
daughter met them and claimed him. When they got near the
Raja's palace, the Raja's daughter recognized him and caught
him. So the policeman could do nothing, but take the five of
them before the Raja, and said : "Your Majesty. Here is a
curious case. Four young women are fighting over one man."

The Raja made an enquiry and heard all their stories.
Finally he said : "There is no doubt all four of you are his
wives. So you better all live with him." So all ended happily
and *murkha's* destiny was fulfilled, in that he married the
daughters of the Badshah, the Raja, the Sahukar and the Nat.